SEVEN LIVES FROM MASS OBSERVATION

SEVEN LIVES
FROM MASS
OBSERVATION

BRITAIN IN THE LATE
TWENTIETH CENTURY

JAMES HINTON

OXFORD
UNIVERSITY PRESS

OXFORD
UNIVERSITY PRESS

Great Clarendon Street, Oxford, OX2 6DP,
United Kingdom

Oxford University Press is a department of the University of Oxford.
It furthers the University's objective of excellence in research, scholarship,
and education by publishing worldwide. Oxford is a registered trade mark of
Oxford University Press in the UK and in certain other countries

First Edition published in 2016

Impression: 1

Published in the United States of America by Oxford University Press
198 Madison Avenue, New York, NY 10016, United States of America

British Library Cataloguing in Publication Data

Data available

Library of Congress Control Number: 2016932818

ISBN 978–0–19–878713–6

Printed in Great Britain by
Clays Ltd, St Ives plc

Links to third party websites are provided by Oxford in good faith and
for information only. Oxford disclaims any responsibility for the materials
contained in any third party website referenced in this work.

Preface

What was it like to live in Britain during the second half of the twentieth century? Historical memory is always in a state of flux, never more so than when dealing with the recent past. Younger readers of this book will have impressions formed by their elders, by media representations, by the histories now being written. Older readers, like its author, will combine such influences with answers drawn from their own experience: in my own case that of a septuagenarian left-wing academic and one-time political activist from a secure middle-class background. But very few people can speak with the authority of the hundreds of volunteer writers whose contemporary testimony is preserved in the Mass Observation archive at the University of Sussex. Throughout the final two decades of the century, Mass Observation's correspondents regularly responded to open-ended questionnaires touching on every aspect of their everyday lives, thoughts, and feelings, both as they experienced them at the time and as they remembered them from earlier decades. This book uses the contributions of seven of these people as a basis for biographical essays designed to explore the social and cultural history of late-twentieth-century Britain.

Around 2600 individuals have at one time or another sent in responses to Mass Observation's thrice-yearly directives since 1981. Half of them quickly dropped out, but around 1100 people remained for between two and ten years, 250 for up to twenty years, and a similar number for more than twenty years, a select few writing for the whole period from 1981 to the present.[1] I began by sampling a handful of responses from a hundred or so of the most prolific correspondents, gradually narrowing down my selection according to the vividness and

---

1. These rough totals are derived from calculations based on information in the online catalogue (<http://www.thekeep.info/collections/mass-observation-archive/>). Nearly 3500 are listed there, but 900 of them failed to respond to any directives after registering with MO.

intimacy of the writing, the respondents' engagement with activities beyond the worlds of paid employment and domesticity, and the need to select individuals, both women and men, from as widely as possible across the social spectrum.

Historians usually write about dead people, and about periods of time in which they were not themselves active players. In sampling the Mass Observation writing, I was looking for lives different from my own, lives from which I could get a sense of how my times looked and felt to people with a very different experience of them. The seven people I eventually selected were all—for reasons to be explained later—born before the Second World War:

Caroline (b. 1922). Wife of a small businessman. West London
Janet (b. 1933). Schoolteacher. South London
Stella (b. 1931). Social worker. Surrey and Yorkshire
Helen (b. 1921). Wife of an RAF pilot. Hertfordshire and South Wales
Len (b. 1930). Mechanic and manager. North London and Sussex
Bob (b. 1934). Lorry driver. North London and Essex
Sam (b. 1933). Banker. South-east England

Clearly this is not a representative sample, and no selection from the rather special people who volunteered to write for Mass Observation possibly could be. Nevertheless, despite echoing the disproportionately southern and middle-class composition of the MO respondents as a whole, these seven people cover a wide range of occupations and social situations. And, although all seven were white, people of colour played a significant role in the lives of several of them. By following their life stories there is much to be learned about the history of Britain in the late twentieth century.

Biography has traditionally been reserved for the great men (and occasional women) who are of interest because they had the power, it was believed, to 'make history'. But, as social historians have long argued, this power has never been reserved for emperors, generals, or intellectuals. Where the sources allow us to recover the biographies of 'ordinary', conventionally 'powerless' people, we get to glimpse the processes by which history is made from below by a multitude of individual, personal decisions: to leave school or stay on, to live together, marry or divorce, to have children or not, to rent or buy a place to live, to save or to spend. The choices made by individuals about such things, and about work, lifestyle, political loyalties, or religious beliefs, are always constrained by existing economic, social, and cultural structures, but they are never entirely determined by them. Individuals pick and choose from the resources available to them, and the structures themselves shift under the impact of the choices each of us make about how to live our lives. Politicians think they change the world, and we are all too ready to buy into their delusions of grandeur because they provide a useful shorthand for understanding the times we live through. If anyone changed Britain in the last seventy-five years—so popular historical memory would have us believe—it was Mrs Thatcher. In reality, however, the sources and processes of social change move at a slower and deeper pace than anything determined by the frenzies of political life or the rise and fall of career politicians. The mass observers, carefully compiling records of their own lives and choices, provide us with one way of observing these deeper processes at work.

Mass observers are guaranteed anonymity, and this has been respected—except in the case of Bob, the lorry driver, who declared that he had never done anything he would mind appearing on the front page of the *Daily Mirror*. Circumstantial detail will, unavoidably, make these individuals identifiable to those who know them person-ally, and I have interviewed those who are still alive (or in the case of the banker, his widow) and taken account of their responses to draft versions of the essays. The identity of Caroline, the small businessman's wife, who stopped writing for the archive twenty years ago and died ten years ago, has been more thoroughly disguised. In order to preserve anonymity I have not revealed the codes by which these people are identified in the archive. Bone fide researchers, however, can apply to the archivist for these codes.

My greatest debt is to the mass observers themselves. They wrote because they wanted to contribute to the way that the history of their times would be written, and I hope that they will see this book as some small justification for their commitment to Mass Observation. I am particularly grateful to the widow of Sam, the banker, for allowing me access to his diaries, and for the generosity of her response to my draft chapter on her husband. Without Dorothy Sheridan's dedication and skill over many years the Mass Observation Project itself would probably not have survived. She has been closely involved throughout the research and writing of this book, and she accompanied me with a watching brief on behalf of the MO Trustees when I interviewed the contributors. I am grateful to Fiona Courage and Jessica Scantlebury, current guardians of the archive, for their help and support; and I thank the Trustees of the Mass Observation Archive for permission to quote material of which they hold the copyright. Dorothy Sheridan, Penny Summerfield, and OUP's two readers have given me invaluable advice on the text. And I have learned a great deal in discussing the project with colleagues, friends, and, above all, my closest friend and partner, Yvette Rocheron.

James Hinton
Les Trémoulèdes
December 2015

Contents

I

Mass Observation

Mass Observation was founded in the late 1930s by two young men—a maverick anthropologist and a left-wing poet—in an effort to establish 'an anthropology of ourselves'.[1] A leading objective of its founders was to counter newspaper misrepresentations of popular attitudes by enabling ordinary people to speak for themselves. During its first phase, which ended in 1949, the organization accumulated a rich archive of popular writing which was later to become a major source for historians of mid-twentieth-century Britain. The archive, housed at the University of Sussex, also provided a base from which the second, and continuing, phase of Mass Observation—now known as the Mass Observation Project—was launched by the anthropologist David Pocock in 1981.

Pocock was primarily interested in using the observers to gather factual data about everyday life. Dorothy Sheridan, who had been in charge of the original MO archive since the early 1970s and who took over responsibility for the new project after Pocock's retirement in 1990, came to understand the enterprise as part of a broader upsurge of history from below, inspired by the History Workshop movement, feminist efforts to document the lives of women previously hidden from history, and community publishing initiatives which encouraged working-class people to write their autobiographies. While critics feared that these voices from the margins would remain trapped in a merely celebratory 'alternative ghetto', restricting their impact on mainstream historical narratives, the emerging discipline of oral history (the Oral History Society was founded in 1973) stimulated methodological debate about memory and the value of personal life stories and helped to place such material at the forefront of innovation in the writing of social history.[2] All this provided

Sheridan with an intellectual context for the development of more searching and theoretically informed 'directives' (the open-ended questionnaires sent regularly to mass observers). While some contributors confirmed established historical understanding, others opened up new perspectives on the recent past, and researchers immersing themselves in the material were able to uncover what Annette Kuhn, discussing 'memory work' with family photograph albums, described as 'ways of knowing and ways of seeing the world...rarely acknowledged, let alone celebrated, in the expressions of the hegemonic culture.'[3] Under Sheridan's direction 'writing ourselves' for Mass Observation became a process not only of telling one's own story, but also of doing so in a framework which reflected new developments in both historical study and the social sciences, a shift of focus sometimes referred to as the 'biographical' turn.[4]

Pocock had cultivated a bond of trust with his correspondents by regular personal responses to their writing, but he showed surprisingly little interest in the uses to which the material might be put, or the methodological issues involved.[5] Sheridan, meeting a new generation of researchers in the archive, and herself involved in feminist activity and in community publishing, was more attuned to the spirit of the age.[6] From 1990, when she took over direction of the project, she was able to develop its full potential as an archive of autobiographical writing. Pocock had been cautious about asking intimate questions of his correspondents, but the first directive for which Sheridan was solely responsible asked people to write about their 'close relationships', and subsequent directives (devised by Sheridan or researchers working closely with her) probed the impact of feminism on attitudes to gender; correspondents' experience of childhood, adolescence, education, sex, marriage, work, and aging; attitudes to everything from current politics to death and the supernatural; and the reasons why people were prepared to write for MO. The resulting mixture of descriptions of everyday life, reflection on issues of the day, and fragments of autobiographical writing provides rich documentation of each observer's experience, sensibility, and contribution to the life of his or her times.

Crucial to the quality of the writing fostered by Mass Observation was the trust established between the project and its correspondents. Guaranteed anonymity, they had little reason to dissimulate. The directives were carefully formulated to allow correspondents to choose their own balance between opinion, observation, and autobiography. Those who wrote for MO over many years came to see themselves as 'participants in research rather than objects of research'.[7] Recording the experience of 'ordinary' people for the benefit of future generations, they felt they had a stake in an archive whose value would depend on the frankness of their responses. Many saw themselves as providing alternative accounts of the times they were living through, alerting posterity to experiences and perspectives which might otherwise be buried under the weight of narratives constructed by the powerful. They wanted their voices to be heard, and they wrote in the belief that their own experience of life, however idiosyncratic, had a value in enabling others to understand the history of their times. They knew that history could be written from many perspectives, and saw themselves as contributing to a collective enterprise designed to preserve for posterity something of the range of divergent ways in which the late twentieth century was being lived.[8]

Some reserved the right not to discuss matters—notably sexual ones—that they felt were essentially private; others told things to Mass Observation that they had never revealed to their partners or most intimate friends. Writing for MO, several people remarked, was like talking to a therapist: the normal inhibitions about saying things that might be thought shameful were suspended. And, as one researcher who used MO to investigate 'family secrets' put it, writing to MO also gave them 'the freedom to be nasty'.[9] What people chose to write about was certainly conditioned by MO's questionnaires, but these were open ended, and many respondents felt free to write about whatever was on their mind at the time. The fact that respondents were writing rather than speaking meant that they had time to reflect on the issues raised and to interrogate their immediate reactions in search of an honest response: 'is what I'm writing really what I believe', wondered one introspective observer, or was it 'what one likes to believe one believes!'[10] Writing also meant that responses were not subject to the self-censoring dynamics of even the most sensitively conducted face-to-face interview.[11]

The MOP panel was heavily weighted towards older people, and two-thirds of those writing for over twenty years or more from the 1980s were already over fifty when they began. People writing later in their lives and thus able to reflect on the experience of many decades provide the richest material for historical analysis, particularly as undertaken here in the form of the biographical essay. 'Life', as Kierkegaard remarked, 'is lived forwards but understood backwards'.[12] Many contributors were retired or close to retirement when they started writing for MO and their autobiographical reflections tend to be fuller, richer, deeper, more considered than those of younger mass observers caught up in the throes of establishing a family and making a living. The seven individuals whose writing is discussed in this volume were all born before the Second World War, two in the early 1920s, the rest in the early 1930s. They came to the upheavals of the late twentieth century already shaped as young adults during the war or the immediate post-war years. Their lives spanned years of tumultuous social change—the inter-war depression; war, reconstruction, and austerity into the 1950s; affluence and the cultural 'revolution' associated with the 1960s; and the decisive impact of neo-liberalism as the structures of Britain's post-war settlement crumbled from the later 1970s. One advantage of looking at this history through the eyes of people formed in the mid-century is that it provides a corrective to accounts offered by those (including the present writer) who came of age during the 1960s or later. This does not mean that my subjects were unaffected by subsequent waves of social change. In their efforts to understand cultural change, historians are often drawn to the study of the young, the primary bearers of change—the world as transformed by the baby boomers or by Thatcher's children. But youth does not have a monopoly on history making. Because the people dealt with here engaged with the defining transformations of the late twentieth century as adults, their sensibilities and expectations shaped by an earlier era, their experiences are particularly valuable in helping us to view these transformations in historical perspective.[13] Some of them felt left behind by history, but their disappointment or bewilderment is as much a part of the history of these years as are the fashionable enthusiasms of the young. Others responded positively to the tides of change, and for several the 1960s provided the occasion for life-changing decisions. As self-reflective individuals, they were all engaged in re-thinking the apparent certainties of their upbringing and youth, stimulated not only by the broad currents of cultural change, but also by MO's probing questionnaires which, arriving three or four times a year, insistently confronted them with questions about every aspect of their own identities and values.

Writing about their lives for MO during the 1980s and 90s, they were drawing not only on their direct experience of these changes, but also on a public memory shaped by television, film, newspapers, and books. Although the mass observers offered their personal stories as material for future historians, those stories were already shaped by public memories of the times they had lived through. Indeed aligning our personal memories with public history is part of the process by which we find meaning in our lives, reflexively standing outside ourselves sufficiently to understand ourselves as creatures of our times.[14] But the effect of such reflexivity on memory is far from innocent. Public memory reflects contemporary concerns more than any rigorous engagement with the actualities of the past. Politicians, journalists, social commentators, and even some contemporary historians have a tendency to manufacture and recycle mythological versions of the past. Some of the most powerful and persistent of these myths are nostalgic: 'memories' of lost working-class 'community' or of wartime 'national unity' are used to point up the stress and anomie of modern living.[15] Others, more negative, are mobilized in defence of current policies: post-war Labour's 'never again' myth of the 1930s depression, Mrs Thatcher's myths of 1960s permissiveness or 1970s social breakdown.[16] To describe such representations of the past as myths is not to deny that they contain elements of truth. Historical myths, like cartoons, work by focussing on particular features and exaggerating them. In so far as we think about our own lives in relation to such myths, we tend to privilege some experiences over others. Memory is a complex process, and historians have become increasingly aware of the dangers of relying on autobiographical accounts—whether written for publication, gathered by oral historians, or contributed to MO—to reveal an authentic past unmediated by unconscious pressures to remember experiences which fit with conventional versions of the public history and to forget those which do not fit. As Richard Johnson and Graham Dawson pointed out: 'Private memories cannot ... be readily unscrambled from the effects of dominant historical discourses. It is often these that supply the very terms by which a private history is thought through.'[17] It is all too easy to use the narratives people construct of their lives to lend authenticity to mythological versions of the past. We need to be careful, in handling such material, to listen for the silences, the unconscious avoidance of things which do not fit.[18]

To date the material collected by MO in the 1980s and 90s has been explored by social researchers 'horizontally': used to discuss attitudes and behaviour in relation to the themes raised by a particular directive (or in some cases several directives.) Until now, few attempts have been made to use this material 'vertically': to track the lives of particular individuals.[19] Back in the 1930s the founders of Mass Observation had no intention of using the panellists' responses to construct individual life histories—indeed they were anxious to assure panellists that their purpose was to investigate 'collective habits and social behaviour', not to intrude on 'the private life of any individual'.[20] During the war MO encouraged people to write regular diaries, and this went some way to break down this distinction, but it took the feminist perception that 'the personal is political' and the turn towards life history methods in the social sciences to fully expose the fallacy of counterpoising 'collective habits' to 'private life'. Advocates of the biographical turn in the social sciences have argued that individual life stories can be used not just to illustrate interpretations already established in the researcher's mind, but also to challenge them: 'the luminosity of single cases' can provide a 'point of discovery' and a 'starting point for inferences about social structure'.[21] Similarly for the historian, close study of individual life stories can often alert us to experiences overlooked or marginalized by existing accounts of the larger history, forcing us to revise or re-think.[22]

The panellists themselves often saw what they were doing as depositing successive fragments of what, taken as a whole, amounted to a kind of autobiography. While some feared researchers intruding on their private lives, others worried that their remarks might be being taken out of context to support some researcher's preconceived theory. They wanted to be understood, as one man put it, as 'an individual, a personality in my own right, not a cipher or a statistic to be manipulated and aggregated'.[23] Asked whether they had ever thought about writing autobiographies, several of the people who are the subjects of this volume replied that they saw their writing for MO as a form of autobiography, perhaps a superior form. Because they were not writing for publication and were guaranteed anonymity, mass observers felt free to write about aspects of their lives that they would have hesitated to make public. The intimacy of the observers' relationship with MO was nicely summed up by one panellist, who imagined the future historian reading her responses as 'a kind of historical love affair'.[24]

Writing biography does involve a kind of love affair, 'the creation', as Richard Holmes has put it, 'of a fictional or imaginary relationship between the biographer and his subject...a steady if subliminal exchange of attitudes, judgements and conclusions...'[25] It is through a process of empathetic engagement that I have tried to enter into the experience of these seven people, and thereby to re-imagine the history of my own times through their eyes. There are, of course, dangers in this procedure, above all the danger of projecting one's own attitudes and responses onto the 'character' that one is creating in one's imagination.[26] There is no absolute way of preventing such contamination, but the very detail and intimacy of the MO material acts as a check on the unconscious import of the biographer's sensibility into that of his subject. I have frequently been brought up short in my imaginative construction of a personality by some unexpected association of ideas, or a turn of phrase revealing attitudes I had not guessed at. And, beyond empathy, the attempt to grasp the wider historical significance of each life by going back and forward between the individual life story and the existing historical literature helps to establish a degree of distance and detachment. While empathy can fertilize the historical imagination, harvesting the resulting crop requires a colder analytical stance.

2

Histories

> There are as yet no properly historical treatments of the social and cultural revolutions of the second half of the century, though the mass of comment and documentation is vast, and sufficiently accessible to let many of us form our own opinions...Readers should not be misled by the confident tone of the literature (including my own observations) into confusing opinion with established truth.
>
> Eric Hobsbawm, *The Age of Extremes*, 1994, 613–14

As historians get to grips with the recent past they find themselves challenging myths, but the interpretations they themselves offer are always provisional. In this chapter I sketch out some of the ways in which contemporary historians have understood, and argued about, economic, social, and cultural change in late-twentieth-century Britain. This shifting body of knowledge and argument has helped me to frame the individual life stories re-imagined in the biographical essays which follow. But history is always a work in progress, and I hope that close attention to these lives will help, here and there, to move things forward, the 'luminosity of single cases' stimulating the historical imagination and drawing attention to areas of experience neglected or undervalued in existing accounts.[1]

I

No decade has been more mythologized than the 1960s, seen as a period of 'cultural revolution' in which 'Victorian' attitudes to sex and the family were more or less suddenly cast aside; deference to authority gave way to a new assertiveness, especially among the young, expressed in new kinds of social movement and a 'post-materialist' counter-culture; and all of this underpinned by the welfare state, full employment, and a degree of affluence that enabled a population whose aspirations had previously been held in check by the disciplines of depression, war, and austerity to demand very much more out of life.[2] Recent historical work, while by no means discrediting these characteristics of the period (usually thought of as a 'long decade' extending from the late 1950s to the early 1970s), has attempted to place them within broader patterns of change.

Certainly the 1960s saw a new openness about sexual matters, first announced by the successful defence of Penguin's right to publish D. H. Lawrence's hymn to sexuality, *Lady Chatterley's Lover*. While popular journalism had always found a mass audience for sexual scandals, particularly those involving elite figures, the 1963 Profumo affair broke new ground in the role of Christine Keeler, perceived not as a vulnerable teenager but as a frankly sexually assertive young woman proclaiming her right to promiscuous sexual pleasure devoid of emotional commitment.[3] While most people continued to condemn both promiscuity and adultery, and marriage had never been as popular as it was in the 1960s, attitudes to premarital sex and to unmarried cohabitation shifted significantly during the decade.[4] Philip Larkin's celebrated quip that sex began between the end of the *Lady Chatterley* ban (1960) and the Beatles' first LP (1963), predated the impact of the contraceptive pill (introduced in 1962, but until 1969 only freely available at the discretion of doctors to married women)[5] and neglected the centrality of sexual pleasure to ideas about companionate marriage which had become generally accepted since the war.[6] As improved contraceptive methods unhooked sexuality from reproduction, feminist and psychoanalytical discussion of the complexities of desire gained wider public recognition. More tolerant attitudes to the varieties of sexual behaviour had already been enshrined in Lord Wolfenden's assertion, in his 1956 report on the legal regulation of homosexuality, that 'it is not the function of the law to intervene in the private lives of citizens or to seek to enforce any particular pattern of behaviour', although it was not until Roy Jenkins' tenure at the Home Office in the late 1960s that the legislature caught up with changing public attitudes—liberalizing the law on drinking, gambling, censorship, abortion, contraception, homosexuality, and divorce. While the new permissiveness relieved a great deal of human suffering, it was not an unmixed blessing. In the era of the pill young women found it more difficult to say 'no' to unwanted sexual overtures. The new openness about sexual matters also intensified the problematic nature of the companionate ideal, which—by focussing on the family as a private relationship rather than a public institution and placing emotional intimacy at its heart—made marriage more vulnerable to the ebb and flow of desire. By the end of the century a dramatic rise in divorce, remarriage, and cohabitation had transformed family life, widening the definition of what a family could be, although surveys made it clear that, among cohabiting as well as married couples, the desire for stability and permanence remained even if, in practice, it was less likely to be achieved.[7]

Five of my seven selected mass observers had married in the 1950s, and three of these marriages were relatively unaffected by the spirit of the times, continuing happily, or in one case very unhappily, in modes legitimated by traditional expectations. For the other two, the new atmosphere of permissiveness had life-changing consequences, leading to divorce in one case and profound renegotiation of the marriage contract in another. The cultural changes of the 1960s may have been led by a younger generation born after the catastrophic experiences of the mid-twentieth century, but, as these two examples suggest, older people were not immune to changes in the moral atmosphere. The oldest of my mass observers, who had married during the war, was also profoundly affected by the 1960s, but in her case it was a student son who provided the catalyst of change, and the issues were not sexual but political.

The expanding university campuses of the 1960s provided fertile soil for the growth of a new kind of 'post-materialist' politics. Living independently and free of adult responsibilities, confident of their personal futures in an era of economic expansion and full employment, students could focus their youthful idealism on combating injustice, oppression, and war in the world at large. The so-called 'new social movements' of the period, which took off from the late-1950s mobilization of the Campaign for Nuclear Disarmament, proliferated through the 1960s in campaigns inspired by the civil rights and anti-war movements in the USA, resistance to apartheid in South Africa, and the May 1968 events in France. Although it was the very success of post-war capitalism that underwrote the optimism of this politics, it was informed by a profound critique and rejection of materialistic values, an urgent belief that there was more to life than the stultifying satisfactions offered by consumerism and mass culture. Environmentalists, identifying the unsustainability of limitless economic growth driven by science and technology in the service of capitalism, called into question the viability of traditional social democratic strategies for redistributing the proceeds of capitalist expansion. The radical counter-culture laid bare the operations of power in the psychiatric and medical services, the school, and the idealized nuclear family, insisting that the route to a new society lay through an 'anti-politics' of self-change and communal experimentation at the margins of established society.[8] At a time when the Christian churches were in precipitate decline, those in search of spiritual values to counter the instrumental rationality underpinning industrial society turned to mystical traditions from the East or the pagan past, giving rise to a diffuse and eclectic prolifer-ation of alternative religious and therapeutic practices loosely gathered under the banner of the 'New Age' from the 1970s.[9] But the most successful product of the new politics, embodying fully the trans-formative insistence that 'the personal is political', was the women's liberation movement.

Launched at the end of the 1960s as an outgrowth of student radic-alism, the new wave of feminism rooted itself in the intensive exploration of personal feelings in small groups discussing sexuality, the disputed sources of women's oppression, and, not least, the discrepancies between the rhetoric of liberation and the realities of young motherhood. Consciousness-raising was combined with a creative activism reaching out to women across the social spectrum and giving voice to ambi-tions and discontents which had long been maturing under the impact of improvements in women's education and the contradictory effects of their increasing participation in the labour market. While new pos-sibilities of personal autonomy called into question older virtues of service and self-sacrifice, the path to liberation was held in check by the dual burden of work and domesticity. During the 1970s feminists campaigned in favour of equal pay, provision of childcare, the defence and extension of abortion rights, and access to contraception, and against pornography, sexual harassment, and demeaning stereotypes of women. They targeted male violence, not only with 'reclaim the night' marches, women's refuges, and rape crisis centres, but also by providing a gendered analysis of militarism, when in the early 1980s plans to deploy cruise missiles heightened fear of nuclear war. The women's peace camp at Greenham Common became an emblem of female empowerment against patriarchal structures in private life as much as in the warfare state.[10]

The upsurge of activism from the 1960s generated much talk about 'new social movements' which, unlike the established labour movement, would operate through mass mobilization and direct action to outflank the hierarchical and bureaucratic operations of the existing political system. In practice the influence and staying power of these movements depended on their ability to penetrate as well as to outflank, to combine direct action with the road through the institutions. By engaging with the existing structures of power, the women's movement did much to entrench its values, nowhere more successfully than in the transformative impact it had on the Labour Party: much to the distress, as we shall see, of Bob the lorry driver.[11] The dual strategy was complicated, generating abiding tensions between 'realist' and 'purist' approaches. Similar tensions were apparent among the very wide range of single-issue organizations which, alongside the protest politics of the 1960s, had emerged at an accelerating pace since the 1950s transforming the charitable and voluntary sector with campaigns around overseas aid, consumer rights, education, health, provision for the aged, disability rights, child welfare, environmental protection, the welfare of immigrants, poverty, housing, and a host of other social issues. By accumulating expertise in discrete areas of the welfare system some of these organizations were able to force their way into the policy making process or to operate services contracted out by central and local government.[12] Such engagements with the state held obvious dangers for their critical and campaigning roles. Nevertheless by the end of century membership of new social movements and of single-issue campaigning organizations dwarfed the shrinking support for the political parties, belying pessimistic accounts of public apathy and cynicism by opening up new channels for effective political participation.[13]

Something of the spirit of the new voluntarism was captured by the Labour politician Richard Crossman's 1973 characterization of its typical activist:

a man with the divine discontent in his soul which makes him question the rulings of the establishment, which makes him suspect what he is told, which makes him a pioneer finding out and articulating social needs, which makes him, when he finds a grievance, organise a protest movement against it, and when he has an idea organise a pressure group to promote it.[14]

Crossman's unthinking exclusion of women, characteristic of his era, was symptomatic of what women's liberation successfully challenged— one cannot imagine a senior politician speaking like this today. In fact, amongst my selected mass observers it was the women, more than the men, who translated 'divine discontent' into voluntary activism. Helen, the RAF wife, combined peace demonstrations with volunteering in her local women's refuge. Janet, the London schoolteacher, had joined the Abortion Law Reform Association in 1956, reminding us that the pre-1960s movement for women's rights had not been as inert as the young women re-inventing feminism from 1960s believed it to have been.[15] As a volunteer teacher in a Barnardo's children's home and a black 'supplementary' school she entered fully into the spirit of voluntarism, while also pressing to extend the liberalization of the law governing personal behaviour as an executive member of the Euthanasia Society. Stella, who, more than any of the others, identified with the 'post-materialist' themes of 1960s radicalism and its later 'New Age' dimensions, supplemented her social work with voluntary activity, including playing a leading role in the establishment of a new self-help and campaigning organization around a neglected issue of women's health in the 1980s. Even Caroline, the Tory wife of a small businessman, was not immune. As a member of Mary Whitehouse's campaign against sex and violence in the media she was playing out a right-wing version of single-issue politics.[16]

2

The sense of moral decline that motivated Mary Whitehouse's supporters chimed with broader currents of belief that Britain's glory days were behind her. Retreating from empire, humiliated in the Suez Crisis, clinging to a global role only as second lieutenant to the United States, and slipping down the economic league table, the British looked back with nostalgia to the Second World War, when, in popular memory, a truly united kingdom stood alone against the forces of darkness, and even defeat could be a cause for retrospective pride in the shape of the much mythologized 'spirit of Dunkirk'. To some, immigration from the old empire appeared as a symptom of decline, presaging inner-city turmoil and social breakdown. But others saw Britain's relative success in establishing a multicultural society as a source of satisfaction and national pride.[17] While both views are represented among the mass observers selected for this study, more complex responses to the cultural challenges represented by Commonwealth immigration are also apparent, notably in the case of Janet, the South London schoolteacher.

As the sense of national decline took hold, intellectuals from left, right, and centre fell over each other to explain the deep social and cultural 'origins of the present crisis', each stressing themes designed to justify their own preferred solutions.[18] In 1964 the Labour Party leader Harold Wilson seized on one such explanation, promising to unleash 'the white heat of technology' against the gentlemanly amateurism of an anti-industrial culture so conveniently symbolized in the person of Harold Macmillan's successor as Conservative prime minister, the 14th Earl of Home.[19] Mrs Thatcher's 1979 victory rested on her success in portraying the problems facing Labour governments coping with the consequences of the end of post-war global economic expansion as symptoms of a peculiarly 'British disease'.

While it suited the purposes of politicians to represent the nation as suffering from some chronic sickness that they alone could cure, historians have become increasingly sceptical about the underlying assumptions of the 'declinist' narrative.[20] One of the central paradoxes of later-twentieth-century British history is the contrast between this pervasive talk of decline, and the experience of rising living standards for most of the population. In the era of global post-war economic expansion real wages rose rapidly, almost doubling between 1950 and 1973, and the British economy grew faster than at any time in the past. There was indeed a *relative* decline, since other Western European economies did even better (largely because they were starting from a lower base); but in the later decades of the century, when growth slowed down, Britain's economic performance was roughly in line with that of its major competitors. And, despite short periods of falling living standards in the later 1970s and early 1980s, overall the upward trend of real wages continued into the new century, although at a slower pace than during the boom years.[21]

Like most other countries, Britain had persistent economic problems and there was much for critics to seize upon. In retrospect, however, many of the critics' favourite targets seem poorly chosen, notably the complaint that Britain was being governed by gentlemanly amateurs out of touch with modern technology. In reality, since the triumph of planning during the war years, the management of the economy, the construction of the welfare state, and, not least, the running of Britain's exceptionally large and sophisticated military–industrial complex had been firmly in the hands of a rapidly growing elite of professional experts, many of them upwardly mobile through the expansion of the education system.[22] The central conflict in Britain's elites during the later twentieth century was not between gentlemanly amateurs and technocratic experts, but between those professionals who expected social progress (and status for themselves) to be delivered through the expansion of the state, and more entrepreneurially minded experts who looked to the market as the source of dynamic change (and their own enrichment).[23] When Mrs Thatcher shifted power towards the latter group, their public-sector rivals found their ethic of disinterested service distrusted, and their work subjected to artificially constructed market disciplines enforced by accountants.[24]

Mrs Thatcher's characterization of the 'British disease'—free enterprise stifled by an overextended state, excessive welfare provision, and over-mighty trade unions—was also problematic. Until the global crisis triggered by the collapse of fixed exchange rates and the OPEC oil-price hike in the early 1970s, Britain's post-war settlement had delivered not only the welfare state and an unprecedented rise in living standards, but also full employment, falling inequality, rapidly rising educational provision, and increased upward social mobility. Moreover this success had been achieved while spending less on health and welfare provision (and more on defence) than had most of Britain's European rivals.[25] While the New Right saw the corporatist management of the economy as ceding too much power to the trade unions, other critics, turning envious eyes on foreign success stories, deplored the failure of Labour governments to implement measures designed to promote industrial innovation or worker participation in management along lines long established in Germany.[26] Escalating inflation triggered by the global crisis, together with a drastic cutback in public spending demanded by the IMF as a condition for bailing out sterling in 1976, set the scene for the final crisis of the post-war settlement. With the government set on restoring private-sector profitability by cutting real wages, trade-union leaders struggled to control a membership distressed by falling living standards and infuriated by the attempts of politicians and the press to pin the blame for Britain's economic problems on the workers. The explosion of strikes in the 1979 'winter of discontent' revealed the weakness, not the strength, of so-called trade-union 'barons', unable to hold the line against workers radicalized by the raised aspirations of the affluent 1960s, and the rapid expansion of trade unionism during the 1970s among new sectors of the work-force, especially low-paid women and public-sector workers.[27] Mrs Thatcher's 1979 election victory was a direct outcome of her success, ably assisted by Britain's overwhelmingly right-wing press, in repre-senting the strikes as an attack on the public carried out by greedy workers and over-mighty trade-union bosses.[28] It was, as we shall see, indignation at this misrepresentation that helped to inspire Len, the garage mechanic, to start writing for Mass Observation. He wanted to set the record straight.

While Labour cut state spending reluctantly, Mrs Thatcher seized on neo-liberal economics as the high road to national rejuvenation, abolishing exchange controls, deregulating the City, slashing taxes on the rich, emasculating the trade unions, privatizing industry, promoting council-house sales, popularizing share ownership and consumer debt.[29] A Labour government prepared to face down business resistance to its industrial policies, or a trade-union movement better adapted to working with government to counterbalance such resistance might have delayed the breakdown of Britain's post-war corporatism, but probably not for long. Thatcher's embrace of neo-liberalism was part of a global phenomenon, itself best seen as the resumption of long-term processes of capitalist globalization which had been tem-porarily interrupted by war and revolution during the first half of the century. The fact that Britain took a leading role in this process reflected its own history as a centre of international finance. 'Thatcherism at its heart', argued one historian, 'was simply the admission . . . that Britain's comparative advantage . . . lay in the services, finance, and commerce . . .' Even during the industrial revolution, when Britain had been the workshop of the world, the richest and most powerful capitalists had been bankers, not industrial entrepreneurs.[30]

To those who opposed Thatcher, her enthusiastic embrace of neo-liberalism, far from representing a solution to national decline, placed Britain in the forefront of a global shift to a form of capitalism far less benign than that which had dominated Britain before the crisis of the later 1970s. Capitalism stimulates innovation, but it also tends to des-troy the pre-conditions for its own success. During the 'thirty golden years' of post-war prosperity, the existence of social solidarities outside the market, of motives other than the drive for profit, had helped to stabilize the system. Capitalism worked, on this account, because its more destructive tendencies were held in check by the countervailing forces of organized labour and national governments committed to the amelioration of inequality through progressive taxation and welfare provision.[31] In Thatcher's entrepreneurial society, market discipline and the profit motive were enshrined as the only effective engines of economic success, marginalizing not only trade unions but also the service ethic of the professional middle class, which had previously been central to the operations of the mixed economy. In the private sector, 'organization man', who had once invested his manhood in service to the company, gave way to the mobile hedge-fund manager, privileging short-term profitability over long-term investment.[32] In the public sector, quasi-markets subordinated professional expertise to a new target-driven managerialism, while a similar regime invaded the voluntary sector on the back of contracted-out public services.[33] The impact of these trends on individual lives is apparent in the stories told by Sam the banker, Len the garage mechanic, and Stella the social worker.

The collapse of state socialism in the USSR appeared to cement Thatcher's message—'there is no alternative'—and it was only by embracing neo-liberal 'new times' that the Labour Party was able to regain power in 1997. One place where the narrative of decline certainly did fit the bill was in the fate of the manual working class. As global corporations shifted manufacturing industry to exploit reserves of cheap labour in the Far East, the manual working class shrank, and while living standards for the majority continued to rise, so did insecurity, unemployment, and poverty for those at the bottom of the heap. The thirty-year trend towards reduced inequality was sharply reversed and by the late 1990s the pattern of wealth distribution in Britain had reverted to that of the previous century.[34] With their trade unions in decline, and the Labour Party increasingly run by the same kind of professional middle-class people who also dominated the expanding politics of new social movements and single-issue campaigning, many working-class people (including both the skilled manual workers in this study) felt themselves abandoned, deprived of the political representation that had previously lent a measure of dignity and status to their work.[35] 'Is it any wonder', asks a recent historian of the post-war working class, 'that some of those working-class people who look back on their lives in the middle years of the century regard it as a "golden age"? In many respects, compared with the lives of their grandparents' generation and those of their own children and grandchildren, it was exactly that.'[36]

Thatcher's greatest success, the conversion of the Labour Party to the neo-liberal agenda, ensured that when in 2008 the chickens of deregulated capitalism came home to roost, no coherent political alternative existed. By then whatever restraining power trade unions, the nation state, or the professional ethic had once been able to exercise had been expelled from the arena. The commanding heights of the economy were now in the hands of global corporations operating beyond the effective reach of national authorities, and supranational regulation remained weak.[37] The corporations were in control and, at the apex of power, naked greed ruled unchecked. In neo-liberal times the ethos of the market invaded every pore of the social body—citizens became consumers, patients became clients, students became customers. As older solidarities decayed, 'choice' became the right and the duty of every individual. The entrepreneurial society might empower the rich at the expense of everyone else, but the doctrine it preached was that each individual was in control of his or her own destiny. Collective solutions faded. Your fate was in your own hands. Responsibility for success or failure in life lay squarely on one's own shoulders, while structural obstacles to personal fulfilment were pushed into the background, a situation as likely to generate anxiety and a sense of inadequacy as it was to leave people feeling powerful and in control of their own destinies.[38] Moreover *my* personal autonomy is *your* selfish individualism: so that even those who adapted successfully to neo-liberal values feared the socially disintegrative consequences of the erosion of restraints on purely self-directed behaviour. Despite her notorious observation that 'there is no such thing as society', Mrs Thatcher worried about the impact of unrestrained market individualism on the fabric of social order. She sought to address such anxieties by lauding the family as the engine of social solidarity, while demonizing the cultural changes of the 1960s as a key source of anti-social behaviour. But to play 'the 1960s' against 'the 1980s' in this way was to obscure what they had in common, and harsh words about undisciplined youth or progressive teachers supposedly fostering such indiscipline (a favourite target of the New Right, and of several of the subjects of my study) could do nothing to hold back the relentlessly individualizing impact of capitalist market relations as they penetrated ever further into everyday life.

3

The individualistic tone of late-twentieth-century culture was not, however, simply a product of neo-liberal economics. It also owed a good deal to the cultural shifts of the 1960s. One reason why neo-liberal hyper-individualism was so difficult to resist was that the 1960s had already done much to loosen the ties previously binding individuals into patterns of social solidarity. More than anything else 'the sixties' had represented a freeing up of personal relationships from prescribed roles as the young defied the authority of parents and women claimed a right to autonomy and self-fulfilment beyond wifely and maternal duty. When the women's liberation movement insisted that 'the personal is political', they were articulating currents of democratization in personal life which spread far beyond the circles inhabited by self-defined feminists. Across the whole of society the restrictions and bonds that had woven the social fabric together, often at great cost to personal happiness and fulfilment, were becoming looser. Rising expectations of personal freedom undermined deference towards parents, husbands, professionals, trade-union leaders, employers, and the state.

Personal liberation, however, could come at a price. In the heady aftermath of 1968 youthful idealists saw no contradiction between personal autonomy and new forms of social solidarity—whether expressed in community activism, grass roots industrial militancy, or, at its most utopian, experiments in communal living. But those who saw in the early 1970s eruption of such activities the green shoots of a post-capitalist social order were to be disappointed. All too easily the democratizing impulse of the sixties ran into channels which either offered no resistance to the individualistic culture of neo-liberalism or even actively contributed to its construction. Radical critique of the top-down paternalism of welfare provision was appropriated to legitimate neo-liberal dismantling of the 'nanny state'. Young workers might rebel against a workplace authoritarianism that their parents had accepted as normal, but their militancy provided no coherent alternative to the lure of private routes to betterment offered by neo-liberalism to the more fortunate and the more energetic.[39] 'New Age' exploration of inner spiritual resources fed into notions of social regeneration through 'positive thinking', spawning a literature of secular self-improvement, while spin-offs from Eastern mysticism found profitable niches in the management training programmes of global corporations.[40] Feminist rhetoric was used to legitimate the claims of privileged women to the kind of independence long enjoyed by men, often on the backs of their less fortunate sisters. The implications of 'the personal is political' shifted from *extending* political struggle into the private sphere, to *reducing* politics to the struggle for personal autonomy. Being true to oneself, shaping a coherent identity, and claiming recognition for one's difference became a central preoccupation of radical politics. While the flourishing of identity politics in the late twentieth century—feminist, gay, black, ethnic—served to identify sources of oppression originating beyond the operations of the market economy, it often did so in ways that tended to fragment rather than broaden the forces campaigning for social justice. At the very moment when neo-liberal economics were reversing a long-term trend towards reduced inequality, the new politics of identity privileged claims to cultural difference over struggles for economic equality: the left was 'winning cultural battles but losing the class war', as one commentator put it.[41] While the rise of neo-liberalism was primarily a result of a crisis of capitalist profitability as post-war expansion faltered in the 1970s, its capacity to become the common sense of the era also owed a good deal to the sapping of older forms of social solidarity by individualizing trends which were already flourishing during the preceding years of prosperity. Quite what balance should be struck between these explanations of cultural change is a question that will continue to be debated by historians of late-twentieth-century Britain.[42]

By the early 1990s, reflecting on these ambiguous currents of democracy and individualism in everyday life, social theorists were writing of an epochal change in the nature of the self. The modern individual, socially mobile and dis-embedded as never before from roles laid down by traditional structures of kinship, community, class, and gender, had unprecedented freedom to shape his or her own identity. In our efforts to make sense of our lives we could no longer rely on prescribed roles or external sources of authority. To answer the insistent questions 'Who am I?' and 'How should I live?' we looked inwards, constructing our sense of self in an ongoing biographical narrative, constantly revisited and revised, and it was in this process of reflexive self-fashioning that we defined a character for ourselves, a more or less coherent identity from which to negotiate the proliferating choice of lifestyles offered by modernity.[43] Nothing, it might be argued, better exemplified this new reflexivity than the commitment of the mass observers, willing repeatedly to 'write themselves' in response to searching questions about their lives, beliefs, and behaviour.

In an earlier book on Mass Observation's Second World War diarists, *Nine Wartime Lives*, I suggested that the mass observers represented an advance guard of the kind of self-reflexivity that late-twentieth-century theorists took to be characteristic of their own times.[44] It would, however, be wrong to exaggerate the degree to which the later twentieth century saw a fundamental transformation of the nature of the self. Certainly deference declined, individualism increased, and the idea that individuals had a right and a duty to choose their own lifestyles became culturally embedded as never before. Nevertheless, notions of the free, self-fashioning individual have been around in Western cultures for half a millennium, always associated with the idea of 'the modern' and always contrasted with 'traditional' ways of being bound into patterns of life prescribed by established social norms.[45] While the 'traditional' is constantly giving way to the 'modern', it seems to possess extraordinary powers of persistence. We all start off in dependency, and processes of childhood socialization shape our selfhoods in enduring ways; a fact richly illustrated in some of the following biographical essays. In adolescence and adult life we may rework inherited norms and values to fit the demands and opportunities of our times, but the choices we make about our lives—our ongoing 'projects of the self'—remain powerfully conditioned by emotional bonds of kinship and friendship. Empirical work on family, kin, and friendship networks in late-twentieth-century Britain does not bear out the bolder claims about self-fashioning and individualization.[46]

It is one of the limitations of the Mass Observation writing that, while it privileges individuals' accounts of themselves, it gives us only indirect clues about how they were seen by others. Our sense of self is shaped and confirmed through the eyes of others: we are chosen as much as we choose. Much of what appears to us as self-fashioning, as freely chosen, is in fact determined by social forces of which we are barely conscious. And in a profoundly unequal society there are obvious structural constraints on the freedom of individuals to pursue their own projects of the self. But if we are less self-determining than we like to think, it may also be the case that our forebears were more self-determining than we tend to assume. Accounts of the modern reflexive self often assume a past inhabited by unreflective creatures of habit, providing a convenient foil to the modernity of the self-fashioning individual. Such assumptions, however, may owe as much to the paucity of records of reflexivity in earlier times as they do to any fundamental difference in the ways in which people have striven to make sense of their lives. While to the outsider we may look like predictable products of our social conditioning, that is not how we perceive ourselves. Perhaps what the Mass Observation sources allow us to tap into is an elemental sense of individuality which, if not actually ahistorical, belongs to a far longer history of the making of the modern self whose roots are to be found in the Renaissance and Reformation, if not before. What is new, one might argue, is not so much the way ordinary people think about their self hoods, but the soliciting and archiving of confessional writing which makes their thoughts accessible to the researcher.[47] Such uncertainties about the extent to which the cultural changes of the later twentieth century have transformed the nature of the human self are unlikely to be resolved any time soon. But in speculating about the larger historical significance of the life stories presented here it is as well to bear them in mind.

★   ★   ★

In this chapter I have sketched some of the ways in which the history of the late twentieth century has, so far, been written. Looking back, in public as in personal time, we tend to think in decades: the boring 1950s, the exciting 1960s, the crisis-ridden 1970s, Mrs Thatcher's 1980s. The images and myths clustering around these pleasingly round numbers have been subject to the critical attention of historians seeking deeper currents of social change than those embodied in the 'decadist' imagination. Ideas of national decline fostered by politicians and commentators as a foil to their own proposals for reform have been scrutinized and revised. While opinions differ about the desirability of the shift from the quasi-corporatist structures of the post-war settlement towards the deregulated capitalism of the neo-liberal project, most historians would agree that the late twentieth century was not a bad time to be alive in Britain. Standards of living were rising more or less continuously; the collapse of the debt-fuelled economy had not yet arrived; nuclear war was avoided; and the ecological crunch remained a future nightmare rather than a present reality. Confronted with doom-laden visions of the future, members of my own generation often reflect that we have lived in a privileged bubble both in time and space. The seven individuals whose stories are told in the following chapters were all a little older, closer to the catastrophic history of the mid-century. Some of them, remembering those disasters, lived in expectation of the worst. Some were more inclined to celebrate the long peace, even while anticipating future catastrophe. Some were content simply to embrace their good fortune without too much thought for the future. All seven, in the choices they made about how to live, were helping to shape the history of their times, and the seriousness and honesty with which each wrote about themselves for Mass Observation gives us a glimpse of the many different histories that can—and no doubt eventually will—be written of late-twentieth-century Britain. Contemplating these stories also gives us something more universal: human beings—obstinate, intelligent, creative—making meaningful lives out of whatever fate chose to throw at them. In the end that is the only resource we have to put against the grimmer tides of contemporary history.

3

Housewife

When Caroline wrote for Mass Observation between 1982 and 1995 she was the Thatcherite wife of a small businessman. The business had its ups and downs, but it was successful enough to sustain a lifestyle of some privilege. She lived in a large Victorian house in West London, had a holiday flat in Spain, and a weekend retreat on an island in the Thames. There was money for affluent leisure pursuits, including membership of an exclusive London sports club with a ten-year waiting list, and the couple mingled with high society in Switzerland as members of a group of off-piste skiers. In the course of the 1980s she enjoyed multiple long-haul holidays—touring with her husband in Canada, the United States, South America, Tibet, and China, and package tours on her own in Egypt and India. She was sixty in 1982, and for a woman who had left school to go into domestic service at fourteen, she appeared to have done well.

Her writing for MO tells a different story. 'People think of me as that rich person who has got that lovely big house', she wrote, 'but I have wept tears enough to fill a swimming pool in this house'.[1] Trapped in a loveless marriage, she had used a diary since the 1950s 'to go on and on over the past with its many traumas, seeking explanation and a release from anger, frustration and a kind of intellectual loneliness'.[2] Her MO writing fulfilled much the same function, providing another opportunity to rehearse a life story replete with misfortunes, some of them extreme. A frustrated, unfulfilled sense of herself pervades her writing—a neglected child refused the education of which she was clearly capable; a faithful wife serving an ungrateful (and unfaithful) husband who had only married her for her money (compensation following a serious accident) and treated her with contempt; a devoted mother of five children born during the first six years of her marriage and brought up single-handedly with no help from her husband, unable to divorce when the children were off her hands because the family business (on which some of the children were dependent) needed her property to survive.

But she refused to see herself as a victim, or to blame her misfortunes on an unjust society. If she had become, as she once described herself, nothing more than 'a little robot programmed to serve',[3] she had only herself to blame: 'It is not society that is at fault. The fault dear Brutus...'[4] The quotation, which she truncated, actually continues:

> The fault, dear Brutus, is not in our stars,
> But in ourselves, that we are underlings.

Cassius' message was that he and Brutus did not have to settle for their subordination to Caesar, that they were free to rebel. Caroline, blaming herself for her failure to rebel, took responsibility for her 'underling' status. And there was a certain pride at the root of that self-blame. Unhappy she might be, but, despite everything, she had survived, and had done so by her own efforts. It was to that pride that Mrs Thatcher spoke: stand on your own feet, reject dependency on trade unions or the 'nanny state', refuse the corrupting permissiveness of so-called 'progressive' teachers, resist socialism. Caroline identified with Thatcher's anti-socialist politics not just because her lifestyle depended on her husband's entrepreneurial success, but also because her own life story, as she understood it, exemplified the values of self-reliance that Mrs Thatcher proclaimed. 'I was emotionally right wing', she wrote in 1983, 'long before I found any good economic reasons for becoming so'.[5]

I

In 1928, when Caroline was no more than six years old, her father tried to kill her—or so she believed. Her mother had died two years earlier in childbirth (along with the baby, a much desired son). Recovering from TB, she had been warned that another pregnancy would be dangerous for her health, and that was cause enough for Caroline's maternal grandmother to brand the bereaved husband a murderer. The grandmother, herself Protestant and upwardly mobile from a Lancashire weaving family, had disapproved of the marriage from the outset, since the father was working class (a chauffeur, turned bus driver), Irish, and Catholic to boot. Thrown out from his mother-in-law's house where he had been living, Caroline's father was told to leave his daughter behind and never come back. In desperation he kidnapped the child from a party and took her to live with his sister: she remembered the journey on the open top of a double-decker bus in the rain, her father crying tears of desperation while she huddled under a mackintosh sheet in her shantung silk party dress. The sister, who had a baby of her own, couldn't take them in for long and for the next two years she was shunted from relative to relative.

When she was six her father remarried. Her stepmother, who had previously been employed as a nurse in a mental asylum, had a violent temper and frequently hit her. Forbidden to go out to play after school, she was locked in the coal cellar when she disobeyed. When the boys that her father so much wanted came along, she was treated as 'a slave to [their] whims and fancies'.[6] Her diet was meagre and she was denied the cakes and the ice-creams she was sent out to buy for her half-brothers. When the school started to provide milk, her stepmother was only dissuaded from refusing to pay for her as well as for the boys by her father's warning that 'you can't do that—people will talk'.[7]

People did talk—the neighbours, or perhaps an aunt—and the NSPCC (child protection) sent an inspector. 'I could...have pleaded that I was a beaten-up, locked-up, half-starved cruelly treated child and I knew it.'[8] But instead she lied, telling the inspector that she had nothing to complain of. When her mother was sick, and when she died, no one had explained to Caroline what was going on. So, intelligent and resourceful, she listened to the adults talking and drew her own conclusions. Walking back from the cemetery, aged four, she had overheard them wondering 'what are we going to do with the poor motherless bitch'.[9] By the time her father remarried, having been passed from pillar to post, she was all too aware that the world did not owe her a living. She knew that fledgling birds who lost their mothers starved to death in the nest, and by the time the NSPCC arrived she had also learned that Chinese girls were often killed at birth or 'put out on the rubbish dump for the dogs to get...I couldn't be less than thankful that things weren't worse!'[10] However badly her stepmother treated her, 'my dad was all I had left in the world', and she wanted to stay with him: 'I loved my dad and he loved her. He would hate me if I got her into trouble...'[11]

Caroline was well aware that her father could do little to protect her. There were occasional moments of closeness, when she helped him make a rag rug or build a garden shed, but in front of the stepmother he kept his distance, understanding (she believed) that any affection he showed would only make things worse for her as soon as his back was turned. She even understood when her father tried to kill her. They were, again, on an open-topped double-decker bus, this time returning from a hospital appointment:

The bus stopped under a yew tree when he suddenly invited me to 'pick the pretty yew berries?...Surely he knew that they were poisonous?...Anyway I picked them quickly and put them in my pocket. When we got back he whispered something in my stepmother's ear and she went a ghastly white under her freckles and she said 'Oh B ..., B ... what have you done?' Then she turned on me and said 'What have you done with those berries', and I just turned them out of my pocket without saying anything.[12]

Caroline never spoke of this incident while her father or stepmother were alive, but she was sure that, believing she had nothing to look forward to in life, he had wanted to kill her.

He might have felt differently had he known how she was doing at school, but her stepmother hid Caroline's school reports, on one occasion burning a report and telling him that it was so bad she didn't want him to see it. In fact 'school was my joy',[13] an oasis of freedom. She did well, and hated the school holidays. As she approached school-leaving age—then fourteen—one of her teachers, recognizing her ability, wanted her to sit for a scholarship and even offered to adopt the girl herself and pay for her to stay on at school and go to university.[14] Her father would have none of it, partly, she believed, because 'my stepmother wouldn't have wanted me "preening myself" in my college uniform right under her nose in the village'.[15] Her own later observation on missing an opportunity that would surely have transformed her life was characteristically dismissive: the teacher was a childless war widow whose inflated expectations of her she would never have been able to fulfil. So she left school in December 1935, two weeks before her fourteenth birthday, and went into domestic service.

2

She didn't mind. She had long looked forward to escaping the tyranny of her stepmother. Her employers appreciated her domestic skills, and she was overjoyed to be earning ten shillings a week in place of the one penny she had previously been allowed for pocket money. When her maternal grandmother found her a job with a nearby family she was encouraged to take evening classes, learning French and studying accounting and business economics. She spent her afternoons off in the local library reading about ancient Egypt, participated in amateur dramatics, and even found time for a first boyfriend. By the age of sixteen she had completed a correspondence course and taken the exam qualifying her for a job in the civil service. Not expecting to pass she moved into central London to train as a telephonist, supporting herself with what savings she had managed to accumulate, part-time jobs in Woolworths and a restaurant, and help from her paternal grandmother, a tough and independent woman who had been a source of moral support for Caroline throughout her childhood. 'Irish Gran', she wrote many years later, 'was a true realist with whom I could identify...as much a lone traveller as I was...Both of us seemed to be "victims" but in truth neither of us ever was, and we both learned well enough how to capitalise on our assets when the occasion presented itself.'[16] This was true enough of her grandmother, who had started work as a scullery maid at the age of eleven, borne two illegitimate children (one of them Caroline's father), married twice but never stopped working, accumulated savings in a Swiss bank account (one of the husbands was Swiss), and, anticipating during the 1930s that the mechanization of housework would undermine the demand for domestic servants, re-skilled herself as a cordon bleu cook.

Happily at work as a trained telephonist, Caroline was surprised to find that she had passed the civil service exam. At first she was inclined to turn down the offer of a job in the National Savings Bank, but what convinced her was the promise of long-term security of employment: 'The government service was made for me. As long as I was a good girl I would acquire a permanent daddy so to speak...':[17] dependable, unlike her real one. Economically secure, she developed a passion for skating, running a club with her workmates at the Earls Court ice rink and mixing with a rather wild clique whose flamboyant leader, a star on the ice, adopted her as his dancing partner. She also had a vigorous intellectual life. At sixteen, having abandoned religion, she discovered Marx and communism: 'the nearest...I ever got to crusading...until I realised that there was no way I was going to kill my bosses for the sake of some sort of instant equality...'[18] Subsequently she read Freud; flirted with the possibility that Hitler had all the answers; and finally found an abiding faith in economic liberalism by reading Herbert Spencer. After the outbreak of war her social life got increasingly out of hand. She had been raped by her dancing partner, but she blamed herself for trusting him and pretended that nothing had happened. Many of the girls she mixed with were sexually active, and she feared she was 'going to become some sort of tramp if I didn't get out of it all'.[19] It was her new daddy, the savings bank, who came to her rescue, asking for volunteers to set up duplicate files in Harrogate in case the London records were bombed.

In Harrogate she went dancing at weekends meeting plenty of predatory males, but, determined not to compromise her independence by getting pregnant, she fended them off before things got serious. Then, in 1942, she fell in love for the first and only time in her life. Mac was a miner's son, four years older than her, a bomber pilot who loved poetry, didn't press her to go to bed with him, and hated war. Although convinced that Hitler had to be stopped, he found it impossible to reconcile himself to dropping bombs on German women and children trapped through no fault of their own in an evil system. To minimize his guilt he took pains to hit the military targets, putting his own life and that of his crew at greater risk. He was killed over Cologne in 1943, the day after the couple had announced their intention of marrying once the war was over. Mac told her that if he did not survive she should find herself 'a nice English boy to get married to and have children, because that is what I will have died for'.[20]

She wrote little about her life during the six years following her lover's death. Back in London she had plenty of suitors, and was haunted by Mac's notion that she owed a reproductive duty to the nation, but she had no desire to get married. Later she was to look back on these years as a happy time when she was 'independent and beholden to no-one'.[21] There was an affair with an older, divorced American officer who offered her marriage if she would join him in the States, but there were complications in his own life and she declined.

In 1949, in a bizarre accident, she suffered brain injuries when a woman fell on her through a glass roof at the local hospital. For some time, 'inarticulate and grunting like an idiot', she was unable to communicate.[22] But she understood what was happening and was determined to stand on her own feet, accepting help from a friendly neighbour, but saying nothing to her relatives and crossing the street to avoid workmates whose well-intentioned sympathy she could not abide.

Unable to continue in the civil service job, she soon found work washing-up in a café and subsequently as a secretary and wages clerk. With a small civil service pension, a flat with security of tenure, the prospect of substantial compensation for her injuries, and in line to resume her civil service job once the doctors gave her a clean bill of health, her freedom and independence seemed set to continue; all the more so since her periods had stopped and her doctors told her that the injury to her pituitary gland meant that she would be unable to conceive. Writing for MO at various times in the 1980s and 90s she gives divergent accounts of her reaction to this news, no doubt reflecting the ambivalence she felt at the time. If the doctors were right there was little point trying to be virtuous: 'why not relax about it all and think about really enjoying a relationship, like everyone else seemed to do. Sex included.'[23] On the other hand she was reluctant to accept her infertility and 'set out to prove [the doctors] wrong'.[24] Ambivalent, like many a single woman approaching thirty, about whether or not she wanted children, her efforts at contraception were half-hearted.

William, four years younger than her, had been demobbed in 1948. A charming and ambitious young man, he was building up a metal-working business in a couple of rented garages when she met him some time after her accident. They had few shared interests, but she enjoyed his company and admired his entrepreneurial drive and self-confidence. Though not very interested in him sexually, she let him have his way, and to her delight and dismay found herself pregnant: happy to be a fully functioning female again, but reluctant to marry a man she did not love. An older ex-lover, arguing that she needed time to fully recover from the trauma of the accident before taking decisions that would affect her whole life, urged her to have an abortion. But in the absence of risks to her own health or genetic reasons to fear for the baby's health she could find no moral justification for an abortion. (Years later she discovered information which, she felt, would have justified an abortion and spared her a miserable marriage, when William's mother confided in her that he had been epileptic in his childhood.) So she chose instead to accept William's offer of marriage, an offer she had not expected to receive when she told him she was pregnant. He had a long-standing obsession with an older woman, and, as soon became clear, no intention of abandoning his other sexual pursuits. It seems clear from her account that William's response was largely mercenary: he needed her money to expand his business. She half knew what she was getting into: 'The night before I had to go to the registry office . . . a little man at the back of my head kept telling me not to do it.'[25] But, having ruled out abortion, the only alternative would have been to follow the example of her grand-mother, who had borne two children as a single mother, refusing offers of marriage. However much she admired Irish Gran's defiant inde-pendence, the difficulties of such a course were obvious, and, believing that many of her own father's inadequacies stemmed from his shame at the stigma of illegitimacy, she felt duty-bound to avoid imposing the same burden on her own child. So the years of freedom and independence ended. As earnest of her intention to commit herself to the marriage she burned her correspondence with her gentle bomber pilot, the only man she ever loved.

3

The marriage was unhappy from the start. A charmer in the world outside, William treated Caroline as a convenience, not a person. He shared none of her cultural or intellectual interests and looked down on book learning with contempt. After forty years of marriage to him she still had no idea of something as fundamental as whether or not he believed in God (she didn't). 'William would never talk to me about anything at all personal . . . His pet phrase has been "I'm not going to discuss it." . . . If I ever got too fierce with [him] . . . he would just flounce out of the door and drive away.' Which, she added stoically, was 'better than being hit'.[26] The sex was plentiful, expert (he 'knew his onions and had read the books'), but impersonal: 'sometimes I felt like I was an unpaid prostitute as there was no caring attached . . . He cared about his sexual performance, but not about how I felt about the rela-tionship in the first place.'[27] So she was left to speculate about orgasm, which she experienced as 'rather like a glorified sneeze': would imagination have transformed it into something which made the earth move had they been in love? But they were not, and she got no joy from her sex life.

What she did get was five babies in fewer than seven years, four boys and finally a girl. For the first three years of the marriage she was marooned in her top-floor flat, while William left for work at six in the morning and seldom returned before eleven at night. After the second child she wanted to stop, but before the pill and without some co-operation from her partner she found contraception impossible. Her use of suppositories was ineffective and when she acquired a Dutch cap after the fourth pregnancy her husband would not allow her to use it. His reasoning, she reports, was strategic. He understood that it was only the children that kept her in the marriage, and that (as she later learned he had boasted at the time) 'the secret of controlling me was to keep me at the kitchen sink'.[28]

However bad their relationship, she continued to admire and trust William's entrepreneurship. He used her compensation money to buy the lease on premises for the business and, after three years, to put down a deposit on the large Victorian house where she was to spend the rest of her life. By this time the business owed her so much money that it was officially bankrupt and to regularize matters he set up a company in their joint names. In theory this gave her equal rights, but as the solicitor acting for them explained to William, his control would remain untrammelled: 'you have your wife as company secretary and you hold a meeting once a year in bed'.[29] In practice her role as company secretary was a mere formality; but she remained powerless, terrified of rows, and unable to challenge his authority.

It was motherhood that gave her a purpose in life, although managing five small children—the oldest was only six when the youngest was born—was no bed of roses. Things did not improve when the three older boys went to the local secondary modern school where discipline was lax and, she believed, the teachers were more interested in allowing them to develop their egos than in inculcating useful skills or knowledge. As teenagers in the late 1960s they played around on motor bikes, experimented with drugs, truanted from school, went joyriding with friends in stolen cars, and engaged in petty crime. She knew, more or less, what was going on, talked to a social worker about the drug problem, and was pleased that the police harassed them and occasionally caught them in the act. On one occasion she went through their pockets and 'relieved that little gang of six different kinds of knives when I sensed that they were hyped up and up to no good at all'.[30] Somehow she kept on top of the situation, and, with support from her doctor, she stuck it out with the most seriously delinquent of the boys, refusing to reward behaviour she believed to be the result of drug-induced schizophrenia by calling in psychiatric help until, in his early twenties, he eventually came to his senses.

While all this was going on William, cheerfully indulging his sons, was no help whatsoever. He frustrated her efforts to make them help around the house or garden, or even to make their own beds. 'Boys don't want to do things like that', he said, overruling her in front of them and leaving her feeling 'right back where I was in my stepmother's home. A servant for my own offspring.'[31] She tried to make them do their homework, but the boys, identifying with their father, refused. As adolescents William paid their fines, saying 'boys will be boys', and refusing to believe that they were seriously delinquent. Although she coped, there were times when she came close to breaking point, and on one occasion in the mid-1960s she tried to commit suicide. William had arrived home one afternoon to find her, ill with a high temperature, struggling to get her two eldest sons down from a tree where they were scrapping and in danger of falling onto the concrete path below. Instead of helping he demanded his dinner, and when she angrily insisted that the boys' safety came first, he cut her short: 'I can see what sort of mood you're in. I'll go and stay in a hotel for the weekend and come back when you are better.' (His code, perhaps, for visiting a mistress?) When he said this she reached down a bottle of phenobarbs which she kept above the kitchen sink and took enough (she was later told) to kill three people. Undeterred, he walked out saying: 'Oh go and make yourself sick you silly woman.'[32] After he left, with 'clouds of nothingness sweeping over me', she got herself to her doctor who lived in the same street and rushed her into casualty. Caroline attributed her survival to the fact that her six-year-old daughter came into the kitchen 'and it dawned on me that I would be leaving [her] to the mercies of five uncaring males—and a stepmother no doubt. One might call it a call back to duty.'[33]

Duty continued. The three older boys left school with no qualifications and two of them, barely literate, remained dependent on the family firm for employment. Supported by their father, they resisted her attempts to enrol them at a further education college, and when she tried to push them out into the real world William, basking in their admiration, found excuses to hang on to them. Until she was able, as she put it, to offload them both onto decent women, she remained their domestic servant, and William would not even allow them to contribute from their earnings to the household expenses. Caroline's fourth child seems to have set out to be as good as his brothers were bad. He was 'born calm and easy'[34] and grew up much closer to her than to his father. Both he, and the final child, her daughter, did their homework, got into the local grammar school, and emerged with A-levels. Although he went on to do a degree in business studies, her youngest son had little interest in making money and no time for the philistine materialism of his father's world. William, she wrote, could not understand people who, like herself and her son, wasted their time with poetry, music, or literature. Perhaps Caroline found in her fourth son an echo of the gentle bomber pilot she had once loved.

Her second son left school at fifteen, but showed more independence than his brothers, putting the skills he learned from tinkering with motor bikes to good use in building up a successful garage business. But the boy was a carbon copy of his father, and gratified though Caroline was that he could stand on his own feet, her heart went out to his unhappy wife:

Like me, [Rosemary] was miserable from year one. The boy's charm was now only what other people saw. We were supposed to be wives and mothers. Not persons anymore. And 'they' held the purse strings...[35]

When her own children left school, however, Rosemary, still in her thirties, broke free with a divorce that caused bitter arguments in the wider family. The garage business had been dependent on her administrative skills and collapsed when she quit. Caroline kept in touch with her ex-daughter-in-law and was pleased when she remarried happily. She would have liked to have followed her daughter-in-law's example, and frequently dreamt of divorcing William, but nothing came of it. The difference between her situation and Rosemary's, she remarked in 1991, lay 'in the generations and [in] ideas about what women could or should do'.[36] Her break for freedom, in so far as it occurred, took a different form.

4

Since childhood Caroline's greatest pleasure had been in learning. She loved school and had taken evening classes while working as a domestic servant, not just to improve herself but also 'for the sake of learning itself'.[37] As a clerk in Harrogate during the war she was introduced to

art, ballet, Shakespeare, and poetry by a left-wing flat mate who became
a life-long female friend. In 1966, after her suicide attempt, she started
attending foreign language classes one evening a week, brushing aside
her husband's objection that as a mother she had no right to any such
self-indulgence. Before the war she had briefly studied German in
order to help her Irish Gran read letters from her Swiss relatives, and
in the early 1980s when she spent three weeks with these relatives she
knew enough to enjoy discussing politics with them. She also took
classes in Spanish and French, keeping the languages alive by reading
with the aid of a dictionary. In 1970 she enrolled on a four-year diploma course in sociology at the local technical college, progressing
four years later to an Open University degree in social sciences which
she finally completed in 1981. After that she continued to make time
to read history, autobiography, and historical fiction and to keep up
with public affairs with the local paper, the *Daily Telegraph*, and the
Economist. Up against William's scornful opposition to her 'silly courses'
she insisted that one reason for persisting with her studies had been to
set an example to the children, to demonstrate that there was more to
life than mere getting and spending. Burdened with domesticity and
her work for the company it was hard to find time or space to study,
or later for her MO writing. Much of her OU work was done at night
after the others had gone to bed, although sometimes, during the day,
she was able to work undisturbed by hiding in the attic or the toilet.
At some point—but perhaps not until the later 1980s—she finally
acquired a room of her own, with bed, desk, phone, and TV: 'It doesn't
save me from interruptions', she wrote in 1988, 'but they do have to
walk upstairs and won't do that unless they really need to'.[38]

However much she enjoyed learning for learning's sake she felt a
need to express her commitment in utilitarian terms. Although advised
by her OU tutor to take an arts course, she chose social sciences
because she saw economics and politics as more relevant to her needs:
'Any sensible animal', she wrote, 'tries to "keep both eyes open in the
jungle"'.[39] And jungle it was in the difficult circumstances of the 1970s
when she combined parenting, domesticity, and study with a full-time
job helping to manage the family business. She kept the books, dealt
with wages and invoices, and kept abreast of relevant employment
legislation. At its height the business employed fifteen workers. None
of them were trade-union members, but the 'family firm' atmosphere
was no protection against rampant inflation. Wages could not be held

down if they were to retain their skilled workers, and the firm had to quote for long runs when there was no way of telling what their raw material costs would be. Eventually, hit by the loss of a major customer and a swingeing increase in the rent for the works premises when the lease fell due, they went into voluntary liquidation: 'We were working-class bosses who didn't understand much about high finance and we didn't want to lose everything we had striven so hard to get. We retreated to the square one from whence we had expanded.'[40] During the years she wrote for MO there was no new expansion: in 1989 they had only two workers, plus their otherwise unemployable sons.

The business might have retreated to square one, but Caroline did not. Already in the early 1970s her letters to the local paper attracted the attention of the Conservative Party, and she was invited to join their ward committee. Whether she found time to work actively for the party in the 1970s is unclear, but during the 1980s she served as a school governor, ran an annual fundraising event in her large garden, attended party conferences, and canvassed in elections. In the Tory Party she was never made to feel inferior or awkward about her working-class accent, and she was dismissive of the sociologically fashionable notions of deference as an explanation of working-class Conservatism that she came across on her OU course: 'In my family . . . we are all what you might call working-class Tories. We were all very poor once but we are not daft.'[41] There was nothing deferential about Caroline's Conservatism. It reflected, rather, values of independence and standing on your own feet that she had internalized since childhood. Reflecting on the miners' strike in 1984 she took pride in the fact that, unlike Scargill's men, an earlier generation of working-class girls brought up to domestic service had accepted the inevitability of economic change (in their case the mechanization of housework) and retrained themselves, as she herself had done, as shop girls, clerks, telephonists, or secretaries. When, following her accident in 1949, her trade union and her colleagues urged her to live on disability benefit rather than seek employment, she preferred to pick herself up, dust herself down, and make her own way. She told with relish a story of her Irish Gran in old age refusing to be patronized by a well-meaning welfare worker, muttering as the visitor left the house, 'That lot'll be the ruin of us all', a remark Caroline took as prophetic of the scourge of welfare dependency which she believed engulfed Britain from the 1960s.[42]

However unhappy she was about William's materialistic philistinism she always admired his entrepreneurial drive. Thatcherism spoke to values of working-class independence, values central to her own experience as a self-defined 'working-class boss'.[43]

Equally important to her politics was her hostility to much of what the 1960s stood for: secondary modern schoolteachers neglecting literacy in favour of letting her boys develop their egos, or trendy vicars turning a blind eye to sin and blaming everything bad on social deprivation. As a parent of unruly adolescent boys she knew better than to explain away crime as a product of material deprivation, and was all too aware of the ability of young delinquents to lead sympathetic social workers up the garden path. In 1973, horrified by discovering hard porn imagery in her sons' magazines, she signed up with Mary Whitehouse's crusade against the portrayal of sex and violence in the media. She disliked what she saw as the loosening moral climate, but she had no problem with the changes in British society brought about by Commonwealth immigration. Among her sons' friends were people from West Indian, Nigerian, Pakistani, and Indian backgrounds, but race had nothing to do with the delinquency she deplored: 'No hint of [racial] prejudice ever came from me.'[44] Believing that intermarriage was 'the right way to break into the "laagers", of any class or colour', she was delighted when her eldest son married a Chinese Malaysian woman. She replied in the affirmative to the question posed by an MO directive in 1990 about whether she would choose to sit next to a coloured person on a bus, adding: 'I am an old white lady wearing a hat, but it doesn't mean I am like the media says I'm likely to be ... I am categorised by my skin, my age and hat, from the start. I understand. I am sad about it.'[45] And sad also about the viciously anti-immigrant opinions she overheard while waiting for the bus.

Ever since learning about Darwin, aged eleven, Caroline had 'accepted the "fact" that I was only a sophisticated monkey', although she knew better than to let on that she doubted the existence of God to teachers in her Church of England school, to her Catholic father, or, later, her Protestant grandmother: 'I kept my intellectual arguments to myself and people like me—and I still do.'[46] Though not religious, she approved of religious education as moral training for the young, and tried to live by a Christian moral code. Caroline was far from subscribing to the ultra-individualist implications of Thatcher's much misunderstood remark that there is 'no such thing as society'. On the contrary, her powerful sense of duty was underpinned by a belief in the sacralized authority of the society into which one is born: 'If for God one thinks "Society" as a whole then the whole is greater than its parts... As far as I'm concerned society *is*... the God that we serve.'[47] She was clear-minded enough to acknowledge the moral relativism implicit in this stance: she would have 'tucked myself and my children' as readily into the dominant ethic of Nazi Germany had she had the misfortune to be born there.[48] Growing up unwanted and 'out of place' she wanted above all to be normal, to fit in, to be a conforming member of a larger normative order.

This desire to conform was, no doubt, one reason why she failed to divorce William, something she had long fantasized about doing once her youngest child left school. The 'dream of divorce'[49] continued to haunt her into her seventies, until she finally resigned herself to the fact that it was not going to happen. For a decade and a half she had repeatedly asked for a divorce, only to be met by William's blank refusal to discuss it. She herself was all too aware of the difficulties that would have to be confronted in disentangling the assets tied up in the family business, on which two of her children continued to be dependent. Despite the collapse of the firm in the late 1970s, the assets were considerable, but they did not give her the 'peaceful and pleasant plateau' she had hoped for in old age, with time to read all the unread books on her shelves and to become fluent in her several languages.[50] She was still working as company secretary and trying (in vain) to get William to take seriously the need to put things in order for a smooth transition of control to the children once they became too old to carry on. Declining physically, her time filled up taking care of house and garden (gardening was, alongside child-rearing, the one subject in which she felt she had some expertise); coping with William (also in decline); hosting frequent gatherings of her children, all of whom lived nearby; and looking after the grandchildren. Any thoughts of breaking free were trumped, now as before, by motherhood: 'I had to be a stable mother once and now I have to be a stable granny person', she wrote, despondently, in 1994.[51]

5

Writing for Mass Observation played an important role in Caroline's self-management, although she struggled to find the time to do it, always feeling that her first duty was to the family. Trapped as she was by domestic chores, at least they left her mind free to wander (unlike her work for the company). But 'a wandering mind has lots of ideas it would like to have time to communicate to someone'.[52] Her closest friend, with whom she shared everything, had died in 1979 and in her writing for the OU she played safe, not always saying what she really thought for fear of disapproval from Trotskyist tutors. When she took up MO, shortly after graduating from the OU, there was no such need for self-censorship, and she justified spending time on it on the grounds that it enabled her to give back to society something of what she had received through her subsidized adult education. MO helped to relieve her intellectual loneliness and, because it could itself be seen as a kind of duty, it also served to legitimate the time she 'stole' for her writing. Just as she'd justified her commitment to adult education by saying she did it to set an example to the children, so, with MO, she needed a sense of larger purpose to justify the time spent 'doing what I want to do as distinct from what I feel that I ought to do'.[53] Desire and duty were inextricably entangled in her mind. But neither the adult education nor the work for MO would have happened unless, somewhere inside her self-constructed cage of duties, there still burned a spirit which delighted in learning, and in writing, for its own sake. And, no doubt, the same went for motherhood. Caroline had a lot to bear, but the affluence of her life style—the travel, the second homes—must have provided some compensation. It is difficult to resist the conclusion that she was, much of the time, rather happier than she let on when she was writing for MO.

4

Teacher

Janet had something in common with Caroline. Both women lost their mothers to tuberculosis at a young age and suffered a childhood whose miseries they rehearsed at length in their writing for MO. But where Caroline wanted above all to fit into what she saw as the prevailing respectable social norms, Janet, by contrast, placed herself relentlessly on the outside, and she used MO to give voice to the oppressed and excluded kids to whom she devoted her professional life as a self-declared 'scum class teacher'.[1] Where Caroline took responsibility for her fate upon herself, Janet raged against social injustice and the elites who sustain it. One of her greatest pleasures, she revealed in a list of pleasures prepared for MO, was 'cursing, i.e. externalisation of painful affect rather than offering it up to him up there'.[2] Quiet reflection serving a confessional purpose was common among mass observers: but in Janet's case the therapy lay, precisely, in the 'cursing'. She rants and she raves. Frequently she expresses herself in angry, undisciplined tirades, polemic edged with paranoia. It would be easy to dismiss this writing as self-indulgent and incoherent and I have been tempted to do so myself. But it pays to restrain one's irritation. The cursing is not as undisciplined as it appears at first sight: it reflects the working through of a coherent world view, a strange amalgam of residual Marxist–Leninism, anti-communism, radical feminism, and a Hogarthian vision of corruption, the lower depths, and evil in power. Behind the cursing is a woman whose energy, resilience, intelligence, and acid wit throws vivid light on the darker side of late-twentieth-century London.

Aged fifty-one when she started writing for MO in 1984, she worked part time, usually combining several different jobs. For many years she had taught sociology and, later, English in 'a clapped out, 57%

ethnic...girls school in a run-down area' of South London.[3] Forced
to take early retirement—so that the local education authority, she
alleged, could replace her with cheaper foreign teachers on short-term
contracts—she found work teaching sociology to adolescents at one
technical college and to adults at another. Alongside this she worked
with delinquent youths in an out-of-school unit—'the Last Hope
School', she called it—and as a home tutor to school refusers. She also
made time for voluntary work, teaching reading, writing, and 'life
skills' at a Barnardo's community home; and English and sociology at
a Saturday supplementary school run by parents of Black British
children. 'It is quite hard', she remarked in 1992, 'to teach at home and
in three other places; one has to keep a firm grip on the kinds of
knowledge and the discourses floating about the place these days'.[4]
Early in the new century, well past retirement age, she was still working
in further education and (now paid) at the Caribbean supplementary
school; and as late as 2011 (aged seventy-eight) she was still doing some
part-time teaching.

'Do not think that I base my remarks on my opinion only,' she
wrote; 'I subsume the opinions of my various classes.'[5] Subsumption
meant sympathy, and she writes not as a detached observer, but as a
passionately involved participant able to see the social world through
the eyes of her pupils. She used her contributions to MO to give voice
not only to her own grievances as a 'scum class teacher', but also to the
attitudes of the black, Asian, and white working-class young people
whom she encountered in her work. Her career coincided with a
rapid decline in the status of teaching and, latterly (she believed), in the
efficacy of schools. Letting off steam to MO, she frequently painted a
picture of an education system laid waste by the combined impact of
a minority of thuggishly disruptive pupils and an almost equally disruptive management, expert only in deploying the trappings of 'theory'
to disguise its own ineptitude. But these were irritants to be borne, and
she never allowed them to sour her dedication to her work as a teacher.
The cursing worked its therapeutic purpose, and her fury never turns
to despair. In 2010, aged seventy-seven, she explained that the purpose
of her writing for MO had been not only to 'tell about teaching and
our sad state schools', but also to record 'how some children win
through.'[6] Although she seldom says so, it is clear from her detailed
accounts of classroom life that she was a gifted teacher, adept at establishing rich and mutually rewarding relationships with her pupils. 'It is

a good little job if you can hack it; never mind the worsened image; do what you think is right.'[7]

I

Born in Belfast to English parents, Janet's early childhood memories were of a mother in and out of hospital dying slowly of TB and a 'depressive, bossy bully' of a father who paid her so little attention that she became jealous of his pet budgerigar and was glad when it died.[8] Among her earliest memories was the occasion, aged four or five, when, overflowing with delight and pride, she ran home from elementary school, to announce that she could read, only to be met by indifference from parents too immersed in their own miseries to respond to their daughter's achievement. Her father had risen via grammar school from a working-class background to become a 'small time manager' in an engineering company. Her mother, daughter of a watch mender, who, before her marriage, had dealt with foreign correspondence in a textile mill, died when Janet was eight, after which the girl was shuttled back and forth between Ireland and Rochdale, in Lancashire, Northern England, where her maternal grandmother and much of the wider family lived: 'any time you're passing, pass' was the bleak greeting of one Rochdale relative, a phrase long remembered as summing up the loneliness and insecurity of these years.[9]

Her warmest memories were of a Plymouth Brethren couple, neighbours in Belfast, with whom she lived for a year or so towards the end of her mother's life and kept in touch with for the rest of their lives. She had been led to their house by their dog, Peter, which seems to have been as thoughtful and kindly as its owners. On one occasion, she recalled, when her father was about to hit her for cheeking him: 'Peter got up and took dad's hand in his mouth. Very nicely . . . I loved the dog and my "foster" mother.'[10] And her foster father, surprisingly for a member of the sect, had interesting books in the house: it was there that she first came across Mass Observation's founder, Tom Harrisson, whose anthropological book on South Sea cannibals was published in 1937.

She wanted to stay with the Brethren couple, but when she was eight, following her mother's death, her father—'ever anxious to do the least he could for the least expense possible'—dispatched her again to England, this time to 'a cheap boarding Roman Catholic nun-run hell-hole' in Lancashire, where she suffered for the next three years, caned for persistent masturbation (a symptom, she later wrote, of anxiety not, as the nuns alleged, of the sin of lust):

and for other indiscretions such as denying the existence of Father Xmas the great gift giver...a fanciful part of the RC nuns' belief system. Perhaps he is a bit like the Blessed Virgin May and there to mollify the strictness of the original father.[11]

She was also punished for reading the King James Bible, not the author-ized Catholic translation. Caught between the ideological tyranny of the nuns—the 'pizdi' as she calls them (a very rude Russian word)—and the Unitarianism (and lower-middle-class status anxiety) of the Rochdale aunt with whom she spent her weekends, Janet decided that she much preferred the Protestant fundamentalism of the Brethren, especially since her foster father, 'seeing I was a nervous and sad child [, had assured her]...very kindly that people under the age of 14 could not go to Hell'.[12] It was the Brethren, she wrote after she had given up religion altogether, who gave her 'a smallish base of emotional security' and whose values she internalized.[13]

Things looked up after she was expelled from the convent, aged eleven. Her father sent her to a Protestant grammar school in the Irish Republic, where she thrived academically and eventually won a schol-arship to study English at Queen's University in Belfast. Although her father would have preferred her to go out to work, he was eventually persuaded by her stepmother and a female neighbour to allow her to take up the scholarship. While she writes in some detail about her unhappy childhood, she gave MO only occasional glimpses of her life during her twenties, thirties, and forties. After graduating from Queen's she taught briefly in Ireland and then went to London to take a post-graduate teaching certificate at the Institute of Education. But, as for many women, it was her sex life rather than her professional qualifica-tions which did most to determine the shape of her career. An early affair ended after an unwanted pregnancy and an abortion whose trauma remained raw fifty years later:

I managed to abort myself though I had some assistance, which was inadmis-sible. At that time abortion was illegal unless you had two signatories, 200 guineas and were better class than I was. Once the bleeding began then you had to endure the pains, which are like mild contractions, nasty for you cannot have your true reward, a lovely child at the end. If the clerical/medical/legal chaps got to you, then they 'patched you up'. You had to hang about, in my case a fortnight, until the waters and blood had mostly drained then the foetus would be dead in the womb...The ambulance men were very nasty but the male docs were OK and a packet drained was delivered in Hendon. The nurse refused to say if it was a boy or a girl so as to punish me. FUCK HER BITCH-FACED SLAG. After ten days I was discharged and went and did my exams a few weeks later... [14]

Much later, reading a medical book, she realized how near she had been to septicaemia and death.

Two years after the abortion, pregnant again after a two-night stand with a married man on leave from his job in Russia, she decided that more than anything else she wanted to be a mother. Having a child out of wedlock in the late 1950s was 'very dodgy, practically a crime, as well as a big sin...like wanking it showed an untoward degree of female independence.... To conceal the disgrace...I emigrated [as 'a £10 pom'] to Australia and never let on to Daddy.'[15] She found work in Brisbane and had the baby there. Returning to London, she got her old job back and set her sights on a teaching career. But in 1963, having failed to get a senior post in a leading South London comprehensive school, she decided that the only way to ensure a reasonable economic future, and a house, for herself and her son was to get married to a long-standing friend: 'We married for liking, not sex, and for the bourgeois thing of the house...it was nearly impossible for an unmarried mother to get a mortgage...If I had got the classy job I would have been able to get a mortgage and would not have got married.'[16]

Janet made friends easily, and from her student days onwards seems to have been drawn especially to refugees from Nazism and Communism. She had been fascinated and horrified as a child by the war news, and one of the first books she read was a gruesome account of the deportations—'people...swapped about in the usual cattle trucks'—that followed the 1939 Nazi–Soviet pact.[17] Her first boyfriend, in Belfast, was a displaced person from Czechoslovakia; she learned Russian (and taught it in school) and had long-standing dissident friends in Moscow; one of her Polish friends had spent his childhood in camps of one sort or another in the Soviet Arctic, Kazakhstan, Iran, Poland, and Uganda; another Pole, one of her closest friends when she was writing for MO, was a woman whose father had escaped from Katyn and who herself got out of Poland in 1956 when the Hungarian uprising opened the borders for two weeks. The friend she chose to marry in 1963 was a Czech Jew, born like her in 1933, who had escaped from Auschwitz as the Russians approached in January 1945 and walked back to Prague. His parents were marched to Belsen where they died. In England he became a clinical psychologist, but died in 1974 in 'an accident at sea'.[18] He had suffered from depression, the marriage had not been happy, and, given his history, the 'accident' may well have been suicide. It was, she wrote thirty years later, 'a relief when he died'.[19]

Through her friendships and her marriage Janet linked herself to the most catastrophic events of twentieth-century history, and she understood her own experience in the shadow of these events. With her husband she talked about the parallels between childhood in Auschwitz and in the 'convent hell hole for girls': the dehumanization, but also the networks of friendship and solidarity hidden from Nazi guards or Catholic nuns. Janet was a survivor, but she lived in the expectation of catastrophe, heir to a history that offered little by way of comfort. In the run-up to the 1967 Arab–Israeli war, now with two young children (her daughter was born in 1965), she offered to work full time so that her husband could go and fight: but he was turned down on medical grounds. 'The Jews, like the Kurds', she wrote during the Gulf War, 'have a fair idea what they can expect if they falter for a second in legitimate self defence'.[20] She was not optimistic. When her husband died she presented her wedding ring to Israel: 'They weren't half surprised . . . My ring should buy one micro-second more before the PLO and Arab oil-money wipe out Israel.'[21]

When her husband died, Janet was left with a second house, originally intended as an investment for the children, which she rented out to supplement her income as a part-time teacher. In her forties she had a six-year affair with a hard-drinking, bisexual pathologist, sharing him, without jealousy she says, with his schizophrenic wife and his occasional Canadian boyfriend. He came for dinner, stayed overnight, took her out to gay clubs, and sometimes they went on holiday together:

. . . with our children, his and mine, or alone . . . The reason [that this time was] so good was that I felt like a proper woman, had good company, food and drink and no-one hassled me or told me how bad I was, or that, by implication, it was my fault that my mother died or that bloody Jesus Christ did not love me . . .[22]

He left her in 1981, and although there were other men, she chose to remain single. She had her work, her cats, and her friends, and 'to marry at the age of fifty when one has sufficient goods and has done with childbearing seems just mad'.[23]

After her husband died, Janet went back to college, studying sociology for a BEd at a polytechnic, graduating in 1978. Subsequently she did an MEd, and, in her sixties, an MA in women's studies, continuing a process of life-long learning that equipped her for her self-described role as 'a low grade dealer in high class ideas'.[24] She also became active in the Voluntary Euthanasia Society which she had joined in 1973, having long been convinced by a vacation job in a geriatric ward of the cruelty of keeping terminally ill elderly people alive against their will. In 1980, when a crisis arose in the society over a decision to publish a 'Guide to Self Deliverance' which included practical advice on lethal pills, Janet organized local meetings and was elected to the executive in a coup against an older generation of leaders who thought the society should confine itself to campaigning for legislative change, rather than actively seeking to test the limits of the existing legal framework. News of the forthcoming 'Guide' triggered a sixfold expansion of the society's membership (to 12,000 by 1981). Deluged with phone calls from desperate people seeking advice on 'self deliverance', and frustrated by delays in publishing the 'Guide', the general secretary teamed up with one of the society's volunteers to offer immediate relief. Between 1978 and 1980, Mark Lyons, a lonely old man (he had been born a Hassidic Jew in the East End in 1912), may have helped up to 400 people to end their lives.[25] Variously described as scruffy, eccentric, sinister, kindly, humane, and compassionate, he posed as a retired doctor and believed himself guided by a spiritual 'puppet master' to bring comfort to the suffering. After being rumbled by a researcher making a TV documentary about euthanasia, Lyons was held on remand for eleven months pending a sensational trial in which both he and the general secretary were convicted of aiding and abetting suicide. The conviction and jailing of the general secretary dealt a major blow to the society's reputation, and in 1983, intimidated by legal threats, the VES withdrew the controversial booklet, thereafter settling back to conventional campaigning: 'very consensus and respectable', as Janet put it.[26] Although she remained on the executive for sixteen years—there was 'no mad rush for the job'—and acted for a time as a regional organizer, the excitement of the early 1980s confrontation with the authorities (when she believed her own phone was bugged) did not return. Her main contribution, she wrote modestly in 1990, was to serve tea at the annual general meeting, although the VES news-letters show her as rather more active than this suggests. Among those she worked with in the VES was the novelist Celia Fremlin, of whose leading role in the original Mass Observation she was unaware.[27]

2

Janet found it difficult to give a coherent account of her politics. Writing for MO in her fifties, she declared herself 'very set in my ways', but her outlook had been 'very different when I was young.'[28] As a student in Belfast she encountered Marxism in the Young Communist League, and in the later 1950s attended lectures at the Communist Party's Marx House in London. When it came to under-standing how the capitalist world works, Lenin's analysis 'of advanced monopoly finance capitalism in its last stages, worldwide, inordinately greedy and destructive' remained the guiding light throughout her life: 'It is wrong morally that those who produce no real value should be filthy rich while the rest who have only their labour power live either in the shit in some countries or in our country, [earn] far, far less than the unproductive, say 5%.'[29] That was written in 1991 during the Gulf War, which she understood in classically Leninist terms. Her sympathies lay, not with Saddam, but with the Kurds whose national aspirations would inevitably be betrayed, she believed, by a capitalist world which had no place for an independent Kurdish state. During the financial crisis of 2008 she remarked that 'Gordon [Brown] is doing his best and [is] less duplicitous than others...[But] it's not really up to him, is it?...Those who thieved will escape punishment as the state is no longer the ringmaster. Shame and guilt cultures don't apply nowadays, it's just take de money and run.'[30] Since the Thatcher governments had 'reduced honest decent labour to its knees' and exported manufac-turing industry to the Far East, the City was—apart from the equally immoral arms trade—all that the British had left: 'What really makes things tick', she had written twenty years earlier, was women working for twopence halfpenny an hour in the Far East, rendering the British as a whole 'like the bourgeoisie [living] on expropriating the Third World's surplus value via the City and its operations'.[31]

This was not an analysis which left much scope for political solutions. She had never had any time for proletarian revolution (too closely tied to IRA terrorism for a woman of her Protestant Unionist upbringing) or for the idealization of the USSR: 'all my life... even at a Party meeting, I truly thought this is a load of guano because it is not to do with England and England's ancient liberties'.[32] She admired the values of the 'old-style genuine Labour' that she associated with the 'respectable working class'—and had always voted Labour until the late 1970s.[33] But, as party politics polarized and fragmented, she became an eclectically floating voter. Believing that any future Labour government would be captured by the hard left, she briefly joined the Social Democratic Party, but voted Conservative in 1987 on the grounds that the sitting MP, despite his party, served the constituency well. Subsequently she joined, and voted for, the Greens, before turning, in the 1997 and 2001 elections, to the anti-European UK Independence Party—'though I know it's a wasted vote'.[34] Despite her best efforts she found no party able to command her lasting allegiance.

While Marxism might do a good deal to explain the world, it had little to offer by way of changing it in desirable ways. The Marxists she came across in the 1970s and beyond—Trotskyist councillors in Lambeth, Althusserian sociologists at the polytechnic—only confirmed her revulsion for the politics of revolution. Not only did some of these people ally themselves with IRA—and later Islamic—terrorists, but, just like the 'pizdi' at her convent school, they ran their own regimes of intellectual terrorism. A mature student with the temerity to refuse to 'lick the jackboots' of the polytechnic's 'Marxified' sergeants of 'grand theory' could, she believed, expect no more than the third-class degree that Janet was eventually awarded.[35] A teacher could lose her job if she refused to 'jump through hoops made of post-Marxist ideological trash' devised by ex-revolutionaries making careers for themselves in educational management or by the lecturers at the Institute of Education who used in-service training on multicultural education to 'force feed' their hapless victims with Marxist ideas.[36]

Faced with this unholy mixture of rampant capitalism and an educational apparatus staffed by bullying ideologues, Janet's resistance—like that she perceived among the white working-class kids she taught at the technical college—took the form of 'interstitial survival... they know that they cannot alter great structures too much, if at all, so they keep going to survive on a micro-level'.[37] Partly this was a question of evasion, like switching off pictures of terrible things during the Gulf War, or removing one's glasses in the violent bits of movies, as she did regularly in the cinema with her best friend. Too much dwelling on the state of the world 'can make you ill and dwelling does no good...there is so much sadness to see...that it could get too much for a person...one has to pace oneself in the management of sadness...'[38] But evasion was not enough: the minimum requirement for self-respect in the face of triumphant evil was to think illegitimate thoughts. 'In the Catechism...it says one can sin in thought, word, and deed, well, my word, I'm a thought criminal through and through and have been all my life.'[39] At the convent school, aged ten, she had invented a secret code to defend the privacy of her thoughts against the prying eyes of the nuns: 'To keep a diary in the face of persecution...is a way of maintaining identity and keeping control of one's own self.'[40] And she saw her MO writing in a similar light. Secure in the knowledge that her anonymity was guaranteed, she frequently ended her contributions with more or less jokey remarks inviting MO to report her to the thought police.[41] At the time of the 1987 election she said she was afraid to talk politics openly in the street in 'the socialist-nuclear-free-zone of dereliction and thuggery' [Lambeth] for fear of losing her part-time job in a local school.[42] But fear and paranoia had its limits. During the Gulf War, provoked beyond endurance by a report that 'the Communist connivers in IRA/Sinn Fenian murders in Lambeth Council [had] disciplined an...employee whose son is in the army in the Gulf for displaying a Union Jack printed in the *Sun* on the grounds that this was racist', she took to wearing a Union Jack brooch, put up the flag in her window, and offered free lodgings to people with relatives serving in the Gulf: 'were I in a Council flat in Lambeth/Haringey I should be well victimised for my impertinence/level of politicisation/incorrect consciousness/wrong thinking à la Orwell 1984'.[43] This gesture of resistance was aimed at the far left, but, like her later subscription to the Soldiers, Sailors, Airmen and Families Association, it was intended to express solidarity with the troops rather than with their political masters, let alone support for the war for oil. 'I want to redress, in a tiny way the inequitable distribution of power: Gaddafi and Sodom [sic] have pots of money so they fund the killers and not a particularly grateful bourgeois state lets [the troops] get on with it and there's not a lot I can do about it.'[44]

In fact there was quite a lot she could, and did, do—not as a landlady with a Union Jack in the window, but as a teacher with thoroughly subversive ideas to put across to her pupils; above all the feminist ideas which she discovered in the course of the 1970s when 'women writing, mainly in America...[were] saying things out loud that I thought all my life'.[45] In 1955 she had joined the Abortion Law eform Association, and from the early 1960s, impelled by her own unwanted pregnancy, she had felt it her duty never to 'let her classes go without teaching them the facts...about sex and contraception'.[46] It was a struggle, amidst the cacophony of feminist theorizing, to find a perspective capable of making sense of her own womanly experience: 'Women's space/time/identity are all closely linked', she wrote in 1992, 'in ways that it takes an incomprehensible grand theorist to unpick'.[47] She attended the women's caucus of the British Sociological Association in 1982 and for some time wrote abstracts of articles in women's journals for a company employed by the women's studies team at the Open University.

Central to her thinking, and her practice as a teacher, was the deconstruction of those patriarchal 'ideas of religion, female roles and duties [that] get screwed in really early on in life', and—taking issue with Lévi-Strauss whose distortions, she thought, matched those of Freud— she offered MO a reading list of radical feminist writing about 'the original robbery, that of women having power and control over their own fertility and having a mother goddess to worship'. Against the Marxists she insisted that 'the original motor of society was not class-conflict or technological change. I think the original motor was male/female conflict and the men won'.[48] Although matriarchy was nowhere to be found on the sociology syllabus she made space to explain these ideas—after writing 'inadmissible problematic' on the blackboard—to her pupils on the grounds that 'belief in a powerful goddess might be more useful for a young female than in a father bully prick in the sky; not just the fertility and sexuality of the goddess, but also her capacity for control of her life and the earth around her'.[49] It was not that she herself wanted to worship the goddess, but rather that, drawing on her experience with the Brethren, she felt that 'the iconography and the social aspects of religion can comfort [a child] and lay down a foundation of emotional security'[50]—a view that got her into serious trouble when, as an active member of the Humanist Teachers Association in the 1960s, she sent her own daughter to Sunday School. While critical of atheist dogmatism— she preferred (and frequently quoted) Samuel Beckett's ambivalent dictum: 'God, the bastard, doesn't exist'[51]—she was second to none in her loathing for the patriarchal core of Judaeo-Christian and Islamic religion, the source, she believed, of the oppression of women since the eclipse of 'the great mother/universal earth goddess'.[52]

She was far too rational a woman to yearn for a revival of matriarchal religion: after all, as she wrote in 1996, 'if there is no god then why should there be a goddess?'[53] The war on patriarchy could be conducted in secular terms through sociological enlightenment.

She was impatient with the socialist feminists of the Open University women's studies programme and drawn to a radical feminism which placed motherhood at the core of female identity. What women had, and what men envied so much that they had been driven to invent art and culture to compensate for their own lack, was the power to give birth. With Havelock Ellis, she believed that childbirth was the supreme sexual experience for women, citing the two days on which she herself gave birth as the best two days of her life: 'If it's a boy you get a mini penis. If it's a girl you get yourself again. Either way you are justified by WORKS. Not faith works, just works.'[54] Why would women need a goddess when they had the power to create and nurture life? Maternal love was instinctive and embodied 'for one's breast milk squirts out on hearing a child's cry... even if the child is not one's own'. But these, she well knew, were heretical opinions not to be deployed by students looking to pass their exams: 'under patriarchal mark schemes that sort of anecdote gets 0/10'.[55]

Much of what passed for anti-racism was, she believed, patriarchy in disguise. She did what she could to support girls from Pakistani homes who were 'continually forced back into their own culture... a load of shit for women... But watch out for the Race Relations if you think you might have a go at reaching Ethnic women.'[56] On one occasion she got into trouble for encouraging a fourteen-year-old Muslim girl to resist the marriage that her parents were arranging for her. A female 'conniver with patriarchy' from the Commission for Racial Equality, the girls told her, had been assuring their parents that arranged marriages were perfectly acceptable in Britain.[57] But inside the classroom— 'part-time and of no importance'—she was generally left with 'lots of autonomy once the door is shut', and she used this to 'put over a version of "critical/emancipatory reason"'.[58] As 'a low grade dealer in

high class ideas'[59] she set out to deconstruct patriarchal norms in discussions triggered by news items like the story of a woman threatened
with deportation when her husband reported her as an illegal immigrant after she had been to the police because he was beating her up;
or by the girls' own experience of a local Pakistani doctor who did his
best to turn every consultation into a discussion of sexual problems.
('Of course he is doubly secure as he is a professional male person, very
highly qualified and also a Paki, so if they said owt [anything], he'd
get help off the MDU [Medical Defence Union] and the CRE
[Commission for Racial Equality] and they'd be up on a charge of
racism.'[60]) She opened her white pupils' eyes to their prejudices with
the aid of 'England in the Eyes of the Immigrant', a (very funny) racist
jingle from Lancashire purporting to offer an immigrant's thanks for
the generosity of the English taxpayer in enabling him, his extended
family, and his friends to live a life of luxury on social security benefits.
(She sent a copy to MO: it ends, 'If English don't like the coloured
man/Plenty of room in Pakistan!'[61]) During the Gulf War she used
a pamphlet which reproduced the anti-semitic 1898 Protocols of
Zion—a text known by young Muslims at the technical college—'to
de-construct [both] racism and so-called Council/Gadaffy-funded,
anti-racism'. Anti-racism, as promoted by 'the intellectual loonies in
power', was opening the way for the imposition of sharia law, something already occurring, she believed, in 'Bradistan' (Bradford) or
her own Rochdale, 'where the flagstones are painted in the national
colours of Pakistan'.[62]

While critical of patriarchal values among south Asians, she felt
much more at home with black culture. She encouraged debate in her
classes between Caribbean and Asian girls on the (un)desirability of
arranged marriage, sympathized with Pakistani girls cold-shouldered
by their peers because they refused to cover their hair, and approved of
a Muslim 'who is best mates with a Jamaican girl and goes to her house
for refuge from the familial/patriarchal tyranny she suffers at home'.[63]
Responding to the directive which asked mass observers to say whom
they would choose to sit next to on a bus, she said she would try to avoid
sitting next to a man, *unless* he was black. Several other observers—
including Caroline—who said the same thing explained it as a kind of
white guilt: to avoid sitting next to a black man might be interpreted
as racism. But for Janet things were more straightforward: 'I very much
like black people as they are outgoing and often from a fundamentalist

background that has some points in common with the Brethren, but [with] a much more jolly concept of the Spirit.'[64] It was among black people that she found a spirit of resistance to match her own:

... when upset or treated badly, I will resist to the utmost of my capacity. I would not apologise and turn the other cheek. I would take example from the Black British whom I know, like and teach and I would resist and never apologise if I am not in the wrong and I'll be the judge of when I'm in the wrong.[65]

Several of her friends were black ex-pupils, of both sexes, including a woman ten years older than her own daughter whom she came to treat as her adoptive daughter, giving her money and visiting her relatives in Guyana. At the Caribbean Saturday School Janet was declared 'an honorary wog' by her pupils and teased by the other (black) staff as the culprit when parents complained that the kids were getting too much 'black consciousness'.[66] In fact, as she noted, these young people were negotiating complex multiple identities. Reacting to BBC campaigns to raise funds for the relief of starving Africans, her pupils combined Rasta notions of Ethiopian dignity with bad taste jokes proclaiming their own critical Englishness: 'What is the heaviest part of an Ethiopian? His Blue Peter badge.'[67]

None of this tempered her indignation that the rapper Linton Kwesi Johnson's 'Inglan is a bitch' should have been adopted as an Open University text, or her hostility to the 'tiny minority of blacks here [who] would be likely to cause violent dissention/trouble...'[68] She took seriously complaints about aggressive black men made by white trainee postal workers at the technical college, and encouraged them to express their feelings freely—'Go on, drop yourselves in it':

Teacher remarked on the past and the British Empire, defended Blacks, stated her fear of Paki men, admitted the class had some points and advised that they should claim self-defence when accused of a racist remark. As they pointed out, some coloured people can be very nasty and the State might give judgement in their favour since they are non-white. Self defence is no offence, said Malcolm X.[69]

But she was clear that rising levels of crime had nothing to do with colour. It was the IRA which had first made her feel unsafe on London's streets in the later 1970s, and since then crime had escalated to the point where she felt it necessary to carry a paint spray, drive with the car doors locked, put bars on the windows, lock internal doors as well as bolting external ones at night, and install an arson-resistant doormat.

This was not, she insisted, just the anxiety of a vulnerable aging widow. She knew all about the criminally inclined minority—'black, white and spotted'—not only from the Last Hope School, where teachers dealing with the most violent kids had to be accompanied by minders trained in physical restraint, but also from her college of further education where the police were called in to break up gang warfare. In the Caribbean supplementary school friendly pupils assured her that 'we wouldn't steal off you miss, we don't steal off people we know'.[70] In her late sixties she gave up reading the local newspaper because 'it was too sad to know so much of crimes', some of which were being committed by her own students.[71]

While deploring the use of taxpayers' money to support 'Albanian pimps, Islamic Terrorist preaching mullahs & imams, and all the beggars and Roma of Eastern Europe', she knew that most crime was home-grown and was not blaming immigration as such. Her quarrel was with the perverse behaviour of the authorities who let in 'thugs, drug pushers and killers from abroad' while harassing her own African students who 'though not the brains of Benin...are decent kids'.[72] Nor, unlike many other anxious older people, did she see young people in general as a threat. While 'a few violent thugs—hardly any thugesses as yet (live in hope)—can make it impossible to teach or learn...most kids are still quite OK' and even in the Last Hope School 'some of the lads can be very good indeed'.[73]

Back in the 1950s she had encountered deeply disturbed children and adolescents while earning a nursing auxiliary certificate with weekend work at the Maudsley psychiatric hospital, but thirty-five years later:

the unchecked violence in say 5% of children...looks more like moral failures, not only psychiatric/organic states...It seems that some younger persons... have no internal boundaries whatsoever...One can see [the] adult culmination [of this] in the Strangeways, Broadwater Farm riots. Such an idea [she added, characteristically] would get the utmost ridicule and contempt if voiced at a meeting these days but thought is still fairly free in spite of what the experts tell us.[74]

Similarly impermissible, she believed, was her conviction that:

some families are a bad influence and dangerous to all and sundry, likewise their sad, genetically engineered, Rottweilers and pits and Staffs...It's not always the social structure, it's sometimes evil around the place, quite unchecked (as far as I can see) if you have a good lawyer. That goes for both black and white thugs.[75]

Nothing angered her more than liberal intellectuals who sought to excuse the crimes of delinquent young thugs by reference to their unhappy childhoods. The courts, cowed by civil rights lawyers—among whom the prime minister's wife, Cherie Blair, allegedly 'sympathetic to suicide bombers and other thugs', came to stand out for Janet as a particular hate figure—handed out ever lighter sentences.[76] Marxist and liberal intellectuals had joined forces to promote 'laws to prioritise thugs and killers' making it difficult for the police to collect the evidence needed to convict them.[77] 'The ailing bourgeois state has lost the courage of its convictions', and those who ran it, secure in their well-guarded private estates, were content to allow the police and ordinary decent people to take the strain of rising crime.[78] The one thing to be thankful for in all this was that most of the thugs were 'without benefit of politicisation…a lumpen ragged group, not [like IRA or Islamist terrorists] a troublesome thinking band of brothers looking for something to kill'.[79]

It was her indignation about crime and its apologists that inspired her most bitterly satirical writing:

In the case of muggings, of course, a victim who successfully defended herself would go to quod [jail] for violence and the mugger would get the GLC [Greater London Council] Peace Prize; he was only expressing his disgust at the social structure and/or his alpha rhythms were dancing funky chicken.[80]

In the late 1980s she gave up reading the *Guardian*, house journal of the liberal intelligentsia, and later offered MO a paraphrase of its approach:

Mr Shamus O'Stroopock was found to have a scratch on his nether regions and his lawyers claimed that this had been inflicted on Mr S O'S as a result of polis brutality. In the course of his arrest 2 soldiers were killed by…but in view of the grave nature of the wound on Mr S O'S's nether regions, the Court threw out the case and we, the Pinko Politically correct have set up a fund for his support and that of his 2 wives and umpteen kids because we think old England's a bitch and that what happens in other countries won't never happen here. And Lenin said the capitalists would pay for the rope to hang themselves and Lenin was right.[81]

Bitterest of all, and more seriously intended, was the figure of 'Judge Alzheimer' presiding over the fate of the most disadvantaged of children, in league with the well-organized groups of 'renters and child-fuckers' who abused them.[82] Some of the boys at Barnardo's and the Last Hope School picked up money by 'renting their botties', and Janet tells the story of one such boy she tried to help who ended up in a home for delinquents while an MP, from whom he had a compromising letter, remained 'too important to touch'.[83] Now, in 2016, we know that this story was all too believable. It was experiences like this, not homophobia, that underlay her complaint, on seeing questions about anal intercourse in a biology exam, that Clause 28—banning education about homosexuality in schools—was not being enforced.

3

Writing for MO helped Janet to work out her ideas and gave her a platform on which to express her anger. Beyond that, however, she reveals little about her inner life. Despite the centrality of motherhood in her thinking, for example, she says little about her children or her relationship with them. Even a woman as committed, intelligent, and energetic as Janet did not always find it easy to keep going in face of the thugs, rich and poor, and those mid-century historical catastrophes with which she felt intimately connected through her friends and her marriage. She was prone to depression, which she thought she had inherited from her father, and at times she felt weak and vulnerable, 'nervous inside myself'.[84] It was not an inside she chose to explore in her MO writing, beyond attributing it to the 'misery and tyranny' of her childhood. Towards the end of her student years in Belfast, overwhelmed with anxiety about her future, she had sought professional help; but she mentions this only to dismiss it in a matter-of-fact phrase: 'I betook myself for out-patient treatment – four electric shocks...'[85]

In later life Janet drew pride and self-confidence from her work as a teacher, work she often regarded as 'to some extent coterminous' with motherhood; 'in my real heart, I think it is the same' (although she was well aware of the contradiction between such an attitude and the teacher's claim to professional status).[86] The children and young people she encountered in her work often took centre stage in her responses to MO directives. In her role as teacher she strove to deliver enlightenment—'high class ideas'—deconstructing received dogma, fostering 'critical/emancipatory reason', and inculcating 'a residual morality' capable of withstanding the sadness, corruption, and evil surrounding the lives of many of her pupils.[87] In her role as mass observer she wanted to put their voices on record, peopling the indignant torrents of her writing with stories of individual kids, sharply, warmly, precisely observed, each story, in its very particularity, helping to provide 'an answer to the preponderance of grand theory ... which has caused so much harm in the world'. Writing like this for MO served to affirm her own identity: 'It has not changed me', she remarked in 1990, 'but it helped to maintain me'.[88] Immersed in the 'real' world of the poor and the powerless she could tell it how it was, and in so doing help to puncture the controlling narratives of religion, patriarchy (in whatever guise), or well-heeled liberalism.

5

Social Worker

Although she had no fixed political abode, Janet understood the world in the language of politics. For Stella, by contrast, politics never held much interest. Instead, it was the pervasive influence of psychological ideas during the late twentieth century that did most to shape the ways in which she came to understand her life and times. This difference is reflected in the uses to which the two women put their participation in Mass Observation. Janet, as we have seen, used MO to expound her idiosyncratic take on the ideological confusions of the era, to represent the views of the disadvantaged children whom she taught, and to externalize her existential fury. Externalization, for Janet, functioned as an alternative to any inward journey: her MO writing reveals little about her intimate life. Stella, who became an adoption worker, also dealt with disadvantaged children, but she did not choose to write as their spokesperson. Altogether calmer, she places her professional life alongside a remarkably full and frank account of emotional and erotic experience informed by her immersion in 1970s New Age humanistic psychology.

I

Born in 1931, Stella grew up as a single child in a comfortable middle-class home. Her father, borough treasurer in a small Dorset town, cycled home for lunch every day, gave his daughter her evening bath, and read her bedtime stories. Her mother sang in a local choir, played the piano, and took in some pupils at home. Both parents were musically gifted, danced beautifully, and were active in a range of sports. Nevertheless, looking back, Stella found it hard to imagine what her mother did with her time. There was a gardener, an occasional cleaner, and a succession of teenage live-in maids who did the washing and the daily housework and doubled as nannies. Mother took charge of the cooking, dusted, picked and arranged flowers, and 'popped under the eiderdown' while the maid took the child out for her afternoon walk.[1] There were bridge parties, tea parties, and, in summer, tennis or the beach.

The idyll was not without its dark side. Throughout her childhood Stella was plagued by nightmares, the most vivid of which she privately entitled *The Crutch Road*:

An army of men, all hideously disfigured, limbless, swung silently on crutches through the town centre. No sound at all, save for sombre music and sobbing. My mother came to my side and explained: *This is the noise that goes round the world, dear.* In the dream she appeared, as usual, unmoved.[2]

Unmoved in the dream, but irritated by the wakefulness of the terrified child, who, if she woke too often, would be sent back to bed 'with a good smack'.[3]

From as early as she can remember Stella was sensitive to the traumatized collective unconscious of 1930s Britain:

As a very small child I cringed in terror when forced to pass by grossly mutilated and disfigured ex-service men from WWI crouched on the pavement to sell matches or dusters. I wept silently in the shoe shop whose proprietor swung on creaking crutches, clutching the boxes under his chin or armpit. I dreaded the inevitable *You'll need new shoes this Winter,* and pleaded unsuccessfully, to visit a different shop. I couldn't comprehend why or how adults appeared outwardly unmoved by these ever-present terrors. I felt they knew something I did not.[4]

On the contrary: it was the child who knew, the parents who were in denial. During the war, encouraged by her parents 'to chortle at news of [German] casualties . . . I once asked my mother if Germans were sad when their children got killed in a raid, [and] she didn't know how to answer.'[5]

By then everything had changed. Dad, working as an air raid warden, was out several evenings a week. The maid, the gardener, and the cleaning lady had disappeared into war work and, capping her mother's misfortunes, she found herself at forty unexpectedly pregnant. Two babies followed in quick succession, separated by little more than a year. For ten-year-old Stella home lost its charm, her years as a single child giving way to screaming babies and stressed, short-tempered parents. School, however, opened new horizons. She passed her 11-plus and started in the local grammar school. After a couple of years her parents put her in for a scholarship to an independent girls' boarding school in Bournemouth. Maybe they thought she needed respite from the miseries at home, although Stella believed that class was the key motivation. Both sets of grandparents had made their living as shopkeepers, and her parents, having 'put "trade" behind them', were anxious to cement their own upward mobility in the lives of their children. At grammar school Stella had been picking up the local accent; at boarding school she would mix with children of a higher social status (including, for a few months in the last year of the war, the future Social Democratic politician Shirley Williams). But the mixing did not have the result that her parents expected. They wanted a daughter 'more sporty, active and charming, to match their own social milieu', and well prepared, after a few years as an air hostess (her mother's idea) or a secretary (her father's preferred option), to settle down as the wife of a professional man. But teenage Stella, not pretty 'compared with other more impressive females of my age', was messy, bespectacled, unfeminine, 'intelligent and bookish'.[6] She was intent on going to university and thoroughly at odds with parents who, despite priding themselves on their 'educated' BBC accents, placed little value on education for its own sake. Her anxious mother nagged about 'hair, eyes, BO, shoes, smile, complexion' with the constant refrain: 'you'll never get married if...'[7]

In the spring of 1948, aged 17, Stella's world fell apart. Following some disappointing internal exam results, the school withdrew the scholarship which had been paying her tuition fees. Later she suspected that this was part of a cost-cutting exercise designed to force better-off parents to pay the full amount. Her father—'a red-head with a red-head's passionate rages'[8]—was furious with both the school and his daughter, and refused to sell shares in order to pay for her final year at school. Her hopes of university were dashed. Resourcefully, she decided that the next best thing was to train as a speech therapist, and having secured a deferred place at the prestigious Central School of Speech and Drama in London, she registered meanwhile for a one-year secretarial course at the local technical college. Her father ruled out speech therapy, acting on the advice of a much revered older brother, a Harley Street surgeon who (on the

basis of a once-a-year visit to the family) declared that Stella lacked
the necessary personal qualities. After scraping through her course at
the tech she was shipped off to Bristol, where her father had found her
a job as a typist.

Writing for MO fifty years later Stella still found it hard to understand these events. Whatever she may have done to provoke the loss of
the scholarship—'I was rather an anarchist at the time often challenging established procedures, but had never done anything seriously
wrong'—it was the 'monstrous' repercussions at home that were most
difficult to come to terms with:

I returned home from school after one year in the Sixth and *my parents never
spoke about it.* I was more or less sent to Coventry. I never dared raise it. It was
never discussed—occasionally I heard them having shouting matches after
I was in bed about what to do with me. I was most utterly disgraced; how
could they explain to friends why I had suddenly left half way through the
Sixth form? Of course I knew *nobody must ever know* I was sent to the local
tech on a shorthand-typing course... My parents were much into *what will the
neighbours say.*[9]

Silence and secrecy were her parents' way of coping with status anxiety, and they probably saw their daughter's intellectual ambitions as a
threat to her marriageability.

But there may have been more to it than that. While Stella was away
at school a sixteen-year-old girl—'shy, lonely and very pretty'—had
arrived in her father's office and quickly adopted her boss as a substitute father. Her own father was dead, and her elderly mother's job, as a
housekeeper for a succession of employers, meant that the girl had no
family home of her own. Flattered no doubt by the calf-love, Stella's
father took Barbara in hand, inviting her to join family holidays and
social events. While his wife preferred not to know, Stella's aunts were
convinced that the relationship with Barbara was sexual, and local gossip
concurred. Stella, who knew that her parents had stopped sleeping
together after the birth of her siblings, was bewildered, not knowing
what to believe. Barbara became a life-long family friend, but Stella
never knew whether it was as the accepted mistress or the adopted
daughter. Fifty years on, both parents dead, she was 'thunderstruck'
when Barbara told her that 'she had always pretended my parents were
her parents, referred to them in her mind as *Mummy and Daddy.*' But
she still did not know what to believe: 'Were those years of mutterings,
scandal, my mother's sneers founded on nothing but a near-orphan's

longing for parents? Or was this the final smoke-screen? I bet I never find out!'[10]

Stella herself does not think there was any connection between her father's angry refusal to find the money for her last year at school and his entanglement with Barbara. Perhaps not. But her own account of her relationship with her father could suggest a different reading. Was her father shifting his affection from his difficult adolescent daughter to a substitute daughter—pretty, devoted, unrebellious, and, maybe, sexually available? Stella's description of her own childhood sexuality points to a strong sexual component to the relationship between father and daughter:

[My parents] told me I began masturbating at about six months; initially my parents found it funny, assuming it wouldn't last... However my father became agitated when the practice continued beyond the toddler years, and would beg me to stop...[He] gave a private name to the shameful performance I conducted nightly under the bedclothes, even today I cannot bring myself to utter that word!... *You'll do yourself a damage* he cried, again and again; as I grew older he'd listen outside my bedroom door to catch me out. In summer he'd even listen under the bedroom window. I found the activity wildly exciting and pleasurable, but loaded with guilt, believing this pursuit to be exclusive to myself...[11]

By the time she was writing for MO Stella was neither prudish nor ignorant about sexuality, yet she reports her father's behaviour with no comment on its peculiarity. Being prevented from going to university, she writes, was the biggest disappointment of her life. Is there an element of smoke screen here too? Was that disappointment masking a still deeper disappointment that she could not articulate: her own displacement by Barbara in her father's complicated affections?

2

On her own in Bristol, living in a hostel for girls, Stella quickly made her escape from the typing pool into more congenial secretarial employment. By February 1951, still intent on getting as close to university life as she could, she had landed a job as personal assistant to the retired colonel employed to oversee the students' union. Although this gave her access to Saturday dances, her schooling had left her 'awkward, red-faced [and] lumpen'[12] in the presence of young men, and it was the accountant working in her office, seven years her senior, with whom she struck up a friendship. After a year Phillip moved to a better job in London. They corresponded, got engaged, and in September 1952 she quit Bristol for a typing job, and another girls' hostel, in London. Four months later they married, but she continued to work until shortly before her first child was born in July 1954. Although she had reverted to the role of typist, the work was in an academic environment at University College, and it exposed her to ideas that were to play a significant role in her personal and professional life a quarter of a century later.

The job itself was mundane enough—transcribing tapes of group discussions among medical students. But the project of which this was a part was exciting, innovative, and controversial. Stella's boss, Jane Abercrombie, was experimenting with substituting small discussion groups for lectures as a means of encouraging medical students to explore their preconceptions and critique positivist understandings of scientific method. Her pedagogic experiments were informed by discussion with a psychiatrist who, during the war, had pioneered group analytic psychotherapy with traumatized soldiers.[13] After participating in one of his groups Abercrombie 'felt that if one could transfer to a teaching group something of the atmosphere he had established in this therapeutic group, new ways of seeing and thinking might be encouraged'.[14] Looking back from 2004, Stella understood how fortunate she had been to find herself in the midst of an intellectual revolution, although at the time she only dimly grasped what was at stake:

It's difficult today to conceive the vast gap between traditional sciences and psychology/sociology/social psychology. My boss was respected in her original field, biology, with a string of publications to her credit...Most of the more traditional academics in the Department of Anatomy thought she was quite mad to abandon her former discipline. The idea that students might learn from her little groups aroused hostility in fellow academics. Such concepts as peer group pressure, group dynamics, the way our observation is modified by the context were not the common currency they are today...She was perceived as woolly-minded, soft in the head.[15]

Stella, by contrast, found her boss 'fascinating and inspiring', and Abercrombie herself was as friendly to her clever typist as mid-twentieth-century formalities allowed. She invited her to attend some of the group sessions as an observer, lent her literature on Freudian group therapy, offered sympathy at a time of loneliness and distress during the first year of Stella's marriage, and allowed her (unusually for the time) to remain in post until the eighth month of her pregnancy.

The marriage was difficult from the start. Within six months of the wedding Phillip had been diagnosed with TB. Through most of her pregnancy he was away in a rural sanatorium, while she gave up their flat and returned to hostel living. When Phillip was released, just before the birth of their daughter, she found a flat in Guildford, but it was another year before her convalescing husband, 'utterly dependent and self-centred', was fit to return to work.[16] These were lonely years for Stella, despite the joy she found in her children. In the later 1950s Phillip switched from accountancy to financial journalism and his career took off, but it was not until her daughter went to primary school in 1959 that Stella, now with a two-year-old son as well, was able to poke her nose beyond domesticity and rekindle her intellectual interests.

The Guildford Workers' Educational Association, which she first joined in 1959, became 'my university . . . a lifelong source of friendship and stimulation'.[17] During the 1960s, comfortably off in a large Victorian house, she had the time to read widely, studying philosophy, psychology, literature, and art appreciation. From 1961 she acted as secretary of the local WEA branch, organizing up to sixteen courses each term for its 400 or so members. With the children at school she could nip up to London in the daytime to an art gallery or a film, and from the mid-1960s she was a regular attender at a variety of summer schools.

None of this brought her closer to her husband. In the early years their friendship had been deep and absorbing: 'we talked about everything, talked and talked, knew every detail of each other's lives, history. Discussed books, films, theatre, friends.'[18] But Phillip had not wanted children and showed little interest in them when they arrived. He was also indifferent to her desire to get some kind of professional training, not believing, she wrote caustically, that 'a wife had a life beyond the Hoover'.[19] The hours he kept as a journalist separated them further: he not in bed before 2 a.m., she (with young children) exhausted by 10 p.m. Their sex life, which she writes about in considerable detail, had never been very satisfactory. When they married they were equally ignorant, and it took them several weeks of clumsy experimentation to achieve intercourse, not helped by the messy business of Dutch cap contraception. It was not until the early 1960s, alerted by the *Lady*

Chatterley trial and a daring BBC radio *Woman's Hour* discussion of the female orgasm, that Stella discovered that the pleasure she gained since childhood from masturbation could accompany sexual intercourse as well. At this point, tired of being woken up in the middle of the night by her husband's attentions, she went off sex altogether.

But not for long. At her first WEA summer school in 1965 she met a Frenchman, 'Jewish, clever, handsome, romantic, and . . . happily married'.[20] For the eighteen months their affair lasted, her daytime trips to London took on a new excitement, and she delighted in 'the secrecy, the phone calls, the poetic letters, assignations in hotel rooms, or on the wild heath, and occasionally in each other's homes'.[21] A second affair followed—'less romantic, more pragmatic'—with a man she met on a WEA psychology course. Her big worry was that Phillip would find out and that she could lose the children as the guilty party in a divorce.[22] But he was, apparently, oblivious, and in 1969 she realized, to her relief, that he was involved in an affair of his own. One Sunday lunchtime in 1970 he announced, out of the blue, that he was going to leave and set up house with his previously unmentioned lover.

3

The divorce was acrimonious because Stella, with two children and no qualifications beyond her shorthand-typing certificate, was determined to get the best financial deal she could. She took much pleasure in the children's teenage years, the house filled with their friends and 'almost enjoying a second teens' herself as she set out to demonstrate that she could manage perfectly well as a single mother.[23] But she was also looking for a career. In 1968, with both children at secondary school, she had started a part-time social studies diploma course at the local technical college and, in 1971, she got a job as an unqualified social worker in the local children's department. Four years later, having been seconded for a year on full salary to qualify as a social worker, she gained a diploma in applied social studies. Alongside these conventional qualifications Stella also found a way of reconnecting with the ideas that had so excited her twenty years earlier as Jane Abercrombie's typist.

So far as I am aware Abercrombie's work had no influence on the development of 'humanistic psychology' in Britain. But Stella certainly saw a link, and it was her good fortune that Surrey University, which opened in Guildford in the late 1960s, played host to the leading light of the emergent discipline. The Vice-Chancellor, Peter Leggett, was an ex-mathematician passionately convinced of 'the need for a new meta-physic, based on experiment and experience, embracing psychological insights and some practices of the East and the scientific disciplines and knowledge of the West.'[24] Alongside establishing a technocratic univer-sity with excellent business links, Leggett was keen to foster work beyond conventional academic paradigms,[25] and he lent his support to the establishment of a 'Human Resources Research Project', described by its leader, John Heron, as the first academic base for humanistic psychology outside the United States. Heron was a lecturer in phil-osophy at the time, but to avoid antagonizing more conventional colleagues the project was run through the adult education department. Starting in 1970, Heron organized a weekend programme of 'Human Relations Training Laboratories' in which, 'through exploratory action-inquiry within the unfolding dynamic of the workshop', participants acquired 'new intrapsychic and interpersonal awareness, insights and skills'. His guiding principle was 'to provide conditions within which people can in liberty determine their own true needs and interests in co-operation with others who are similarly engaged', a practice, he argued, which fosters 'the interdependence of *autonomy* and *co-opera-tion*... within a fertile context created by the *hierarchy* of benign facilitation'.[26] The emphasis on guided peer-group and experiential learning had much in common with Abercrombie's work with med-ical students twenty years earlier.[27] Alongside these 'laboratories', Heron also ran a training course in co-counselling, a practice he described as 'peer self-help emotional development' which he had learned from a Californian sociologist visiting Britain to study the anti-psychiatry work of R. D. Laing.[28] Most of the participants were local people rather than students at the university, many of them recruited through the WEA.[29] Stella became involved, and Heron's workshops were to have major consequences for her future in both her professional and her personal life.

In 1975 Stella was redeployed to the county council's adoption department, and from then until her retirement seventeen years later she worked with parents and children involved in adoption and fos-tering. Keen to apply humanistic psychology in her social work, she enrolled on a part-time diploma in group work at Goldsmith College in London, but in the 1970s group work among adoptive parents was still in its infancy and her colleagues were not interested in any such new-fangled experimentation. The impact of her extra-mural studies on her personal life, however, was more immediate. During the later 1970s she was:

swept up in the Human Growth movement, encounter groups, Co-counselling, New Age—which encouraged greater sexual openness, freedom and activity than I'd previously enjoyed. The children were at University, I was a free agent... Love affairs, previously *sub rosa* could emerge into daylight without wounding anybody.[30]

The most important of these was to lead to radical changes in her life.

In the summer of 1977, her involvement with the encounter group movement—'fashionable at the time'—took her to a weekend sexuality workshop at the university: '... we acted freely. Part of the contract was that any activity between participants behind closed doors would be shared with the group later.'[31] The man she went to bed with on that occasion 'refused to consummate the act', but a week later another participant, a married university lecturer from Yorkshire, phoned her, anxious to develop a relationship. She went to York, met Alec in a hotel, and fell 'violently in love... blindly adoring'.[32] Subsequently she joined him when he had conferences in various parts of the country, and he visited her during occasional trips to Surrey. Looking back she marvelled at her inability to understand 'his utter dominance':

our relationship hinged completely on his time-scales/availability. He did the phoning. I mustn't phone him. When we were together he required an ardent listener to matrimonial difficulties, work complexities, etc. etc.... His marriage was 'dry', 'dead'.[33]

She, on the other hand, was happy in her work, her various courses, her local friendships, her independence. But none of this could withstand the intensity of their occasional meetings, and 'years of quiet humour and commonsense flew out of the window' as Alec:

piled anguish on passion, beg[ged] me again and again to join him in Yorkshire. We would make a home together, while he would remain near enough for access to his children... [He] wept down the telephone, COULDN'T LIVE without me. My children were grown up. I could leave my job (he couldn't leave his!)[34]

Overwhelmed, she got herself a job with Bradford social services, sold her Guildford flat, bade goodbye to local friends and, at the end of December 1978, 'with sinking heart...drove North...I must have been mad!'[35]

4

1979 was a terrible year. Not because of the 'winter of discontent' or the election of Mrs Thatcher in May for which it paved the way—Stella was never very interested in politics—but for more personal reasons. Isolated in temporary accommodation in Bradford, 'I seemed stripped of everything that made me who I was, and missed my Surrey friends who seemed a thousand miles away.'[36] With no telephone—one had to wait in those days for a new line—and months of snow making car journeys difficult, she had less contact with Alec than before she moved. She went down with flu, was burgled twice, and Alec was unsupportive. It was distance that had lent enchantment, and now that she was on his doorstep he got cold feet, worrying that they might be 'seen together', redefining her as a threat to a marriage that he now wanted to protect. In May her father died unexpectedly and she toyed with the idea of moving back to Dorset to take care of her mother. In the autumn she and Alec were able to spend some time together on a residential course—'yet another growth group'. But hours of 'analysing our relationship from the thread to the needle'[37] got them nowhere, and, far from rekindling their passion, they both found themselves more interested in other people in the group. By the end of the year the relationship was virtually over.

Mad though her reasons had been for moving north, in the long term she did not regret it. Bradford had a go-ahead social services department, and she joined a unit pioneering the use of professional (paid) foster parents to keep difficult teenagers out of institutional care.[38] Building on an experiment conducted during the 1970s in Kent, social service departments were now developing group work with foster parents, who came to see themselves more as fellow professionals than as clients. Social workers, finding their authority challenged, had to learn to act as 'convenors and enablers' as much as professional experts.[39] In this situation what Stella had learned from both Abercrombie and Heron came into its own. Initially employed as a specialist caseworker, within nine months she had been promoted to team leader. After 1981, as a senior social worker, she was dealing with both fostering and adoption. She loved the work, which involved assessing the capacity of families to take on 'the most wounded and damaged children and young people it is possible to find', preparing them for the task and supporting them through whatever the child chose to throw at them.[40]

As an adoption worker she frequently found herself counselling couples unable to conceive, and developed an expertise in infertility counselling, on which she published a couple of booklets. One particular cause of infertility—a congenital absence of female sexual organs—struck her as so distressing, and so badly handled by existing services, that she took the initiative in introducing sufferers to one another. For these women, psychologically damaged since childhood by the secrecy, shame, and dishonesty surrounding their condition, simply being in touch with other victims was a help. The account Stella gives of her efforts, with the help of a sympathetic gynaecologist, to establish a network and support group and to influence public and medical attitudes to the condition is a model of forceful but sensitive intervention in a neglected problem mired in ignorance and taboos. Her efforts in Yorkshire fed into initiatives elsewhere in the country, and by the early 1990s a national network of people with Androgen Insensitivity Syndrome had emerged. After she retired she continued to run a local support group and to counsel women suffering from the condition.

This work had been done in a voluntary capacity, and full-time though her job was, Stella also made time to pursue her interest in the human growth movement. Although her move to the north meant abandoning the networks she had enjoyed in Guildford, she was able to continue her involvement with humanistic psychology by undertaking a two-year diploma course—a big commitment of time in evenings, weekends, and summer schools.[41] Run by Heron's Institute for the Development of Human Potential, the course involved 'group work practice and alternative therapies—e.g. Gestallt Therapy, Transactional Analysis, psychodrama, Encounter, Bio-Energetics, Hypnotherapy, Psychosynthesis as well as "tasters" of other therapies...'[42] Later on she started training as a hypnotherapist, although she never practised. Another outcome of the diploma course was that she began to keep a regular dream diary—it ran to nineteen volumes by 1993—and joined a group of women listening to and helping to analyse each other's dreams. Although in all this, 'personal development' was her primary aim, her continuing involvement with 'holistic therapy...provided...a good background for social work, counselling, and group work'.[43]

Immersed in work and the world of alternative therapies, she soon overcame her initial sense of isolation. Friendship was vital to Stella's well-being and during the 1980s she built a rich network of friends in Yorkshire, although her closest friends remained those she had made earlier in life with whom she kept in touch on the phone and with occasional visits. Nothing gave her greater pleasure, she wrote in 1993, than:

to sit down with a friend, gaze at her, take in how she looks (especially if we've been apart for some time), to hear how she is and what she's doing, to exchange news...then as we become centred in the present to start discussing ideas, thoughts about other people we know, books we've read, and especially feelings...I feel a glow of warmth, eyes light up when I contact a friend, when her name is just spoken. Present in my thoughts, in the back of the mind—an underground river just below the surface, such love is never far away, contact instantly rekindles the spark days or decades later.[44]

Her friends spanned the range from 'way out' to people almost as conventional as her own mother. Friends, she wrote, were more important to her than family, nurturing, each in their own way, the different facets of her personality.

Her sense of belonging in Yorkshire was further enhanced when she moved to a terraced Victorian stone house nestling under a hillside in a small town within commuting distance of Bradford. The street held a pleasing mixture of long-term working-class residents and recent professional immigrants, and the house itself seemed to exude a soothing atmosphere of 'calm and wisdom' when she first saw it on a wet afternoon in November 1984:

Later in the cliff-like garden I felt presences. After moving in I had a dream of three beautiful women dragging themselves on their bellies through thick mud—but this was not an unhappy dream—rather they seemed to be rising out of the mud. Later still I attended a course where a medium...explained that I had encountered the 'Devas'—spirits of the place. These are not ghosts exactly but some manifestations in Nature. I certainly want to believe in them. Sometimes I just stand in the garden and feel the weight of the hillside, my breathing slows down and I feel satisfied of their presence.[45]

In 1992, aged sixty-one, Stella decided to take early retirement. Three years before, frustrated by the increasing complexity of her management job in the constantly reorganizing department, she had stepped down from her senior position to become again a hands-on social worker. But she found the loss of status at work difficult, and the driving and long unsocial hours left her with little time for her many other pursuits. Not that she lost interest in her professional work. In retirement she took on paid work: covering for sick colleagues; short-term research, reviewing, and training projects; writing booklets on infertility issues. She also did a lot of work for a voluntary after-adoption counselling service which she had helped to establish. The organization, run by parents and adoptees and financed by Barnardo's children's homes, was entirely independent of the statutory authorities (with whom some clients had experienced such painful relationships that they refused to talk to them), and was designed to meet post-adoption needs that social services had no time to handle. As with her continuing work with victims of Androgen Insensitivity Syndrome, she used her professional expertise to help clients organize to fill gaps in the statutory provision. But she also made time to develop non-professional interests, running courses on 'working with dreams', joining a choir, attending classes on painting, pottery, and sculpture, and writing fiction: before retiring she had joined a creative writing class and she continued to belong to a writing group well into her seventies.

Her other main activity in retirement was providing bed and breakfast accommodation for walkers and cyclists. She had been doing this on a small scale at weekends ever since discovering, shortly after buying the house, that the previous owners had done likewise. It was a way of supplementing her income, and she enjoyed her light-hearted encounters with the guests, 'however varied...and however peculiar'.[46] One such encounter, however, turned out to be life-changing. One evening in the autumn of 1988 a man of roughly her own age turned up, having confused her place with somewhere he had stayed previously. Second-hand clothes from Oxfam, his belongings in a plastic bag, the pockets of his jacket bulging with odds and ends, speaking with a rough Lancashire accent, this was no weekend-walker. They chatted, watched a video together, and in the morning:

gazing out of the French windows he said: 'Your garden needs doing, want any help?'. I learned he had just moved to rooms in Halifax and taken a job 'with the council'. Later I learned he worked as a road-sweeper.[47]

Jim turned out to be a wonderfully imaginative gardener, sensitive to the same magic of the cliff-like garden which had captivated Stella. Over the next few months his love affair was with the garden, but he and Stella seldom met. Out all hours at work, she gave him a key, and their relationship was conducted largely via notes on the kitchen table: 'Done two hours. Peas podding up nicely. Calling in Sat. J.' When they did coincide she offered him 'first a cup of tea, later a drink, later still a meal'. Occasionally she took him in the car to get things from the garden centre, and then for the odd day out to visit other gardens. For some time she had been celibate, 'resigned to life without sex', and it took a message he sent when away on holiday for her to realize what was happening:

A picture postcard arrived, unsigned, depicting deep woodland. The message. 'I hope to take you into the woods myself before too long.' 'Ah well', I thought, 'and I thought I was past it!'

Nothing was said, but he started staying more often for meals. And then:

One wet Sunday afternoon when a planned garden visit just couldn't take place. 'Oh well', announced Jim, 'we've got to do it sooner or later' and he calmly escorted me to my bedroom and began removing his clothes without, honestly, one other word.[48]

They had very little in common, apart from music and the garden. Jim was a loner. He had no contact with his family and no friends. From a working-class Catholic background, he had worked in forty-two different jobs, lacked all ambition, and never planned ahead. His standards of bodily cleanliness fell well short of hers; he had no interest in people; and he took no pleasure in discussing his opinions. 'We have very, very different ideas about what constitutes a conversation.'[49] Politically they were worlds apart. Since becoming a social worker she had always voted Labour—'a natural outcome of the training, and of the experience'—whereas he read the *Daily Telegraph* and saw Mrs Thatcher as 'a tonic to the country'.[50] But the sex was marvellous, more fulfilling than anything she had previously experienced. Six months later, she came back from holiday in Greece to find that Jim, having been evicted for non-payment of rent, had moved in. And there he remained until shortly before his death twenty-five years later.

Stella wrote more explicitly and at greater length about her sex life than any of the other mass observers whose work I have read. She had first realized that the pleasure she derived from masturbation could also be achieved with a man in the early 1960s, but despite at least fifteen affairs during the next thirty years, it was not until she got together with Jim that she found complete satisfaction in sexual intercourse. It may not be entirely fanciful to suggest that one clue to her relationship with Jim is to be found in the event that originally alerted her to the possibilities of heterosexual sex—the *Lady Chatterley* trial. Jim was, after all, her gardener. Stella, 'brought up to be a terrible snob', knew very well that, confronted with popular taste, she had the reflexes of her class—'an inwardly raised eyebrow, so to speak'—despite her professional ability to suspend such prejudice in her dealings with working-class clients.[51] There is more than a whiff of Lawrentian class transgression in the way she writes about Jim:

I get deep pleasure from his physical presence: the look, feel and smell of him. If I'm out in the town shopping and I come upon him round a corner, limping a bit, with his feet turned out, wearing an old corduroy jacket with bulging pockets, I just can't help grinning from ear to ear, I'm so pleased to be taken by surprise by him ... He is not fussy about soap and water, but I love the smell of him.[52]

And not only Jim. One of the compensations for being an elderly lady was the freedom it gave her to indulge a lustful gaze that had excited her since adolescence. As a young woman on her daily trips to the local technical college she had found herself 'eyeing with extraordinary intentness the occasional passing male as I hurried through town. Blushing and ashamed I ... fixed my eyes upon the flies of any approaching male ... I probably passed the same blokes each day, but would never have known them from their faces.'[53] Sixty years later the only difference was the absence of shame:

One advantage of being an oldie is that one becomes invisible. Nobody thinks the half blind elderly lady at the front of the bus or quietly enjoying a coffee might be having sexual thoughts. I watch men in overalls, dungarees, aprons and especially those pouched garments favoured by painters and decorators— now I can get an eyeful with impunity.[54]

Class is surely at work here. But so is gender, and in an equally transgressive way. Stella did not see herself as an active feminist, having been content to leave campaigning for women's liberation to a younger generation: 'I accepted the goods that came from it with a reasonable degree of pleasure, but I myself did nothing...I was sort of too immersed in other things.'[55] Nevertheless, attending a feminist workshop in 1991, she reflected that among the sixty women present, 'all shapes, sizes, ages, attributes I thought "all I want is here"—in terms of relationships, friendship'. The long-term friendships that sustained her in life were all with women—although, despite offers, she was not interested in them sexually—while men came and went. Women, she felt, 'have a deeper range of feelings and behaviour available to them', they are 'the more "whole" sex, more fully capable of possessing the full range of qualities—in spite of that "extra six inches", in which men take such pride, being missing!' 'Why bother with men?', she asked herself, rhetorically.[56] The answer, clearly, lay with the extra six inches. Stella's objectifying gaze nicely subverts the gender order: it is men, not women, who are reduced to sex objects, faceless bearers of what she knew awaited her beneath their overalls.

When, in 1989, Jim moved in he did so with no prior discussion and, although she was furious at his presumption, she let it happen. For some years after her retirement they worked together to expand the bed and breakfast business before abandoning it in the late 1990s. They shared daily routines: the *Telegraph* crossword, watching TV, squabbling over the radio, and, of course, bed. But her relationship with her 'eccentric, shabby, awkward, irritable partner' was never easy.[57] He was too dependent on her 'emotionally, practically and financially', and, she felt, he resented his dependence. 'Warm and lovely at times', he could suddenly, for no apparent reason, become 'monstrously angry, cold, taciturn, critical of everything', and as he aged his irritability increased.[58] As with her decision to move to Yorkshire ten years earlier, she found it hard to understand why she had so meekly accepted him into her home. She had been happy on her own, and while she had enjoyed him staying at weekends, she had also valued having the house to herself when he left. She regretted not having kept it like that, and came to envy friends who sustained passionate but semi-detached relationships of this kind over many years. Still, she wrote in 2006, 'I love my partner [and] it's pointless regretting life's choices—with one different step, all would have been different. I wish I'd gone to University—but then I wouldn't have had the same life. Each life is a journey—what might transpire if we took the other path?'[59]

5

'Each life is a journey...' What can be learned about the culture of late-twentieth-century Britain from the journey that Stella made? For someone like myself who grew up assuming that the key to any desirable social change lay in politics of one kind or another, it is instructive to encounter a thoroughly engaged citizen for whom politics was largely a matter of indifference. She didn't read a daily paper, and shocked colleagues when she told them that the only part of the *Guardian* she didn't find boring was the Arts section. Although an avid listener to BBC Radio 4—especially *The Archers*, which she had followed since it began in 1950—she avoided news and current affairs programmes, which made her feel 'stupid, helpless, angry: HATE anything political...just point scoring games'.[60] Although pleased by the outcome of the 1997 election, she was not hopeful that New Labour—'a blind date...they are continually re-writing their own "truth" '—would save the welfare state or the National Health Service. At a time when many saw Blair as a fresh new start, she was perceptively disconcerted by his performance: 'glazed eyes, puppet grin, body movements give a lie to the message...'[61]

For some, like the woman we will encounter in the next chapter, political engagement offered a sense of purpose, a glimmer of hope for the future, a site of human contact and friendship in the present. While Stella found all these in her work, it was her engagement in the world of alternative therapies that did most to inform her understanding of life's larger puzzles. Some have linked the centrality of psychology in late-twentieth-century culture to 'the fall of public man', citizenship giving way, in the therapeutic society, to a malign narcissistic individualism.[62] Others, by contrast, have argued that the growing influence of psychological expertise has served to diffuse norms of behaviour required by liberal democracy, shaping the soul to the needs of modern society.[63] Stella's story suggests another reading, in which the explosion of alternative therapies from the 1970s fostered values which were neither individualistic nor normalizing. For Stella the therapies of the New Age embodied a critical practice with the potential to create a more egalitarian, caring, and co-operative society.

One thing that Stella learned from her work with disturbed children, and the families involved in fostering or adopting them, was that 'the pressure to appear *normal* is a tyrannical social force'. Nothing did more harm than the 'secrecy, shame and misinformation' surrounding deviations from assumed norms in the families it was her job to assess; or indeed in the lives of her own parents, 'their eyes and ears perpetually cocked for the social norms'.[64] The alternative therapies with which she experimented were geared not to adjusting the individual to predetermined social roles, but to freeing them from the tyranny of norms so that 'any problem can be looked at honestly out in the open'.[65] Freedom from norms was not, however, a recipe for anti-social individualism. Whether in Abercrombie's experiments in 1950 or Heron's humanistic psychology, the core of therapeutic practice lay in the work of the group, listening, and sharing, breaking down the barriers between people. The ethos was co-operative, not individualistic, and Stella saw herself as participating in a human growth *movement*, in its own way a politics of social transformation, paving the way (as Heron put it) for:

a self-generating culture . . . a society whose members are in a continuous process of collaborative action research, in which all forms of association are consciously adopted, periodically reviewed and altered in the light of experience, reflection and deeper vision.[66]

In the meantime one of Heron's leading objectives was to inform the everyday work of the professionals—doctors, teachers, social workers, etc.—who participated in his workshops. Although Stella described her participation as 'not directly linked to my work, more for personal development', she also believed that her professional practice owed as much to what she learned in the humanistic psychology movement as it did to her conventional training.[67] In Heron's philosophy of 'integral learning', personal, professional, and spiritual development were inseparably linked.[68]

In the week that Stella retired she found herself answering an MO directive about 'the pace of life'. In a mood to reflect on how her life might change now that she was no longer in full-time work, she explored the issue using the contrasting experiences of two friends—a stressed-out eighty-five-year-old workaholic psychologist all too happy to '*fill the unforgiving minute, with sixty seconds worth of distance run*'[69], and a Buddhist living on benefits who spent so much time listening to his inner voice that the things he was always 'about to do' were rarely started and never finished. While hoping to situate herself somewhere between these two extremes, she remained puzzled: 'As we don't have clear ideas about the purpose of life it is hard to know whether we lose out by rushing about or by sagging [sic] about.' Was the Buddhist wasting time; or was he escaping it altogether as she herself did in sex, never a 'waste of time because time becomes timeless in lovemaking'? This was, for Stella, more than just a figure of speech: 'to me there is another world where time is not of importance, and we live in that world as much as we live here...a parallel world where time doesn't exist— perhaps it's more important than what we call the "real" world'.[70]

One reason she paid such close attention to her dreams was that, as with her glimpse of the garden 'Devas', they gave her access to another reality in which 'I certainly want to believe'. As a child, fascinated by gothic tales, she had joined with friends in a 'Ghost Society': 'for some three years we regularly frightened ourselves with twilight visits to churchyards, lovers' lanes, old beach huts—anything dilapidated, dark, isolated, or ancient...'[71] She never did encounter a ghost, neither then nor later, but she continued to believe that they might well exist. As an adult she dipped into a variety of psychic activities, visiting astrologers and a clairvoyant; learning about Tarot cards and psychic healing; taking part in 'regression' workshops where hypnosis was used to make contact with previous lives. Ideas of reincarnation, she noted in 1996, had 'gently seeped into our way of thinking—working forward from the Beatles and the Maharishi, no doubt', but she remained unsure of their validity.[72] She attended the regression workshops 'in a spirit of enquiry' and enjoyed being in an altered state of consciousness, but 'always I came out at the same door as in I went...Alas, uncommitted.'[73] And when I asked her about the Devas in 2014 she had forgotten them: 'I'm much less spiritual than when I came here...'[74]

Alongside her openness to unconventional ideas and her willingness to explore, Stella was aware in herself of a 'hard core of cynicism or self-protection [which] prevented me from going the whole way'.[75] Charlatans abounded in the world of psychic practice, and many phenomena that New Age enthusiasts embraced as evidence of the paranormal—dowsing, out-of-body experiences, lunar and seasonal influences on behaviour, body auras—either were, or would eventually be, explicable in scientific terms: 'yesterday's supernatural', she wrote, with electrical and biochemical processes in mind, 'is today's science'. But ultimate mysteries remained. She had no time for Christian or other religious doctrine—projections of our deepest terrors and yearnings, myths made in the face of 'forces quite beyond our understanding'. Awed by our cosmological insignificance, 'we hope desperately that we are of importance and value, but we don't know'.[76] She wanted to believe in some other dimension in which life and death would make sense. Longingly she quoted Francis Thompson's evocation of a universal interconnectedness:

> All things by immortal power,
> Near or far,
> Hiddenly
> To each other link–ed are,
> That thou canst not stir a flower
> Without troubling of a star...

'That's what I want to believe', she wrote:

the web of being of which we ourselves form an infinitesimal part...our lives are woven into a giant tapestry, thread by thread, but...all we can see on our present plane is the tangle at the back of the tapestry...In some other time and place we may go round to the front, and see the glory of the pattern.

But in the end we simply don't know:

We are bound by space and time, our minds limited by our physical, biological make up...If there is some meaning or purpose we cannot grasp it. It is far, far beyond the capacity of our rigid, limited earth-bound mind. Like tadpoles in a pond for whom the concept of frog-ness is inconceivable.[77]

In old age, with death approaching, these ultimate uncertainties mattered more and more. Practical as ever she joined a University of the Third Age philosophy class where, once a fortnight, she could gain the 'blissful relief' of knowing 'without a shadow of doubt' that the others were 'as full of questions as myself. For two hours I know that there is no right answer waiting to be discovered and take comfort.'[78]

6

RAF Wife

Helen took up mass observing in her mid-sixties after reading Nella Last's wartime diaries.[1] Like Nella, she writes with great emotional intelligence—words, she had always understood, 'only resound in a healthy way when they chime with feelings'.[2] And no doubt she found in Nella's 'brave and insightful' account of her own 'gradual maturity' an echo of her own experience of a mid-life awakening following many years of constricting domesticity as housewife and mother.[3] In both cases the personal awakening was interwoven with, and partly triggered by, larger historical events: 'in so many ways', Helen wrote, history 'impacts on our lives and is vital for our feeling of self'.[4] For Nella it was the war; for Helen, the impact of the cultural shifts of the 1960s. In both cases it is a story of female emancipation, but Helen, born in 1921, thirty years later than Nella, enjoyed her new-found freedoms with none of the ambivalences that restricted the older woman's challenge to patriarchal authority. Nella, thrust back into domesticity after the end of the war, led a rather miserable old age. Helen's later years, by contrast, were a time of activism, satisfaction, and fulfilment; an exemplary case of the late-twentieth-century invention of the 'third age'.

I

Born fifth of seven children to a well-off, but philistine, family in the Wirral in 1921, she had a difficult childhood. One of her most vivid memories was of lying behind the sofa reading, over and over again, an account of William Wilberforce, 'The Man who Freed the Slaves' in Arthur Mee's *Children's Treasure House*, the twelve leather-bound volumes of which were the only books she remembered from an otherwise 'completely uncultured' home.[5] She would hide there to escape what she later referred to as the 'background noise', the fraught relationship of her parents, and 'the great quarrelling mass of kids whom they surely never meant to bring into their world'.[6] She described her mother as 'an ill-informed and shallow woman...only at ease with babies', who became 'distant and uninvolved' as her children began to acquire independent identities of their own.[7] A shop assistant from a humble background, she struggled in vain to 'move herself up' in order to please her husband; while he, a volatile, womanizing businessman brokering in dairy produce, bitterly regretted having succumbed to a shotgun wedding and took consolation with the live-in 'mother's help'. Helen, aged seven, caught them kissing, but kept the secret, 'knowing somehow that this was a taboo activity'.[8] Her father sent his children to private schools and thrashed them when they got bad school reports. Helen herself was spared the attentions of the cane which hung by the side of the grandfather clock, but when a teacher, spotting her potential, suggested he should keep her on at school beyond fifteen, he just laughed and said, 'You'll be just like your sisters. You'll get married.'[9] Her feelings about him were confused: 'here was this vital, humorous, loving man who could "turn nasty" and clip you over the ear or worse seemingly for nothing'.[10] But she treasured an infant memory of stuffing seaweed into his shoes—an assault which he not only accepted with good grace but also memorialized for the rest of his life in the nickname he used for his youngest daughter—Tiwi, the three-year-old's version of 'seaweed'.

Helen's childish obsession with the story of Wilberforce was not just a means of escape. Looking back from her eighties she felt that this early engagement with the horrors of the slave trade—in particular a memorably 'grim lithograph picture' of people packed like sardines in the hold of a slave ship—had an important impact on her own sense of identity, and one that acquired critical poignancy later in life when she discovered that the distinguished ancestor said to be at the apex of her family tree—Elizabeth I's favourite privateer, Sir John Hawkins—had been personally responsible for inventing the Atlantic slave trade, from which his descendants profited for several generations.[11]

At school she was outgoing, popular among her peer group, cheeky to teachers, and, at first, academically successful, excelling in English. She had little in common with her siblings, except for one older sister, who also 'read books and thought', and ran away from home aged thirteen only to be found in Birkenhead docks hiding in the hold of a ship bound for South Africa.[12] Subsequently Miriam stayed on to get her school certificate, before escaping to London to train as a nurse. Helen's rebellion was more self-destructive—neurotic stomach pains, becoming very thin, plummeting school performance, getting her thrills by stealing money from her mother and shop lifting without ever being rumbled. After leaving school she worked for a year or two in her father's office—until in 1940 the war enabled her to make her own escape.

Retrospectively she characterized her eighteen-year-old self, an auxiliary in the air force stationed at a Norfolk airfield, as 'feckless, irresolute, ignorant, intelligent, musical, manipulative, greedy'.[13] Her experience of the costs of war was both intimate and strangely 'disembodied': she 'would sit in an officers' mess laughing and talking to a breakfast table full of young pilots and the next morning a group of them were dead'.[14] Seventy-five years later, when I met her, she was still moved to tears by the memory of those young men. There were plenty of flirtations—'innocently talking and kissing'—but she resisted anything more and was teased by her women friends for being 'the only unsullied young girl in the Services'.[15] When she fell in love it was not with a man of her own age, but with an 'immensely cultured' twenty-seven-year-old Australian airman. Previously a Franciscan monk, he was 'handsome, unusual, highly intellectual . . . way, way above my own experience', and determined to marry her. Fired by 'a deep and abiding need to learn and grow', she was head over heels, but terrified. 'Overwhelmed by this knowledgeable and beautiful man . . . I knew instinctively that my uncultured background . . . would only be acceptable—to me and to him—when my sexual inhibitions were overcome. They never were.' Flouting the rules, absent without leave, they took a room for the night in a pub, just 'holding each other and talking'. As punishment—he missed a bombing raid—he was transferred 'to another part of the world. End of love story.'[16] In later years, looking back to this moment, she remained unsure whether their marriage would have been 'a total disaster or the beginning of a new life, a lifelong learning'.[17] For years afterwards, both by then married to other people, they continued to write to each other until his wife put a stop to it. Perhaps the awakening she was to experience in her forties could have come twenty years earlier, but 'it was all too much for my pathetic unformed mind to go to Australia and marry him'.[18]

2

As it was, in 1943, she played safe and married a 'childhood sweet-heart', a fighter pilot, who gave her the unwavering love and finan-cial security which was, eventually, to underpin her awakening, but only after a twenty-year 'decline into a life that didn't suit me'.[19] She wrote little about her years as a peripatetic service wife—'we moved 30 times in 20 years'—living in RAF married quarters, her two sons at boarding school, never staying long enough in one community to put down roots, trapped in a life of domesticity and dinner parties with 'silly, shallow...RAF wives' and their boring husbands ('all cloned').[20] When, aged forty-two, seven years after her second son was born, she found herself pregnant again, she felt 'a crushing sense of bewilderment...a rat in a trap'.[21] The birth of her daughter was a delight, but sleepless nights and the renewed demands of childcare left her deeply, if inarticulately, angry with her fate. She wrote off her peripatetic years as 'a dull and constricting experience',[22] relieved only by the two or three educated people she came across, including an intellectual landlord who lent her the book that she long remem-bered as opening her mind to the joys of serious reading: 'God bless *Catcher in the Rye*.'[23] In fact those years were not quite as empty as they came to seem to her by the time she was writing for MO. She took a couple of O-levels during this time and passed them with top grades.[24] And her literary horizons were extended in the early 1960s, when her husband was based in North Devon, and she became friendly with people in the bohemian circle around the Liberal MP Jeremy Thorpe. Her son, aged fourteen at the time, remembers novels by Hemingway, Fitzgerald, and Updike as 'the first books to come into our house'.[25]

From the mid-1960s her husband had a desk job at the Air Ministry in London and she was at last able to stop moving about. They settled down to civilian life in an urban community in Hertfordshire and 'within a year...I was a different person'.[26] Enclosed in her RAF cage, hearing 'on the periphery voices which spoke of a wider world', she had shared in the anxious dinner party talk of the collapse of all values. [27] But now, getting to know a new circle of people, she discovered that the shifting moral codes of the 1960s could be embraced, and need not be resisted. 'This was a new life and I loved it; being "out in the world" meant theatre, interesting films and discussions and learning about people and books.'[28] She discovered that there was no need to condemn one-parent families, the cohabitation of unmarried couples, or homosexuality. And, above all, she learned about politics, abandoning, 'without a backward glance', her previous Conservative attitudes and finding like-minded people in the local Labour Party. Reflecting on this moment, and her later involvement with the 1980s peace movement, she explained:

all these experiences...open you up to the sort of things that you've denied, whether personal, social, sexual, you name it...things you've denied all your life...I'd gone into a whole different life with a whole lot of different people and I...felt that I was the innocent abroad, it dislocated me...I didn't know quite where I belonged.[29]

Among her *Daily Express*- and *Telegraph*-reading siblings her overnight 'transition from Tory lady to Socialist firebrand' remained an abiding source of astonishment.[30] Her own children, on the other hand, were instrumental in her enlightenment: 'my greatest source of intelligent learning.'[31] In sharp contrast to accounts of the 1960s, which emphasize the generation gap—unprecedented according to Hobsbawm— Helen's story shows how cultural transmission can flow between the generations, and not only in one direction.[32] Her eldest son, able to escape from a hated minor public school to do his A-levels at the local grammar school when his parents settled down, became fully engaged with the revolutionary politics of the late 1960s and early 1970s.[33] Radicalized by the civil rights movement in the US, the Vietnam War, feminism, and gay liberation, he brought his politics home: 'I couldn't wait', Helen recalled, 'for new ideas to come home from College!...As parents we "grew up" with the children, with their revolution-on-the-streets, the injustices, the disparity between rich and poor.'[34] She went on marches, sold papers for her son's libertarian Marxist group, and helped out in the crèche at the group's summer school 'where they all slept in dormitories and talked all day'.[35] Later, in the early 1980s, she was a firm supporter of the leftward swing in the Labour Party. Her husband, a conservative monarchist until he retired, seems to have taken the domestic revolution in his stride. It cannot have been easy for the decorated air force group captain to adjust to a far-left son and a born-again socialist wife. He was 'a bit right wing', she remarked, 'but we pulled him over...' and later, in his sixties, he became affectionately known as 'the only Tory in our local Labour party.'[36]

Alongside the politics, film, theatre, and reading—'Virginia Woolf was an eye-opener'[37]—Helen took evening classes in English and psychology, did basic training in youth work, and took an intensive course in counselling. After volunteering in a local youth club she spent eight years employed as a part-time youth worker dealing with severely disturbed adolescents and discovering a 'hard and hopeless' world of deprivation. She loved the work, but after eight 'life enhancing' years her husband retired and, at his insistence, in 1982 they moved to a remote Welsh cottage in an isolated coastal area.[38] She 'died an emotional death', terrified that, deprived of work, politics, urban life, and company, she would be plunged back into lonely domesticity.[39]

There were few like-minded people among her immediate neighbours, as she discovered when taking turns to deliver newspapers to their remote houses: 'I keep up with the Terrible Tabloids by delivering them to my neighbours . . . and furtively scan the headlines to be suitably shocked!'[40] More to her taste was a nearby centre giving activity holidays to young children. She volunteered and joined the governing body while her husband, a keen sailor, helped with the outdoor pursuits. But it was the county town, half an hour away, that provided her with congenial company and an outlet for her energies. She put her experience as a youth worker to good use on the management committee of a women's refuge, working mainly with the children, and 'in contact almost daily with emergencies in the house'. Faced with the suicidal despair of some of the mothers she found herself 'alternating between exasperation and compassion', but she stuck at it.[41]

She also held office in the local Labour Party, respectful of the local MP, but depressed by New Labour's relentless pursuit of the marginal voter. 'I listen and listen and read and read and feel more and more debased', she wrote in the run-up to the 1997 election:

Everything has become so trivial in the urgent need to be elected . . . Are we sure we would lose votes if we said loudly and clearly that taxes must go up to pay for decent education, training, NHS?[42]

For Helen the high point of the local campaign was a visit from the Labour leader, Michael Foot, to canvass a local council estate:

We all stood in the sunshine to greet him (just a handful) and I couldn't resist putting my arms round the old war horse from Socialist days. Of course he had his scruffy little dog with him and he looked like a down and out in his terrible clothes as usual. People like that remain themselves.[43]

Her delight at Blair's 1997 victory was tempered by the fear that Labour's pursuit of 'middle England' would leave it unable, in government, to undo the depredations of Thatcherism.

Alongside the Labour Party, Helen was active in the peace movement. She was a member of the Campaign for Nuclear Disarmament and several times joined protests at Greenham Common: 'quite a remarkable experience', she wrote later, 'for someone brought up in complete political ignorance, and a huge turn round in my whole life...a dislocation which I embraced with enthusiasm...': although, along with many of the original Greenham women (one of whom became a life-long friend), she disliked the separatist politics that came to dominate the peace camp.[44] During the crisis that followed Saddam Hussein's 1989 invasion of Kuwait, mass observers were asked to keep a daily diary. Helen followed the build-up to the Gulf War with increasing 'anxiety and despair'. She joined her children and their families on a large demonstration in London a few days before war broke out, argued 'strongly and loudly' against the war—'too loudly: I was told to shut up!'—at local Labour Party meetings, and was pleased when even the neighbours—'the little group in our post office'— agreed that 'if the politicians had to fight these wars they would soon find other means'. During the war she listened all day to the radio, faithfully recording events and feelings in a diary she was 'beginning to detest'. The 'terrible inevitability of all this', she wrote, 'is like a huge weight on my spirit', giving her nightmares, sleepless nights, and a 'churning stomach'.[45]

Twelve years later watching the huge London demonstration against the Iraq War, she was proud that her children—and grandchildren— were there to represent her, and she was delighted when school students joined the protests:

If nothing else this terrible crisis has provoked an unprecedented response throughout the country. In small villages there are candle vigils—and certainly in our own local small towns there are many demonstrations. NOT IN MY NAME. That's how I feel.[46]

Despite her age (eighty-three) she twice joined local protestors on the five-hour journey to the Gloucestershire base where B52 bombers were taking off for Iraq:

...we had a Granny-Against-The-War demo with lots of singing and daffodils and rather ridiculous policemen/women standing passively all day in the sunshine. Two people were arrested but they left the grannies alone. We circled the base and came home feeling despair...[47]

Whatever comfort was to be found in the rituals of protest—and on this occasion the knowledge that her feelings were so widely shared—she remained profoundly disturbed by the horror of war.

Helen's husband died unexpectedly following an asthma attack in 1993. Although once, early in the marriage, she had been tempted to 'make a run for it', he became her 'absolute rock'. She had married for security—financial and emotional—'and that's what I've got'. Despite differences in their attitudes and ways of life—'I had nothing in common with him at all'—they were able to live 'fairly peacefully together' in 'an absolutely honest relationship'.[48] He had offered none of the challenges of her lost Australian lover, but she had 'no regrets . . . no bitterness . . . Being loved', she wrote in 1998, 'is a great compensation for anything more exciting'.[49] Her children, worried about how she would cope alone in her isolated house, urged her to move back to urban living. But, involved in politics and her voluntary work and with an extensive network of local friends, she was content to stay put.

Friendship—mainly with people who '"talk my language"...the books we read, the politics we share, the newspaper we read'—was central to her life.[50] She loved 'the warmth and intelligence of Labour Party people', and however 'debased' she felt by the triviality of New Labour's 1997 election campaign, she revelled in the company of fellow party stalwarts:

Today...in the railway club...stuffing envelopes...sitting round a huge table with committed, cheerful, decent members of the Labour Party...So much fun, banter, political complaints for five hours non-stop. A local member sent in trays of delicious sandwiches and tea and coffee were on board. Lovely atmosphere, win or lose.[51]

Her friends were of all ages, ranging from young paid workers at the women's refuge to a ninety-two-year-old friend, twenty years her senior, with whom she could talk about everything, including sex and politics. As a peripatetic RAF wife it had been difficult to make deep and lasting friendships, but she retained a few from those years, including one which she came to regret. Helen had been overawed, an 'unwitting stooge' to this woman, but now, 'grown up and away from feeling inferior', she found her boringly obsessed with domestic trivia. Although they were both in their eighties and living 150 miles apart, the 'friendship' lingered on:

Our children were brought up together, our husbands were friends, all those old memories. But the inherent misjudgement all those years ago would be too painful to try and untangle now, in old age, and it's pointless.[52]

By contrast, among like-minded people in Wales she was able to learn and to grow:

It's a wonderful experience for me [she wrote aged eighty-seven] to find younger people in their 50s and early 60s with whom I can have wide-ranging discussions and a warm and affectionate relationship and feel that it is a friendship.[53]

Most of her friends were women, and she confessed to feelings of 'unease and discomfort' in the company of men whose intelligence was seldom matched by their capacity to articulate or share their feelings: 'I've long been fascinated by the emotional immaturity of some of my intelligent friends.'[54] One of the good things about being a woman, she had learned as a young mother, was 'having real women friends with whom one could share...anger and frustration.'[55] Such friends fulfilled her own needs less problematically than the long-standing (and undiscovered) affair conducted by a young friend starved of warmth and intimacy by an intellectual husband, 'witty and attractive' but 'emotionally stunted'.[56] Helen had no religious belief, and confessed herself 'amazed that people close to me' could believe in fairy tales about God and the after life, but she understood 'the relationship my religious friends have with "their" God [as] the Best Friend contact, that beloved person who listens and loves me without criticism and advises me. I prefer the human bit', she added, 'but it's not so different? It's just that spirits have never attracted me.' She was, however, deeply impressed by the daughter of a friend, a parapsychologist gifted with insight into the collective unconscious of the earth, Helen believed, dismissing her own scepticism as a lack of imagination: 'Because of my temperament (ordinary) I think that these revelations will never come my way.'[57]

Writing in 1991 Helen described herself as 'a liberated woman...speaking the truth as I understand it, not what I was programmed to do and say', although she hesitated to embrace 'feminism', a word she associated with man-hating women, 'strident and out of control'.[58] She had, nevertheless, been a member of the National Abortion Campaign since its inception in 1975, and had joined mass lobbies in London in defence of abortion rights. She was quite happy when her children decided to live in stable relationships without getting married, accepting their view that marriage was now an outdated ritual. Among local friends in trouble to whom she offered 'support and affection and a sympathetic ear' was a young Catholic married woman involved in a lesbian relationship, and a gay man who finally dared to come out aged forty; both of them deeply upset by their parents' extreme hostility to their sexual preferences.[59] The warmth, intelligence, and generosity of Helen's attitudes were clear in her reaction to the Rushdie affair in 1989, when the book-burning reaction of some British Muslims provoked anti-immigrant sentiments among some mass observers—Len for example—and among most a deep unease. Helen, whose sensitivity to issues of race was informed both by her childhood horror at slavery (and her own ancestor's part in it), and by her acquisition of a West Indian daughter-in-law and (later) a mixed-race grandchild, interrogated her own reactions to the affair with an unusual degree of honesty:

I am stirred to anger when I see crowds of fundamentalists baying for Rushdie's blood, and I try to imagine this outrage. Then I become a typical racist and think 'well, if you don't like it here and our way of life and our language and our customs, you know what you can do'. Overcome by shame I try to imagine how I'd feel in their situation and I'm pretty sure I'd feel like them. Clustered together for safety, hanging on to their traditions, in a racist and ugly society which patronises them.[60]

3

After she settled down in Wales, Helen looked forward—health permitting—to an enjoyable old age:

...with some feeling of reasonable charity towards oneself, and enough warmth and food and family love to carry one to the end of life, old age for me is not all that bad. The losses are linked with the 'if only' syndrome; why wasn't I mature at 30, why wasn't I brave enough to develop independence? The gains are a gradual acceptance of the losses and a huge gratitude for a wonderful family...[61]

The acceptance was never complete, and her continuing anger is apparent in the way she writes about her mother, in her contemptuous dismissal of the superficiality of RAF life, and in her war-induced stomach pains. But these were no more than dim echoes of the over-whelming feelings she must have experienced when, in her forties, she transformed herself 'from Tory lady to Socialist firebrand'. By the time she took up writing for Mass Observation she had had time to digest and work through her earlier life and could look back on its depriv-ations with relative equanimity: 'The greatest gain' of aging, she wrote in 1992, 'is the result of a long and painful assessment of my own life which brings a sort of serenity which I missed when young... Confidence in oneself is beyond price.'[62]

It was, as she was the first to acknowledge, a serenity underpinned by financial security, good health, the satisfactions to be drawn from family, friendship, purposive activism in the wider community, and, not least, by her delight in her rural situation. In despair during the Gulf War she set off one morning:

... down to the beach through a snow-speckled meadow, over a fence into the woods and along a green path, with the dog racing and chasing all the way. The sea appears through a window in the trees, the sun shining and cold...I blunder down the cliff and onto the wet sand as the tide recedes. Two hours later I climb another path, collect wild watercress, and meet a group of chil-dren [out for a walk from the women's refuge].[63]

Twenty years later, aged ninety, she was still able to walk down to the beach and back, a 'great and lasting joy'.[64]

The years of her retirement were a bad time for a peace-loving socialist—Thatcher destroying everything she had come to value 'and with it my hopes of a decent society';[65] the Gulf War which she found hard to bear; a brief moment of hope with Blair's election, and then Iraq. What is historically significant about her story is that, although she felt these things deeply, she nevertheless lived a happy and fulfilled life in opposition to them. Late-twentieth-century Britain had space for an oppositional contentment, a contentment which deserves to be remembered as balance against more pessimistic accounts of the period. 'Before we get too depressed and negative about old age', she had written in 1990:

let's think of all those wonderful old people who, if they're not poor or dis-abled, swarm onto busses to lobby Parliament, do their bodies a world of good by attending afternoon ballroom dancing; go in droves to Bingo, church, OAP [pensioners] entertainments and are still valued in families when there's a new baby, can laugh and have sex...[66]

What Helen's story exemplifies, above all, is the late-twentieth-century invention of the 'third age'—a time late in life, for those with adequate pensions and decent health, to learn, grow, and be useful to others. As an older man with similar advantages (and views) I have found it easier to write sympathetically about her than about any of the others—but more difficult to find the critical distance necessary for an objective evaluation. Her remarks about the emotional immaturity of intellectual men strike an uncomfortable chord, to which I can only respond by basking in the warmth and generosity of her approach to the world. Unqualified admiration is, perhaps, not the best stance for a biographer with pretensions to contribute to the social history of his times. But on this occasion it is the best I can do.

7

Mechanic

Writing for MO is good therapy for someone like myself that has a
lot of thoughts, ideas, opinions on events and situations . . . As . . . mine
are usually minority views, there is some satisfaction in the thought
that I may be directing future historians to a line of investigation . . .
not universally considered.[1]

Len wrote, quite explicitly, *against* his times. Born into a working-class
family in 1930, he left school at sixteen, apprenticed as a motor
mechanic. Although, after many years on the shop floor, he eventually
made it into management he continued to see himself as working class.
He started writing for MO in 1987, shortly before he retired, driven by
a desire to put on record a dissenting view of recent history: 'I just did
not like the way modern history is being recorded . . . I saw an opportunity to record alternative views and ideas on issues that the press and
media so often distort according to their political dogma . . . My opportunity to stir the pot', he wrote, adding modestly: 'I hope no one
minds.'[2] As a one-time member of the Congregational church—
which, like the working class, was in rapid decline through much of his
adult life—he sought to uphold traditional values against the tides of
history. The world view he expresses—combining a rejection of fash-
ionably progressive attitudes to education, sexuality, female equality, or
multiculturalism, with an ethic of public service, pride in his skill,
hostility to managerial arrogance and capitalist profiteering—serves,
as he intended, to remind the historian of the experience of large
numbers of people caught between the hammer of the 1980s and the
anvil of the 1960s, people who felt themselves and what they stood for
marginalized, excluded, and politically unrepresented.

I

Len had grown up in a 'typical working-class environment' in North London, living in 'an assortment of lodgings and flats' until the family took out a mortgage on a house on a new estate in Enfield in 1937.[3] His father, apprenticed as a textile engineer in Manchester during the First World War and a staunch trade unionist, had moved south after the 1926 General Strike, whose collapse convinced him that 'the working man's worst enemy is the working man'.[4] His mother, like many young women of her generation, had escaped from domestic service to the relative freedom of factory work. She met Len's father, working as a skilled engineer in the same North London factory, and settled into full-time domesticity as a wife and mother after they married. Despite spending the first three years of the war evacuated away from home with his grandparents in Stockport and attending seven different schools between the ages of five and sixteen, Len remembered his childhood as secure and happy, 'blessed with caring parents and a stable family circle'.[5] But wartime exigencies disrupted his education and, to his parents' surprise, he failed the 11-plus.[6] Three years later, to his own surprise, he secured a place at the local technical college in Enfield.

Through the depression years of the 1930s his father had never been without a job and he was determined to hand on the same security to his son by apprenticing him to a trade. Fascinated by cars, Len started his apprenticeship in 1946 in a North London garage. Looking back he wondered whether his father had made the right decision, and he always remembered the words of a family friend: 'You want your arse kicked . . . signing 'dentures for him. You know very well once he puts on overalls and makes his hands dirty he becomes a second class employee for life.'[7] It is, however, difficult to see what other routes were open to the boy, given his continuing difficulties with the academic side of the apprenticeship. And when, three years later, his parents decided to set up a guest house on the south coast, Len, unable to survive alone on an apprentice's pay, was forced to move with them and quit the apprenticeship, making himself liable for National Service. Miserable, cut off from his friends, undermined by his mother's inability to disguise her disappointment at his lack of achievement, he decided to pre-empt his imminent call-up and sign on for five years as a regular soldier in the

Royal Electrical and Mechanical Engineers, most of it served in
Germany. He did well in the army, qualifying as a tank technician and
ending up 'lord of my own little kingdom', in command of a vehicle
repair and maintenance workshop employing 'military, German
civilian, and displaced person mechanics'.[8] Although he toyed with the
idea of making a career in the army, the security that this offered was
outweighed by his desire to find a wife and settle down to family life.

Len's return to civilian life was not easy. Employers were unimpressed by his military qualifications and he was in and out of jobs for
several months before finding employment in the vehicle maintenance department of a south coast engineering firm. The unexplained
suicide of his younger brother at this time rocked the family and
added to his own sense of disorientation. The austere and disciplined
post-war England he had left in 1949 was disappearing amidst teddy
boys, skiffle, and rock and roll. The ballroom dancing skills he had cultivated as a teenager lost their pulling power: 'I found I did not fit in.
At the local palais formality was all but dead. Young men no longer
asked a girl to dance. He just went up to her and nodded . . . At the age
of 24 I had become quaintly old fashioned.'[9] But perhaps this is what
appealed to the young woman he met one evening at the *palais de
dance* and proposed to three weeks later. Marion, a local girl working
as an office supervisor for British Rail, shared his distaste for most of
the cultural changes of the next two decades. Rejecting the 'crackpot
theories' of 'trendy progressives', they brought up their three sons,
born between 1957 and 1962, 'in a disciplined and controlled family
environment'.[10] When the kids went to school Len found himself
in constant conflict with 'progressive' teachers delivering what he
believed to be a substandard education, greatly inferior to his own.
When he complained that inadequate maths teaching would leave the
country short of 'the next generation of mechanics', he was infuriated
by one teacher's response: 'they were not training young people to be
factory fodder. They were being educated to enjoy a richer and fuller
experience of life.'[11] Long remembered and oft repeated, this remark
summed up for him everything that was wrong with progressive
education:

There was no 'learning is fun' ethic at the schools I attended. Learning what
was worth knowing was hard work. I was not being educated to 'enjoy a
richer and fuller experience of life'. I was being educated to be a useful and
productive man in the community . . . I left school well prepared for the

demands working life would make of me. I think I had the right frame of
mind for making my way in the world. There may be those who would say
my horizons were not as wide as they would be to-day, but then in all my
working life I have never been bothered by the threat of unemployment . . . I
do not think the educationalists of to-day will be able to make the same claims
of many of their ex-pupils . . . Thus are the seeds of future unemployment and
industrial decline sown.[12]

2

When the 1957 credit squeeze threatened Len's job in the engineering
firm he found more secure employment as a vehicle mechanic in the
transport department of a south coast local authority, and the couple
took out a mortgage on a bungalow in a nearby village where they
were still living when I met them in 2014. Having a trade brought him
security, but—as his father had been warned—it left him trapped in
manual work. In local government the divide between shop floor and
office seemed absolute, and promotion from one to the other floor
was unknown. By the mid-1960s, fed up with 'grovelling under motor
vehicles', he was casting around for more fulfilling employment.[13]
Taken on as foreman by a farmers' co-operative in 1967 he thought the
breakthrough had come, but found himself 'piggy in the middle'
between the directors who appointed him and a transport manager
who saw no need for a foreman.[14] He quit after a year. Back on the
shop floor he worked in a succession of unsatisfactory jobs culmin-
ating in two years with a badly run bus company which brought him
close to a nervous breakdown: 'I was constantly horrified at the engineering practice that they tolerated and in conflict with my supervisors.
To me it was something a daily miracle that someone somewhere
was not killed by a bus.'[15] The work was demanding, driven by a
crudely designed payment-by-results scheme that sowed antagonism
amongst the workers. Exposure to exhaust fumes in the ill-ventilated
workshop permanently damaged his sinuses. The prospect of another
twenty years in such conditions, 'struggling to keep up with a schedule
that had been designed for younger and stronger men', filled him with
despair. Somehow he overcame his depression—with the help, he later
wrote, of 'a loving, understanding, and forgiving wife'—took a pay cut
and returned to the relative calm of the local government job he had left
five years earlier.[16] Then his luck turned. The 1974 reorganization of

local government led to the amalgamation of several different authorities
whose transport operations were in various states of neglect and the
chief technical officer of the new authority, who understood the
need for men of practical experience to sort things out, appointed
Len as part of a team of superintendents 'responsible for the care and
maintenance of some 130 vehicles, 350 items of garden machinery and
light civil engineering plant, and two workshops and depot facilities'.[17]
Aged forty-three, he had finally made it into a junior management
position.

Marion insisted that they had now joined the middle class. Len
dissented. His family background, formative years, and twenty years
on the shop floor left him in doubt about his class identity: and any
pretensions he might have had to superior status were rudely stamped
on by better-educated superiors who made it clear that they continued to see him as a jumped-up mechanic. He might have a cosy
office to work in, but status was more difficult to come by, and the works
manager—'an officer and gentleman from the RAF'—dismissed him
as an ex-fitter, consistently ignoring his advice in favour of 'the
professional clever dicks in the Civic Centre'.[18]

Despite spending the last seventeen years of his working life as a
manager, Len's understanding of the world of work remained firmly
grounded in his experience as a skilled manual worker. While seldom
impressed by the abilities of his fellow workers—'once again', he
wrote of his return to the local authority workshop, 'I found that
out of a labour force of five mechanics I was the only one with the
skills to undertake the complete range of repairs to all the council's
vehicles'[19]—he had nothing but contempt for the ignorance, arrogance,
and incompetence of managers who lacked experience or understanding of the work they were supposed to be organizing. Worst of
all were the work-study men and the payment-by-results schemes for
which they were responsible. At the time that he joined the bus company the mania for payment by results had been at its height, driven
by the Labour government's belief that it provided a key to reversing
Britain's relative industrial decline. Len's view, on the contrary, was
that the imposition of ill-thought-out bonus systems did more damage
than any number of strikes:

The work study operator knows nothing about the job he is studying and that
is considered an asset. He looks at a job with an open mind and introduces
new ideas. Sadly there are good technical reasons why some things cannot be

done, particularly when maintaining heavy vehicles. Even sadder was the refusal of the work study [men] to listen to those reasons...Payment by results schemes were in fact an extremely disruptive way to measure productivity. Developed from manufacturing industry where it was a simple task to measure the work content of assembly line tasks. The claim that the same technique could be applied to something as complex as vehicle maintenance was absurd. Much of the data produced seemed to many mechanics pure guesswork. Some came from manufacturers all striving to claim that their vehicles' maintenance costs were lower than that of their competitors. No one seemed able to accept that a nut and bolt that had been on a vehicle for three or four years and for some hundred thousand miles was more difficult to remove than one that had been put on last week!

He hoped he had seen the back of such schemes when he left the bus company, but as a supervisor in the local authority where the pay was too low to retain and recruit workers with the necessary skills, he found that the only way he would be allowed to raise wages was by inviting the so-called 'efficiency experts' to devise a bonus scheme:

The clever dicks in work study produced a carbon copy of the...scheme that had been such a disaster [in the bus company]. I was horrified. Their proposals further reduced my already short staffed workshops and substantially increased their workload. The report submitted to chief officers and members began with the following sentence. 'This report has been produced with the use of synthetic data.' In vain I tried to get my chiefs to consider the meaning of the word synthetic.

His warnings that the men would find the scheme unacceptable were brushed aside with assurances that the unions had already agreed to it. Since none of his workers were union members this was of little help, so Len took it on himself 'to convince my staff that if they wanted dialogue with management they had to join the union', something the unions themselves had been quite unable to do. What had long been a non-union workshop became a closed shop and his 'laziest and most militant fitter' became the shop steward, negotiating with management over his head. The men soon found out how to exploit the absurdities of the bonus scheme to their own advantage, earning 'more money with a biro than they could with a spanner'. Abandoned by his superiors and unable to reassert managerial control on the shop floor, Len joined the union himself and took an active part in branch meetings, provoking the chief executive to storm into his office:

'You had better make your mind up. Do you want to be one of my managers or a shop steward?'

'Well sir', I replied, 'for many months now I have tried to present to my chiefs the difficulties their interventions have caused and the reasons why. They have consistently refused to acknowledge my concern, even to talk to me. If I want to know what damn fool decision I am going to have to implement next I have to ask my shop steward. I become active in the union and no less a person than yourself is in my office talking to me. Now you tell me what I should have done.'

Eventually the chief executive realized that the work-study experts had created a disaster:

Within a few months it was costing thousands of pounds every week to put work out to private garages and hiring in transport because so many of the council's vehicles were off the road. Routine maintenance came to a standstill. All my remaining fitting staff were running around like headless chickens fire fighting. Worse still the MOT testing programme came to a complete standstill. Vehicles either did not keep their test appointments or failed miserably.

Expecting disaster from the outset, Len had made careful preparations to ensure that 'when the excrement hit the fan' none of it would stick to himself. He kept a detailed record of his advice, the refusal of his superiors 'to consult my thirty years experience on their proposals' or to admit that things had gone badly wrong. In the event the chief executive sacked the senior technical officer in charge and relied on Len to 'pull the fat out of the fire'.

If the culture of payment by results, initially promoted by a Labour government, was anathema to Len, the Thatcher government's recipe for efficiency in local government was even worse. The Tory councillors who ran his authority were at the forefront of pushing through the privatization of municipal services. Having worked in the private sector Len initially had no fear of compulsory competitive tendering, confident that no private firm would make the heavy investment necessary to compete with the council's direct labour organization on equal terms. Equal terms, however, was the last thing that the councillors— 'dogmatic and bigoted', Len alleged—had in mind.[20] One by one the council outsourced its services, rigging the competitive bidding with such devices as loading an unfair share of central administrative costs onto in-house accounts, while subsidizing private contractors with the sale of under-priced plant and machinery and access to council resources. Len gave MO a detailed account of these manoeuvres, a valuable microcosm of the neo-liberal project as witnessed by a critic well placed to understand its inner workings. Although in the forefront of resisting these moves, Len nevertheless benefitted from them when, in 1986, his immediate boss was headhunted by the newly privatized refuse collection service leaving the chief executive with little choice but to promote Len from supervisor to transport manager. Perhaps he hoped Len would not be up to the job, thus justifying the eventual privatization of the transport department. In fact—although of course we only have Len's word for it—for a couple of years the department did well under his management, winning contracts from other public bodies and returning a sizeable profit. Learning from recent experience, Len took care to build his defences against privatization:

Vehicles and equipment were leased rather than purchased outright. There would be no new equipment to be handed over to contractors for peanuts. We learned to be secretive about the way we operated. That was for us to know and others to find out. Above all we had learned the need to control overheads and how to apportion them in a way that suited us best.

In 1988–9, however, with rising inflation and interest rates denting their profitability, and with the help of 'an amazing display of creative accountancy', outside consultants made the case for privatization and most of what was left of the council's direct labour organization was finally closed down. Len survived the purge and was expected to head up the small surviving works unit, but higher authority wanted him out and offered him early retirement one month before his sixtieth birthday 'on terms it would be foolish to reject':

I did survive a lot longer than most people thought I would, and the pay off, when they finally got me, was much higher than the statutory maximum. Presumably because I had demonstrated an ability to fight back and embarrass authority. After I had been pensioned off I learned that my efforts to protect myself had indeed caused great consternation in high places. There was some satisfaction in that.[21]

3

The failure of the Labour opposition on the council to challenge the dodgy accounting used to justify privatization reinforced Len's alienation from politicians of whatever party. While he was delighted when

Mrs Thatcher got her comeuppance, and again when the Tory government was finally ousted in 1997, he had little faith in a Labour Party
which, in his view, had abandoned its working-class roots decades
earlier. He came from a staunchly Labour home—both parents were
party members—and as a teenager he had joined the Labour League
of Youth, where he helped to engineer a coup against the middle-class
girls appointed to run the organization. When the local party leaders
responded by closing down the youth wing, that put an end to 'my
little dalliance with the Labour party', although he continued to think
of himself as 'a natural supporter of the Labour movement'.[22] It was
the experience of Labour governments in the 1960s and 70s that finally
broke this support. Barbara Castle's confrontation with the trade
unions, 'In Place of Strife', he believed, had set the agenda for Thatcher's
anti-union legislation ten years later and he described Castle as 'a
woman who almost single-handedly destroyed the modern labour
movement'. Experiencing Labour's incomes policies as 'a vendetta
against wages' he could not bring himself in 1979 to vote for a party
'that was always blaming people like me for their failures.'[23] He had no
time for those who blamed the 1978–9 'winter of discontent' on
left-wing agitators in the unions: 'To me it was a spontaneous explosion of anger from a working population that felt betrayed by their
own Labour government...'[24] Of course 'extreme left-wingers' exploited
the unrest, but 'in my experience the unions were doing their best to
keep the lid on pent up working class anger', a role he himself played
in his dual capacity as supervisor and union activist, helping to organize
a token twenty-four-hour strike of his own mechanics carefully timed
to cause the minimum of disruption.[25]

The transformations of the Thatcher years confirmed Len's sense of
belonging to a culture overtaken by history. But he was reacting not
just against the enrichment of the favoured few and the decline of
the manual working class, with which he identified, but equally to the
broader cultural shifts associated with the 1960s. In retrospect two
iconic moments stood out for Len: the *Lady Chatterley* trial of 1960,
which he saw as giving the green light to sexual license and promiscuity, and the 1966 TV docudrama about a homeless single mother,
Cathy Come Home, which, Len believed, had 'opened the flood
gates for the bleeding heart society'.[26] Combining in her person the
twin evils of undisciplined sexuality and welfare dependency, the
figure of the single mother summed up for Len much of what had

gone wrong with British society since the war. Among the unmarried mothers he had come across in his work with the council's emergency services, several, he was convinced, had 'deliberately got themselves in the family way in order to jump housing queues and qualify for state benefits'.[27] Cushioned by the welfare state and encouraged by 'progressive' schoolteachers to expect more from life than it could deliver, young people—boys as much as girls—were no longer able 'to anticipate the consequences of their behaviour' or 'to come to terms with the disciplines of life'. It was 'as if their instinct for self preservation has been wiped out'.[28]

At the root of much modern social evil was the feminist pursuit of an unnatural equality between the sexes:

Being a religious man I do not believe God intended men and women to be equal. I cannot even see how non believers with even a basic understanding of nature could rationally advance the cause of equality...Nature has equipped women to fulfil some functions in life and men others. The diversity of these tasks is so huge it should be obvious, even to a half wit, the mental and physical equipment needed to fulfil them is very different indeed.[29]

His appeal to God and 'nature' was deeply felt, underpinning equally his intolerance of the 'disgusting preferences' of homosexuals and his outrage at the idea of abortion on demand: 'The view that a woman's body is her own to do as she pleases...only serves to degrade the value of a woman's body, it is far more precious than that.'[30]

Feminists messed with nature at their peril. The pursuit of female equality by 'trendy progressives' fundamentally upset the natural, and divinely intended, gender order, causing untold social harm:

Abuse the sexual relationship and the whole fabric falls apart...self restraint, commitment, responsibility, trust, loyalty, all the best characteristics of human relationships.[31]

These values, embodied in his own marriage and that of his parents, were lost to the new generation, leaving both men and women floundering, miserable, and unfulfilled. Female teachers 'obsessed with sex equality humiliate boys by making them change a nappy on a doll', systematically undermining their masculinity. No-fault divorce laws enabled women selfishly pursuing impossible freedoms to shatter the lives of innocent husbands, something he observed when, as part of his job, he supervised a training scheme for the long-term unemployed:

tp: ut *****

:tet

All the men who came to me had been involved in a messy divorce and lost everything. Home, savings, family, job. Their wayward wives had taken everything leaving them with nothing, not even a desire to rebuild their lives... Their motivation to make their way in the world had been taken away from them.

Closer to home, 'wayward wives' had divorced both his sons, leaving them embittered, impoverished, and sadly reluctant to 'enter into any relationship with a woman that involves any commitment'.[32]

Women, no less than men, were victims of the cult of equality. The divorced wives would not find the happiness they were looking for. Just like the boys educated by misguided teachers 'to enjoy a richer and fuller experience of life', girls were being led down a path which would render them incapable of dealing with the realities of life:

It is not clever to indoctrinate their natural inclinations out of young girls in the class room and produce expectations which for most young women will extract a price that is not worth paying. By its very nature feminism can only benefit the more ambitious female, and then only those who have the talent to realize their ambitions. For the rest it will mean the worst of all worlds.[33]

Deprived of the femininity, and the age-old feminine wiles, which enabled women to hold their own ('always... their best weapon in the battle of the sexes'), they were being led to expect more than life could deliver and were likely to end up as miserable and lonely as the husbands they so casually betrayed. And as for the calculating, welfare-dependent 'Cathies', Len was well aware that the pregnant teenager was herself a victim of changing sexual mores which were far from liberating for women: 'Young men expect to have sex on demand, young women seem to think they ought to oblige.'[34]

If feminism had a lot to answer for, so too did the 'trendy progressive' embrace of multiculturalism: 'people who are "politically correct"', he remarked, 'are usually seeking to give away something that is the result of somebody else's hard work', in this case the living standards of the white working class.[35] Racism, he insisted, was a product of coloured immigration. Rather than trying to impose Islamic norms in British cities, immigrants should remember that the 'grinding poverty and deprivation' which they came to Britain to get away from was itself a product of their own culture. The political elite which, from 'Blunder Mac' (Harold Macmillan, prime minister 1957–63) onwards, had allowed parts of Britain to become 'swamped' with immigrants, should remember that 'desperate people turn to the politics of the hard right. It should never be forgotten that Hitler came to power in Germany through the democratic process, elected by a desperate and frustrated nation.'[36] He expressed his own alienation from the mainstream parties by voting for the UK Independence Party, whose Euro-scepticism he fully shared while distancing himself from the party's zanier characteristics: 'I have to admit that I am not sure how much I would like it if such people were ever to form a government.'[37]

A sense of frustrated nationhood had been central to his thinking ever since 'Blunder Mac' first applied to join the Common Market in 1961. He saw British membership, imposed and maintained against the popular will by a conspiracy of leading politicians, as a major source of the economic problems which the conspirators then 'blamed on people like me who worked for a living'.[38] His choice of newspaper—the *Daily Mail* and the *Mail on Sunday*—reflected these attitudes and no doubt reinforced them: but the fit was far from perfect. The *Mail* would hardly have shared his attitude to trade unionism or privatization, and he was often 'nauseated' by the paper's editorial bias towards the Tory Party. Len thought for himself, and his views were rooted not in press propaganda, but in fond memories of the Britain that had already begun to disappear when he came back from the army in 1954:

I have happy memories of my youth, just after the second world war. A time when no doubt to-day's bleeding heart society would claim young people were deprived. I have never seen it that way. True there were a lot of things we could not have or could not do. Yet we lived in a country that had immense pride, having endured a terrible war, overcome many dreadful experiences being the sole defender of freedom for a whole year. We lived in communities that had the clear aim to build a better world from the ruins of war. A sense of purpose and targets to achieve.[39]

Nostalgia, he confessed, was 'perhaps my greatest weakness', a weakness he shared with other working-class men drawn to autobiographical writing in late-twentieth-century Britain.[40] There was so much about modern life that was offensive and distasteful; why would the 'old reactionary', as he sometimes described himself, not turn to the past for consolation? Among the pleasures he listed in the 1990s were the 'sheer magic' of old Hollywood films on TV (romance without indecency) and of listening to the big band music of his youth.

4

He did his best to fight against modern evils, in his family life, at work, and as a voluntary worker in his local community. As a loyal member of the Congregational church in the early 1960s he was 'frog marched' by his minister into running the local scout troop. For the next thirteen years, drawing on his experience in the military, he devoted much of his spare time to the scouts: organizing summer camps; weekend adventures on the South Downs; and swimming, life-saving, first-aid, and other courses 'almost every night of the week'. The work took over his life, and he found it less rewarding and 'more demanding than the job I did to earn a living'.[41] He was particularly distressed by the growing indiscipline of 'a generation of young people ever ready to assert their rights but with no interest in their obligations'.[42] When, on a training course for scout leaders, he spoke about the need for greater discipline on the more adventurous activities, a 'hush...fell upon the group at the mention of *that* word and I found I was no longer able to contribute to the discussion.'[43] Even in the world of scouting, 'progressive' ideas were destroying the old values.

Len was not cut out to be a youth leader. Nothing that he wrote suggests that he actually enjoyed the company of the young, and he often wondered whether 'the aggravation and abuse I got, even from those I was trying to help, was worth the trouble'.[44] He was by nature something of a loner: 'It is the way I am', he wrote, 'I am not an outgoing person...Nor am I the sort of person that makes friends easily.'[45] Responding to an MO directive on 'friendship' in 2008 he said that there was no one from his past with whom he wanted to keep in touch. At work he had always found it difficult to be one of the lads, and was at one time known as 'the isolated fitter'. But he was not lonely—his wife and her large extended family 'offer me all the companionship I need'.[46] Since the death of his brother in 1956 he had had little to do with his own family. His mother disapproved of his marriage and his lack of ambition, and his parents had abandoned their guest house and moved north to live near his elder sister.

His work with the scouts was more a question of duty than of pleasure, driven above all by 'my religious belief that a Christian should serve his fellow man'.[47] At the time he was an active member of the local Congregational church. But, an alien among the middle-class people in charge, he did not find it a comfortable place to be:

being a mechanic I was seen as the right person to help out with the problems of a practical nature, looking after the boiler for instance. Whenever I had anything to say about the administration or policies...they had ways, quite hurtful at times, of putting me in my place. It was not always intentional, it just did not occur to some people that a horny handed mechanic could have anything worthwhile to say.[48]

He gave up both the scouting and the church following the death of his twenty-year-old son in a motor-cycle accident in 1979—a grim echo of his younger brother's suicide thirty years earlier. His son's grave, which he and Marion visited every week, became their church. Sadly, the church had allowed itself to be 'corrupted by modern morality' and no longer stood for the values in which he believed. It was now in the hands of a younger generation who went in for 'happy clappy services...[and] had little time for grieving parents'.[49] Although Len remained a 'God-fearing man', his faith was severely tested not only by the death of his son but also by the affliction suffered by one of his grandchildren, 'locked into lifelong infancy' by Rett syndrome:

She has a twin brother and her condition has made him hostile to all religious belief. 'What sort of God allows such an affliction with no hope of successful treatment?' It is a question I cannot answer...I like to think something better than her life with us awaits her when she dies. I dream about it sometimes. We are walking down a country lane. My granddaughter walks beside me, holding my hand and chatting away nineteen to the dozen. If only.[50]

By this time, in his late seventies, he was deeply sceptical about the value of organized religion, dismayed by its role over the centuries in inciting conflict and war, but still unable to abandon his belief in God: 'Which leaves me wondering. Is God religious? Or is that a silly question?'[51]

5

Len bitterly resented being forced into premature retirement. For a couple of years he picked up pin money as a van driver for a local garden centre and put his training and experience to use on the management committee of a local community bus project, for which he also worked as a volunteer driver. Family duties, supporting his divorced sons and helping with the grandchildren, took up much of his time; and through his wife, who had always acted as a kind of 'agony aunt' in her extended family, he remained in contact with a wide circle of people. But his main activity in retirement was to develop new skills as a writer. Among the courses he had been sent on as part of his management training in the 1980s was one on creative writing, and during his final years at work he followed this up with evening classes. By 1991 he had produced 'one full length work of fiction, several short stories and plays, and some poetry', although regretfully he told MO that 'publishers do not share my high opinion of my work'.[52] What he found most rewarding, however, was delving into his family history—'a fast growing hobby with many older people'.[53] Stimulated by the discovery of some papers which showed that his wife's grandfather had been 'well connected with a wealthy family in Windsor',[54] he threw himself into the research, uncovering 'many fascinating, even dramatic, stories' amongst his and his wife's ancestors: 'material', he wrote in 2004, 'for a whole series of novels. Were I clever enough to write them.' Struck by the paucity of documentary evidence left behind by his more plebeian ancestors, and hopeful that his own grandchildren, 'or even their grand children', might be as interested as he had become in family history, he decided to write an autobiography, 'recording the events that shaped my life, how I was affected by them, and how I responded'.[55] Already by 1994 he had completed a draft of nearly 1000 handwritten pages:

it has been a very interesting exercise. I had not realised how eventful my life had been, though I wonder sometimes how much it will interest other people. Perhaps it is just an exercise in vanity. Anyway as the wife says it keeps the old boy occupied. I have not written my work with a view to publication, well not in my lifetime. It may interest those future generations exploring their family history or perhaps some future social historians. So far ... only my wife has read the completed chapters. It is an autobiography that pulls no punches.[56]

Len's third career—worker, manager, and now writer—must have done something to assuage the sense of unfulfilled potential that had haunted him ever since his father's friend had warned that an apprenticeship would condemn him to life as a second-class citizen. In many ways he had embraced that life, adopting the inverted snobbery of the skilled worker as his core identity, condescending towards the ignorance and impracticality of the 'superior' classes—the bosses, politicians, and the 'clever dick' so-called experts in whom they put their trust—while, at the same time, remaining painfully aware that the values he stood for were rapidly losing purchase in late-twentieth-century Britain. In his writing for MO—which continues to the present day—he sought to redress the balance in an archive which he assumed, rightly, would tend to over-represent people 'inclined to modern progressive thinking'.[57] Second-class citizen he might be, and on the losing side of history, but his running commentary on the follies of the political elite was intelligent and well informed, and by using MO to give future historians pointers to an alternative way of telling the story of modern Britain he was doing something to transcend his own subordination.

As a self-confessed 'old reactionary' who defended education geared to the realities of working-class life against 'progressive' teachers foolishly indoctrinating their pupils with an expectation of 'a richer and fuller experience of life' that few of them would be able to achieve, Len could be seen as a man who had internalized a narrow and life-denying subaltern consciousness. But as an MO correspondent, an autobiographer, and family historian, he found a way of answering back to 'those who would say my horizons were not as wide as they' should be.[58] By the very act of putting on record the experience, thoughts, and feelings of a man who felt himself bypassed by 'progress', he was overcoming his own limits and contributing directly to a 'richer and fuller' account of the history of his times.

8

Lorry Driver

The story told by Len is echoed in many ways by Bob Rust,[1] a lorry driver and one of MO's longest-serving contributors. The similarities between the two men's experience are striking. Both grew up in North London: Len, born in 1930, in Tottenham, and Bob, four years later, in neighbouring Wood Green. Both spent two years at Enfield Technical College, Len leaving in 1946, the year before Bob arrived. Both started apprenticeships as motor mechanics, and both subsequently signed on for several years in the 1950s as regular soldiers in the Royal Engineers. After the army their careers diverged, Bob working as a lorry driver until his retirement in 1997.

Bob defines himself as 'working class from the soles of my safety boots'.[2] Born into a settled working-class community in 1934—at school he had the same teachers as his father and mother twenty-five years earlier—his forebears on both sides were working class as far back as he is able to trace: horsemen, carpenters, railwaymen. His grandfather and father had both been lorry drivers, and Bob followed suit, as, indeed, did his own son. Proud of his occupation and of his class, he became a left-wing socialist and, for much of his working life, a trade-union activist. Shortly after starting to write for MO at the beginning of the new project in 1981, however, he began to have his doubts. Like Len's, his contributions document the late-twentieth-century collapse of a working-class identity formed in the crisis of the Second World War. But they do so from the standpoint of an occupational identity which resists easy classification.

Lorry-driving attracted men who refused the regimentation characteristic of most working-class occupations, individualists who treasured their freedom from supervision in the cab, loners who could tolerate the isolation of driving and nights away from home. At the same time, however, there was a strong sense of occupational identity. Aware of their strategic position in economic life, drivers demonstrated their capacity for solidarity in 1979, when they played a key role in the 'winter of discontent' and again in the fuel tax protest of 2000.[3] At an everyday level, solidarity was manifested in the expectation that drivers would stop to help out with breakdowns and in the companionship of the transport café and overnight 'digs' (lodgings).[4] Bob identifies strongly with his occupation. In 1979 he joined a club for vintage lorry enthusiasts—a club that he still helps to run—and after his retirement he published a vividly anecdotal account of his own working life.[5] His own personal trajectory shines light on the shifting balance between solidarity and individualism as drivers confronted the challenges of the later twentieth century.

I

Five years old when the war began and living in North London, Bob's schooling was a patchy affair. Although he was not evacuated, when the Blitz was at his height his father, a long-distance lorry driver, would take the boy with him on his travels. By the age of eleven Bob was an experienced furniture porter and mechanic's mate (his father repaired the firm's lorries), and often played truant from school when Dad needed a helping hand. He looked back on these trips as crucial to his education, teaching not only practical skills and British geography, but also history. They visited ancient sites together, and his father told him their stories, giving Bob the edge over more sedentary children back at school: 'I had had a pee against the stones of Stonehenge when my mates had never heard of it.'[6] He also learned a technique, invaluable in days of rationing, for appropriating a jam jar full of sugar from their load by inserting a highly polished piece of petrol pipe into the sack. Admitted as 'Bert's boy' to transport café chatter, he felt at home in the camaraderie of the road and knew that he wanted to follow in his father's footsteps when he grew up.

At home, too, he was treated from a young age as a responsible adult, cooking the mid-day meal for his younger brother when his mother went out to work later in the war. She had taught him to read in infancy, and his precocious intelligence is apparent in a story he tells of his puzzlement in the assembly hall on his first day at school. While the others closed their eyes in prayer, he tried to figure out why the light shining through a round window high up on the wall appeared on the floor shaped as an oval. Such curiosity about how the world worked was fostered by the talk around the kitchen table: 'my family were great radio listeners and conversationalists.'[7] Years later, when he brought his future wife to meet his folks, she was bemused by their habit of conducting simultaneous conversations on different topics: 'it took her months to work out who was talking to whom about what'.[8] His father, 'uneducated but extremely knowledgeable', was, in his spare time, a self-taught metal worker, electrical engineer, cabinet maker, French polisher, and 'into DIY before it was invented'.[9] One uncle was a toolmaker, another a bricklayer, an active shop steward, and a Communist, as was his maternal grandfather, a railwayman. The talk amongst these men did much to shape the young boy's view of the world and his place in it.

Native wit and knowledge of the adult world compensated for Bob's disrupted schooling. In 1944, when the VI flying bombs arrived, the classroom windows were left open so that the children could hear them coming and get under the desks until they exploded, thankfully, somewhere else. The brand new 11-plus exam was less predictable. No one had seen an IQ test or a multiple-choice exam before, and Bob's teachers were unable to do anything to prepare their pupils. 'When the General Knowledge paper was opened there was an audible gasp. There were sets of numbers, sequences of shapes, true or false statements…'[10] Undaunted, Bob sailed through and won himself a place at what everyone considered to be the best grammar school in Tottenham.

This was not at all what he had in mind. Not for him the pain and privilege of upward mobility into the middle class: 'I could not see myself as an academic learning French, Latin and the Classics.'[11] Remarkably for an eleven-year-old, he knew from the newspapers that the 1944 Education Act had established technical schools much better fitted to the kind of schooling he had been taught to value: education as a 'supplement [to] manual skill in the pursuit of earning a living'.[12] The grammar school, astonished at being turned down, sent for his mother, but she told them: 'We brought him up to make his own decisions, if that's what he wants me and his Dad will support him.'[13] He had to wait until he was thirteen to join the technical school in Enfield, and then only stayed there for two years, declining a third year and

leaving school for good at fifteen after talking things over with the
teacher of engineering workshop practice:

I've watched you since you started here. You've worked with your hands and
mixed with adults all your life. You treat teachers as equals and are more at
home with the adult college staff than with the boys. Go to work, you'll be
happy there. One day you'll see the need to improve your academic education.
If circumstances permit, then will be the time for schooling.[14]

It was in his late twenties that Bob began to discover something of
the intellectual and cultural world that a grammar-school education
would have opened up for him, but by that time circumstances did
not permit: 'I was married with two young children, working twelve
hours a day six and a half days a week.' There was no time for further
education, although, as we shall see, he found other ways of widening
his horizons.

By turning down his grammar-school place Bob chose to remain
working class. Unlike Len, whose father ignored a warning that by
putting the boy into overalls he was condemning him to life as a second-
class citizen, no one in Bob's family saw his decision as a perverse
embrace of subaltern status. Proponents of the new technical schools
argued that there should be no status hierarchy between the different
kinds of schooling. Explaining her support for the system to the 1946
Labour Party conference, the minister of education, Ellen Wilkinson,
remarked that 'not everyone wants an academic education. After all
coal has to be mined and fields ploughed.'[15] Bob would have agreed,
and with no suggestion that the skilled manual worker was in any way
inferior to his academically trained compatriots. Bob's choice was a
product not just of values inherited from his family, but also of his times.
It was not unreasonable for a politically aware eleven-year-old—he
helped campaign in the 1945 election—to see in Labour's triumph
evidence that the prestige enjoyed by skilled workers, saviours of the
nation during the 'people's war', had come to stay. 'We are the masters
now', declared Labour's attorney general, repealing anti-union laws in
1946. The boy was not to know that the triumphalist mood would be
short-lived. The optimism of 1945 left its mark and it was not until
Mrs Thatcher and the 1980s that Bob, along with many others formed
in that new dawn, was finally to abandon faith in the capacity of the
workers to refashion British society.

2

After leaving school Bob was apprenticed as a motor mechanic before joining the Royal Electrical and Mechanical Engineers as a regular soldier for three years as a (better-paid) alternative to National Service, two of them in Hong Kong. Back home in April 1955 he tried to get a job with British Road Services, state owned and unionized, but was rebuffed at the local depot: 'you have to wait for some poor bugger to die'.[16] For the next six years, interrupted by a spell in Tripoli when he was called up as a reservist during the Suez Crisis, he worked for a series of small private firms delivering TVs, furniture, pianos, and general merchandise, some of them run by owner-drivers and all operating on (or beyond) the margins of legality. Prizing the freedom of the road, and their ability to maximize earnings by putting in more hours than the law allowed, drivers put up with poorly maintained vehicles and, in Bob's case, the inconvenience of unpaid fuel bills which left him 'trekking from garage to garage...trying to find one where your firm was not on the blacklist'.[17] Eventually one of his employers was caught embezzling the drivers' national insurance contributions, and when the firm was taken over by a much larger one Bob was elected shop steward to negotiate with the new management. He did not last long, but his involvement with the union finally opened the door to secure employment in the nationalized industry. In 1961 his union branch secretary found him temporary work with BRS as a holiday replacement paving the way for twenty-three years with various branches of the company, interrupted by six months on the dole after a minor disciplinary offence gave the management the opportunity to get rid of an active trade unionist. Following the normal pattern of a lorry driver's career he had started out doing local deliveries ('shunting') before moving onto long-distance work ('tramping'), delivering and picking up loads all over the country and often spending several nights a week away from home. In the 1970s, re-employed by BRS, he returned to shunting, but on internal work, transporting raw materials and finished products to and from incoming lorries inside the Ford's tractor plant in Basildon, where, by now, he was living. Made redundant in 1983, he returned to the private sector for the last fourteen years of his working life.

Unlike some of the 'cowboys' in the private sector, Bob took pride in the contribution of lorry drivers to economic life: 'I like to go past a building and think I helped to build that, I delivered all the precast or all the flooring.'[18] As a mass observer he was pleased to recall that during the 1960s he had delivered materials for the construction of Sussex University, where the archive was later to be housed. Bob saw lorry-driving not just as a job but as 'a way of life', and one appropriate to a man who described himself as 'a solitary, self-sufficient person, who does not need close human contact.'[19] During the many tedious hours of waiting that were characteristic of a lorry driver's job, he entertained himself with science fiction, thrillers, comedy, and fantasy novels, or, more unusually, knitting—a skill he had learned at school and used to make clothes for his wife and children, including a full-length Arran coat for his elder daughter. And, from the 1980s, there were the MO directives: 'I'm a great muller, sometimes for weeks. I always read the directives through a couple of times and then let my brain get on with it... Thinking about MO's latest topic and for-mulating answers takes the boredom out of a boring job...'[20] What he valued in the cab was more the absence of supervision than the solitude, and he picked up hitch-hikers when he could. The most rewarding were college girls going home for the weekend with bags full of washing for Mum. They were always good conversationalists, and much more fun than their male counterparts who only wanted to talk about 'rugby, booze and birds... I particularly remember a debate on the morality of birth control which lasted from Nottingham to the North Circular.'[21]

Ever since his boyhood trips with his Dad, Bob had felt at home in the social world of the long-distance lorry driver. His definition of a friend—'in the fashion of lorry drivers'—was someone with whom he could 'pick up the conversation from the last time we met'.[22] The hub of the drivers' social life was the transport café. By the 1980s the motorway network had put paid to many of them, but a full quarter of Bob's published memoir of his working life is devoted to an encyclopaedic description of the hundreds of transport cafés he had frequented, each cemented in memory with its own anecdote. Taking breaks in the cafés drivers chatted, joked, played cards, and caught up with the latest gossip. According to one driver, writing in the early 1960s, the great majority of the talk was about the job:

I don't suppose there is another body of men like us for discussing their work...New types of wagon, always a firm favourite. Roads up, roads down, speed traps, sections presided over by unusually tough cops, loads, return loads, firms, governors, foremen...[23]

Sometimes mundane talk about the hazards of the road was spiced with ghost stories. Bob enjoyed these and wrote about them at length. Drivers taking a nap in the small hours parked up near Coventry would hear, but never see, a man walking with a wooden leg. On making enquiries locally Bob discovered that a lengthsman (a man employed to take care of a length of road) who had been clearing a nearby drain in the 1920s had lost a leg after being hit by a lorry. Fitted with a peg leg, he eventually went back to work, only to be hit by another lorry and killed. In another lengthsman story from the A4 road near Reading, drivers approaching a dip in the road notorious for black ice would sometimes see an old man sitting on a wall waving to slow them down. When they stopped to ask what was wrong, the old man vanished. In the 1930s, it turned out, the local lengthsman had been killed by a skidding lorry while gritting the road. People dealing with breakdowns at a particular spot in Warwickshire were terrified by an ancient vehicle which appeared to drive straight through the lorry they were working on: 'The story is always in essence the same', Bob wrote, 'a winter's night and there is some mist or fog'.[24] In 1923 a lorry, just like the one whose ghost appeared from the mist, had crashed in exactly the same place and its driver was killed. Other apparitions warned more directly of danger. The driver and his mate who saw a horse-drawn stagecoach crossing the road in front of them immediately knew it as a 'fetch'—a portent of death. Abandoning their lorry—doors open, lights on, engine running—they walked five miles to the nearest phone box and told the foreman 'they would go no further'.[25] When Bob met them, several years later, neither man had driven again, although a sympathetic boss kept them on as yard workers.

Bob had no doubt about the authenticity of these stories, and on one occasion was convinced that he himself had witnessed a ghostly apparition. At 2 a.m. one night he broke down near the site of the civil war battle of Edgehill: 'As I was sitting pondering the next move, I heard slow footsteps on the road and a sound like a stick being dragged along. I put on the headlights but could see nothing.' As soon as he got out to take a closer look the noise stopped, and he thought no more about it. Eight years later, lunching in a pub near Edgehill, he overheard people talking about 'the wounded Roundhead' whose skeleton had been found several decades earlier and whose ghostly apparition—'a soldier plodding along the road trailing his pike'—was well known in the locality. Bob is a convinced atheist, and, as he himself points out, there is a curious illogic in believing in ghosts while rejecting any notion of an afterlife. Did experience, and the culture of the road, trump logic? Or might there be a perfectly natural explanation for such phenomena? Thinking about the way in which a short-circuited capacitor could violently discharge its energy, Bob wondered whether 'the electrical energy which occurs in one's brain and makes the difference between being alive and dead is somehow captured in the surroundings at the point of sudden, violent death'.[26] He has a fertile technical imagination, and is well aware that there are many things that science has yet to explain. Be that as it may, the sociological function of these stories was clear enough—the pleasures of storytelling helping to cement group identity among men whose work, most of the time, was stressful, boring, and lonely.

Many transport cafés provided overnight digs as well as food and conversation, and their owners were significant figures in the lorry drivers' world. Among the 'transport ladies' who provided digs, there were some for whom Bob would babysit if they wanted to go out for the evening, or who, if a driver was taken ill on the road, would take him in and nurse him 'just like at home'.[27] There was a place on the main road to Scotland, near Penrith, where he several times took the family to stay for their holidays. Bet, the woman who ran it, was a close friend:

She is a wonderful woman and her digs was always home from home. Anybody taken ill on the road or injured in some way would get to 'Bet's' by hook or crook, she would put them up, nurse them back to health, even arrange a driver to unload their wagon or get it back to its home depot...[28]

When he was 'tramping' in the 1950s:

she knew everybody's runs and deliveries and if you had an odd delivery miles out of the way, Bet would know who was going there with a big lot, so you could leave it with her and she would arrange to get it delivered.[29]

In the winter, if the high passes were closed by snow:

Bet would take in anybody who was stuck. I've seen her place with two in every bed, and the entire floor covered with 'shake downs'... Bet used to keep huge stocks of everything come winter and she had an AGA cooker which had not been out for over 30 years. She used to make great earthenware crocks of homemade wine which was strong enough to stun a Cossack. She also went in for herbal cures which all the drivers swore by... The locals used to call her the Witch of Brougham.[30]

Some of the cafés provided other compensations for lonely drivers in the shape of 'ladies of the night'. While Bob did not avail himself of their professional services, he was friendly with several of them and tells their stories (prefaced by an appropriate warning of their pornographic nature) in his published memoir. He made other women friends as well, notably a colleague who was 'so much a driver that it's easy to forget that she's female. One of the most sensible, practical, down to earth people you could meet.'[31] In the 1980s she was founder and chairman (her preferred designation) of the Lady Truckers Club, networking and providing support for female drivers. Another such club, founded more recently, described itself, with a panache appropriate to women intent on gatecrashing masculine territory, as the Mother Truckers. Women were acceptable in this male world if they took on its values, but Bob could not forgive the editor of the road-haulage trade journal in the later 1980s, a female graduate, who transformed what had been a paper 'written by men in the industry for men in the industry' into 'a coffee table magazine for transport cost-accountants'.[32]

3

Bob's self-image as a bit of a loner might well have been disputed by those who knew him best, but it served to protect the safe masculine distance which he had learned from a father he described as 'a very unemotional man'—trusted and admired, but to whom, despite being 'very close... I never felt emotionally attached'.[33] His father figured in his life, above all, as a mentor and a mate in the world of work. Even after his early death from lung cancer in 1962, Bob felt that his Dad:

...was keeping an eye on me; in the fog: in the winter when the roads were bad... When something was starting to go wrong with a vehicle or a load, although there was no physical indication, I got and still get a strong feeling that I must stop and look round the vehicle. It could be that I unconsciously absorbed so much of his knowledge that I sense tiny changes subconsciously.[34]

When, in old age, he was asked to write about 'friendship' by MO, he puzzled over the term and was not sure that he knew what it meant or whether he had any friends. 'Do children count as friends?', he asked wistfully, thinking particularly of his younger daughter, who lives next door.[35] Quoting with approval an old saying—'A son is a son till he takes him a wife. A daughter's a daughter the whole of her life'—he reflected that he had reproduced much the same close but unemotional relationship with his son, based around shared interests in work and domestic DIY, as he had had with his father: 'we are [both] now in road haulage', he wrote in 1989, 'we sit in the kitchen Saturday afternoon, drink tea, smoke and talk shop'.[36] Bob's world was one in which gender roles were fixed, relatively inflexible, and, above all, functional. 'Emotional attachment' was not something that fathers did with sons; and even with their womenfolk intimacy was subordinate to function, not an end in itself.

Bob admires strong women. In childhood his mother had been 'the stable centre of everything', keeping home going while Dad was away on the road. She herself had a tough start in life. Her father vanished in her infancy, probably returning to an earlier marriage, leaving Nan (Bob's maternal grandmother) destitute, with two young children to support. For a time she kept going with 'what must be the most menial job it is possible to imagine, washing sanitary towels for "well to-do" women'.[37] In 1915 she married an engine driver, a violent man who terrorized his stepchildren. Although Bob's mother came top of her class, there was no money to buy the uniform for secondary school, and she escaped home into domestic service as fast as she could. By 1932, when she married Bob's father, she had worked in shops and factories as well as other people's homes. As soon as her younger child, Bob's brother, went to school in 1943, she took on a full-time job in a grocer's shop, and went out cleaning for a couple of middle-class regulars on the side. She was known in the locality as a formidable woman, sorting out other people's marital problems, acting as an emergency midwife:

She was knowledgeable about so many things that women would come to her for advice and support. She was well able to cope with the forms that wartime bureaucracy dreamed up weekly and helped people to fill them in properly. [At the same time] she was the most awkward, cantankerous, obstinate and out spoken person it would ever be your misfortune to meet. She did not suffer fools gladly, nor would anyone be allowed to put one over on her . . . Shopkeepers cringed when she appeared [and] people who knew Mum well, swore that Ena Sharples of *Coronation Street* was modelled on her.[38]

As this characterization suggests, Bob admired his mother for her toughness as much as for her nurture. She was the matriarch who kept the fledglings safe in the nest. Bob's brother never married; he lived with and looked after (or was looked after by) his mother until she died. But when Bob left the nest, true to the old saying, he took his 'emotional attachment' with him; and his mother, in his perception, shrank from Ena Sharples to 'a little old lady contented with her lot'.[39] By getting married, he had replaced her. This was quite deliberate. 'I looked for someone with all the qualities of my Mum', he wrote, congratulating himself on having found her. Within a year of coming out of the army in 1955 he had fallen in love with a 'slim, very pretty girl...with the most graceful walk' whom he met in the local cycling club and who shared his interest in traditional jazz.[40] When they married in 1958, Leslie was clear about the future she wanted—motherhood and domesticity—and, herself the daughter of a lorry driver, she knew what she was taking on.

As things turned out it was almost a decade before the family was able to put down secure domestic roots. Golden years of post-war capitalism these may have been, but for Bob and Leslie money was tight and in the early 1960s they were twice evicted from flats for non-payment of rent. On the second occasion she was forced to 'trek...around relying on the generosity of friends and relations to give her and...our two children somewhere to sleep', while he went back to Mum, who was nursing his dying father.[41] After several months of this they were able to hire-purchase a caravan on a site in Basildon, thereby gaining access to the council-house waiting list in the largest of Britain's post-war new towns, built to re-house working-class families from London's East End. For four years, during which their third child was born, Leslie coped in the spartan conditions of the caravan site, until they were finally able to move into the comfort of a post-war council house in 1967. The struggle to make ends meet continued, and after the youngest child started school, Leslie found part-time work as a home help, later briefly working full time when Bob was unemployed for several months in the early 1980s. By then, however, she was becoming crippled with the rheumatoid arthritis that was eventually to lead, after much pain, to her early death, aged sixty-one, in 1998.

Illness apart, their marriage had been a happy one. Sexually, they were well suited, and, despite the opportunities available to a long-distance lorry driver, he was never tempted to stray. He hesitated to define her as a 'friend'—'somehow wives come in a unique category'—and often called her 'mate', a Cockney habit (his Dad had done the same) which served to emphasize the functional nature of marriage as a working partnership. Much of the time they led very separate lives, with him away several nights a week on the road, and the domestic role divisions clear (although he did not hesitate to take over her duties when she became too ill to manage them). She tolerated his absences and had an uncanny ability, which he attributed to telepathy, to anticipate his homecomings, always having his meal ready whether he was early or late. Herself a 'very non-political person' she had little interest in the political or trade-union activism which absorbed much of his spare time, but she was intrigued by his relationship with MO and 'when the buff envelope with the University postmark dropped on the doormat, she would always ask, "What do your friends at Brighton want to know this time?"'[42] They would often discuss what he was going to write, and after her death, he chose to commemorate her by donating a clock for the archive's reading room.

Bob and Leslie understood their worlds in very different ways. Although his mother was a Baptist, Bob's schoolboy atheism, provoked by his discovery that the aircrew trying to kill him had 'Gott mit uns' inscribed on their belt buckles, had been 'hardened to the point of commitment by the liberation of the concentration camps'. No loving God could have permitted such atrocity. In the army he was known as 'Rust the Unbeliever' and thrown out of Padre Hour for asking awkward questions.[43] Leslie, by contrast, was 'always . . . into religion of one kind or another'.[44] They were married in church and the children baptized. Later in life she became a dedicated Jehovah's Witness, and Bob, without doubting his atheism, admired the friendship and support she received from fellow Witnesses as her disability took hold. Unlike many other mass observers, who saw their spouses as friends as well as partners, Bob's expectation of marriage was modestly functional. Leslie, he wrote shortly after her death, had 'completely filled the old fashioned idea of what a good wife should be . . . Something', he added regretfully, 'which seems to be an alien idea in these days of political correctness and equality'.[45] It is possible that Leslie, if we had her story, might have questioned the desirability of 'the old fashioned idea' of marriage, but recent historical work suggests a more benign view of working-class marriages built on conjugal role separation than has sometimes been assumed.[46]

Although Bob claimed that feminism had forced him to think about issues of gender during the 1980s, he was not given to interrogating the underpinnings of his own gender identity. Rebuffed during a train journey by an angry young woman to whom he offered his seat—'Do I look pregnant or too f... feeble to stand?'—he deplored the way in which feminism was undermining 'the traditional courtesies reserved for women'.[47] He saw positive discrimination as insulting to women, and it was Labour's introduction of women-only shortlists that finally precipitated his resignation from the party in the 1990s. He admitted to being confused about the issue of abortion rights. While well aware of the horror of backstreet abortions, deep down he believed that abortion was murder and sympathized with a fellow driver's remark that, after all, women did have control over their own bodies 'right up to the time they give it up by opening their legs'.[48] His reflections on gender issues seldom get far beyond the kind of the defensive banter he reports as characteristic of his milieu. 'Of course she'll win', he was told by one elderly London docker anticipating Thatcher's third electoral victory in 1987:

Look here mate, 'alf the electorate are women, they'll vote to keep her in power because she's a woman. Pig headed, illogical and never bloody wrong, same as the rest of 'em. My old woman'll only admit to being wrong once in 37 years, that was the day she married me instead of my mate Alf.[49]

'What's all the fuss about equal rights for women?', remarked another man of similar age:

They've always run the world. Starting with my mum, then my sister, the school teacher, the headmistress, the Boss's secretary, my wife, my mother-in-law, my daughters and their mothers-in-law. And now it's granddaughters, meals on wheels, the Home Help, and the District Nurse. Knowing my luck when I pop off God will be a woman.[50]

Brought up in a culture of separate spheres, Bob was never able to come to terms with the radical changes in attitudes to women's role in society that occurred during his lifetime. Women, as he remarked in relation to his own wife, remained creatures of mystery, and trying to figure out how their minds worked was 'rather like doing a Rubik's Cube blindfold'.[51]

4

Bob's account of his home life echoes that of his childhood. Writing
for MO during the 1980s and 90s he would sit at the kitchen table
while, as often as not, 'holding a conversation about something else at
the same time'.[52] He talked shop with his son and son-in-law and
enjoyed 'profound discussions' with his younger daughter, an 'avid
reader...who is very much like me in outlook and shares a lot of my
interests'.[53] 'This is a reading household', he declared:

> Books are consulted in this house as a matter of course, if you don't know it
> look it up...We are all sociable readers, reading out funny bits or interesting
> bits. Including such comments as 'What do you think this idiot's written here,
> he's got it all wrong' and then discussing the author's shortcomings, especially
> on matters of confirmable fact.[54]

His respect for 'confirmable fact' is accompanied by a practical man's
distrust of 'theory', and of the academics who indulge in it. In 2004,
when Dorothy Sheridan gave him a scholarly article based on MO
sources, he was horrified by the way the authors described her role
in the 'creation of the correspondents as...writers of their own lives.'[55]
To Bob, just 'a silly old lorry driver', this sounded like manipulative
mind games worthy of a 'psychological warfare department'. Outraged
by the implication that his self-expression was somehow being
'created' by a woman he had come to know and trust, he wondered
whether 'the relationship which I have had with MO since 1981'
could survive:

> I grew up and live in a practical world...Being drawn into some sort of
> academic thesis does not sit easily with me. To me academics live in a dream
> world of their own making which has nothing to do with real life, just life as
> they interpret it. 'Them as can do, them as can't teach, and them not capable
> of either become academics.'[56]

But this, of course, was over the top, symptomatic of a defensiveness
apparent in the way he chose to describe the intelligence he thought
he had inherited from his father: 'my dustbin memory and grasshopper
mind'.[57] Bob was a mine of information, picking up knowledge wherever
he could get it—radio, TV, the *Daily Mirror*, the *Encyclopaedia Britannica*
(which they had in the house), and the newsagents W. H. Smith's,
which he used as 'the poor man's reference library' (making notes

and then putting the magazine back on the shelf). 'Much of my
dustbin of knowledge', he wrote in the days before the internet,
came from the *Readers' Digest*, which he had read from cover to cover
ever since Leslie bought him a subscription as a Christmas present
in 1962.[58] Despite the magazine's right-wing pro-American editorial
bias, which he loathed, its condensed articles gave him quick access to
a cornucopia of information. But the self-denigration—'grasshopper
mind'—is belied in the reflective and thoughtful responses which,
despite the mind games of academics, he continues to make to Mass
Observation directives.

5

Trade-union organization was weak in the smaller private road-haulage
companies, where individual drivers could negotiate directly with the
boss, and, before recession hit in the 1980s, easily change jobs if their
demands were not met. BRS, on the other hand, was highly organized,
and Bob quickly found himself playing an active role. When, in 1965,
the Transport and General Workers Union branch secretary was promoted to management, Bob was elected to replace him, a post he
continued to hold for the next twenty-five years. As a schoolboy he
had shown leadership qualities, organizing a boycott of the canteen
and taking on a catering manager who was siphoning off supplies
intended for the school to sell in her father's grocery shop. More at
ease with the written word than the average lorry driver, he became
known as 'the glasses' or 'the admin' and, like his mother before
him, people came to him for help 'filling in accident reports, writing
letters, dealing with Disciplinary Procedures, taking statements.'[59]
With training at TGWU summer schools he became expert in representing drivers who fell foul of the law. He regularly attended
union conferences, represented the union on the Basildon Trades
Council, and was blacklisted by the right-wing Economic League for
his pains.[60] He joined the Labour Party when he settled in Basildon,
and was an obvious choice to represent the union in the local party.
Subsequently he was appointed to liaise with the Labour group on
the council. On top of all this, from 1977 he 'took up the cudgel of
the newly formed tenants representative committee' whose success for
a time earned Basildon the title of 'Little Moscow down the Thames'.[61]

Bob served as the tenants' representative on the district council. During these activist years he was spending three weekday evenings plus Saturday afternoons on trade-union and political work and getting 'a great deal of personal satisfaction from what I did helping to better the lot of my fellow man'.[62]

By the time Bob started writing for MO in 1981 his faith in the labour movement was beginning to unravel. The road-haulage workers had played a major role in the so-called 'winter of discontent', successfully challenging the Labour government's attempt to hold wages below inflation. Bob, working inside the tractor plant at the time, was not directly involved, but the years of confrontation between the unions and the Labour government that culminated in Mrs Thatcher's election victory certainly raised questions for him about the credentials of Labour as the workers' party. When the party swung to the left after losing the 1979 election he was briefly hopeful, but the erosion of trade-union power during the Thatcher years made his socialist beliefs seem increasingly unrealistic and eventually undermined his will to engage actively in political life.

As a lorry driver, Bob once remarked, 'you always arrive at the back door…where things really happen and you see life as it is'.[63] He had a close-up view of many of the industrial conflicts of the 1980s and the reports that he wrote for MO reveal his scepticism about the possibility of working-class solidarity in the face of Mrs Thatcher's anti-union onslaught. High levels of unemployment allowed employers to reassert control, driving conditions in road haulage back to the 1950s and leaving him, in 1984, wondering why he had spent 'all those hours on Committees and at Conferences to improve the lot of the lorry driver'.[64] During the 1984–5 miners' strike he reported that many union members among the drivers felt justified in shifting coal because of Arthur Scargill's failure to hold a strike ballot, and, briefly unemployed himself, he confessed that he 'might even be tempted to drive one of those coal lorries for £400 to £500 a week if I lived in S. Wales or Scotland where 30% of Heavy Goods Drivers are out of work'.[65] When the newspaper mogul Rupert Murdoch took on the print workers in 1986, Bob reported that some of the drivers delivering paper to or collecting newspapers from the Wapping plant were themselves active union members who refused to respect the picket lines because they were so fed up with 'the whims and arrogance of the print workers'.[66]

Similarly in 1989, when dockers were threatening to strike against the abolition of the National Dock Labour Scheme, Bob and his fellow drivers had scant sympathy for the militants. He had been in and out of the docks all his working life—and before with his father—and he was well aware of the evils of casual labour which the Scheme had originally been designed to overcome. As a BRS driver in the 1960s he was able to skip queues at the docks 'because dockers were all left wing and when they saw a BRS lorry they would say "oh there's one of our lot" and let us in round the back'.[67] (At that time there were said to be anti-union firms in the private sector which sought to gain privileged access to the docks by hiring one or two TGWU drivers.[68]) By the late 1980s, however, Bob was back in the private sector and, despite having good working relations with men on the wharfs he visited most frequently, he wrote an account of an 'average day' at the docks which suggests that, from the standpoint of the lorry driver, unsackable dock workers protected by the Dock Labour Scheme were far from being seen as comrades in a common struggle:

Arrive at the wharf at 6.40, queue up at the delivery office...lodge the collection order and receive the tally...Join the rank (queue of lorries waiting) to load...At 8.00 the dockers begin to roll in and go to the canteen for a quick cuppa...If you're not loaded or started on by 9.20 it's 'See you after breakfast, driver'. Breakfast finishes at 10.00, so it's 10.10 back at the shed. At 11.20 they're talking about going to dinner...Back from dinner 13.10, do a couple of lorries and it's 14.25 and time for tea. In the canteen they will weigh up how many lorries are in the dock from the number of drivers in the canteen. Back from tea 15.00. There are plenty of lorries so the pace quickens to make the tonnage [and thus earn their bonus]. At 16.00 the last lorry booked in for loading and the decision made on overtime. Once overtime is agreed (a short night 17.00 to 19.00 qualifies for four hours time and a half) all hell breaks loose—gangs rush from shed to shed, lorry to lorry and by 17.30 they're all going home. They know at 16.00 exactly how many lorries they have got to do to get away by 17.30 and still collect their overtime. They even have someone placed to watch the gate and make sure no lorries are sneaked in by management after the overtime has been agreed. For this they average £350–400 per week.[69]

Still worse, he wrote, was the Scheme's 'protection of the useless'. The rundown of the workforce had left the docks staffed by men whose main attributes were 'big biceps and little imagination'. No matter how 'thick, mechanically inept, or alcoholic', these men were all the bosses had to work the new machinery, sometimes with disastrous results. Now driving for a specialist firm importing printing paper, Bob witnessed dockers 'with no regard for anyone or anything' taking nearly an hour to do jobs that a supermarket forklift driver would have done in fifteen minutes, and causing so much damage to the paper that his firm eventually decided to send trailers to be loaded in Finland and not touched until they reached the customer's warehouse.

During the 1980s Bob lost faith in trade unionism and in the capacity of his fellow workers to build a fairer society:

There was a lot of selfishness. The whole situation was heavily hedged around with legislation and no one was prepared to stick their neck out... People were prepared to overlook injustices done to workmates.[70]

The baneful effects of unemployment and anti-union legislation were further intensified by 'Maggie's buy your council house ploy'.[71] New owner-occupiers, snared by deals too good to refuse, were reluctant to risk industrial action: 'How am I going to pay my mortgage', 'What happens if I get repossessed'.[72] When, in the 1990s, media commentators looked for a useful stereotype to explain successive Conservative victories, they alighted on 'Basildon Man'. Basildon, which had the highest percentage of skilled workers of any town in Britain, was a 'bellwether' constituency that voted for the winning side in every general election between 1974 and 2010. Local attitude surveys in the 1990s confirmed not only the popularity of council-house sales— between 1981 and 1996 home ownership in Basildon increased from 53 per cent to 71 per cent—but also the absence of any deep identification with Labour or the trade unions and a belief that it was only through their own hard work, enterprise, and determination, rather than through collective struggle, that working-class people could make something of their lives in a harsh, insecure, and unfair society. With some people, Thatcher's individualistic rhetoric struck a chord, but what the surveys revealed more generally was 'a profound detachment from all forms of collective political process or social agency. Local people are living their lives increasingly in the private sphere', with the family seen overwhelmingly as the most important thing in life.[73]

It was not just Bob's neighbours who lost faith in collective struggle. In 1989 Bob himself became an owner-occupier, buying his council house at a knock-down price. Since 1982 when, in one of the Conservative government's first privatizations, the National Freight

Corporation (the renamed BRS) was sold to its employees, he had, as he put it, 'become a capitalist'.[74] Subsequently he bought shares in the newly privatized British Telecom and British Gas, and his profits from these investments enabled him to buy the house outright. In the absence of a mortgage, owner occupation may not have entrapped Bob as it did less fortunate buyers, but his personal accommodation with Thatcherism nevertheless took its toll:

The 'me first' society [he wrote in 1985] carefully engineered by the Tories in the past few years seems to militate against a caring Socialist Britain in my life time, so barring a revolution (most unlikely) for me realism comes before dogmatism.[75]

He sought to justify himself to 'socialist colleagues' by citing 'Marx's dictum that there is no harm in benefiting from capitalism even if you don't believe in it'.[76]

Realism trumping dogmatism was all very well, but Bob was not immune to the individualist tides that he deplored. Within ten years, shortly before retiring, he was writing: 'I have forgotten everything political and Trade Unionist. I now concentrate on me. I look after my disabled wife and serve out my last two years on the best terms I can get for me.'[77] Already in 1986 he had declared himself 'content . . . to be a middle-aged lorry driver, doing his best to do a good job, pay his way, keep a roof over his head and make the best of what the tide of fortune washes up'.[78] At that time he was still concerned to 'put in my twopen-north [sic] and influence the way things go', but by the end of the decade the satisfactions he had drawn from serving his fellow workers had lost their appeal. After twenty-five years as a TGWU branch sec-retary he resigned and let his union membership lapse. A few years later, after years of doing no more politically than paying his dues, he left the Labour Party.

6

There was one thing Thatcher did that met with Bob's wholehearted approval—retaking the Falkland Islands from Argentina. Along with thousands of other ex-servicemen he volunteered to go himself, 'but they wouldn't have us'. 'There is nothing to negotiate about', he declared as the task force approached the Islands: 'If we "bottle out"...then we abdicate as a world power.'[79] He knew very well how fragile that position was, deeply resenting American plans to use Britain as a dispensable base in a limited nuclear war in Europe, and approving Labour's support for a non-nuclear defence policy. This anti-nuclear position in no way contradicted his investment in British military prowess—abandoning nuclear weapons (whose uselessness as a deterrent was demonstrated by the Falklands Crisis) would release resources for conventional forces. His enthusiasm for Thatcher's war was, like that of the Labour leader Michael Foot, rooted in the memory of the Second World War. Amongst his fellow middle-aged drivers at the local depot, he reported, 'the old Dunkirk/Blitz spirit is re-emerging...our view is coloured by all being able to remember to some degree Neville's bit of paper at Croydon airport'. Although only four years old at the time of Munich, he did remember his mother shushing him when Neville Chamberlain came on the radio a year later to announce the imminence of war. While acknowledging that his readers might think that his views 'merely indicate how well we were brainwashed with "Rule Britannia" in our formative years', he deplored anti-war talk among his children's friends as a symptom of national decline. If this younger generation had its way, he wrote contemptuously, redundant servicemen would find themselves retraining 'as Morris dancers, potters and basket weavers, in fact any quaint pacifist pastime...perhaps we could then be a world power in tourism'.[80]

Britain's future as a theme park for tourists recurs several times in Bob's writing, an echo perhaps of those childhood travels in which his father had taught him to appreciate his country as a collection of 'historic sites'. Asked to fantasize about having the perfect job, 'writing touring guides' came second only to itinerant handyman or canal boatman.[81] There could be worse fates than tourism for a declining empire. 'Our future can be predicted by simply looking back', he wrote in 1983:

We are closely following the pattern of all the colonial empires of recorded history. The smelly 'wog' who tries to sell you his sister in Port Said is the direct descendant of a culture which had art, science, mathematics and medicine while our ancestors were communicating in grunts.[82]

When he was at school 'a liberal history teacher who taught the bits not in the approved books' had impressed him with stories of the decline of the Roman empire:

As the . . . Empire contracted back into Rome, what happened? First there was the good life, wine, food, the acceptance of homosexuality, prostitution, pornography and general living it up. With the drudgery borne by human slaves. Then came the civil unrest as the have-nots began to realise what they had not got . . . so that it became necessary to introduce violence into the arena to provide a vicarious stimulation and outlet for the crowd . . . We already have 'live' shows in Amsterdam and London's West End if you know where to go. We have 'gays' out in the open, even in parliament. All that is left is for Rollerball to become a fact.[83]

The comparison was fanciful, as he well knew. While holding no brief for the permissive society, Bob felt no antagonism towards homosexuals, and he was sceptical about moral panics worked up by the media. Prostitution, child abuse, and the use of drugs or alcohol to escape from everyday misery was as old as civilization itself; and his own grandmother had danced the can-can 'Moulin-Rouge style' (knickerless) for Edward VII.[84] In any case decadence was now beside the point since 'Attila is already ensconced at No 10.'[85]

And Attila was a wrecker. Thatcher's martial spirit, however admirable, did nothing to compensate for the wasteland being created by her preference for finance over industry, her threat to dismantle the welfare state, and Britain's sacrifice of economic sovereignty in the European single market. For a brief moment in the early 1980s Bob had invested his hopes in the left's Alternative Economic Strategy (rebuilding industry, and with it national sovereignty, behind protectionist walls), but Tony Benn's narrow failure to defeat Denis Healey in the 1981 contest for the deputy leadership of the Labour Party put paid to that. Bob and his fellow drivers' enthusiasm for Thatcher's war enabled them momentarily to put to one side their knowledge that the social democracy whose benefits, however limited, they had enjoyed since the 1950s was in deep crisis. Theirs was a working-class nationalism rooted in the memory of the 'people's war'—the apex not only of national pride but also of the social and political power of the organized working class. Writing about aging shortly before his sixtieth birthday, Bob remarked that he was becoming more and more nostalgic, especially for the war years: 'the key time of my life and, I think, of many of my contemporaries. So much of my basic thinking and outlook was indelibly formed then.'[86] But nostalgia led nowhere. Conservatives might wave the flag, but they were evidently not the party of the workers, and as Labour signed up to the neo-liberal agenda it became apparent that there was 'nowhere left for a left wing anti-European socialist to go'.[87]

By the mid-1990s Bob no longer believed in the projection of British power, hoping on the contrary that 'with a bit of luck Britain may stop pretending to be a world power, reduce our armed forces down to a Home Guard, leave the EC [European Community] and let us have what money we've got to spend on ourselves'.[88] But he had no inclination to engage in a more radical re-thinking of his politics. He was unimpressed by what he saw as the 'sea of introspection' invading the media in the 1980s. Confronted by people on television trying to 'find out who I am', 'get into myself and find a meaning', 'rediscover myself', 'think through where I'm going', he wondered whether he was 'fortunate or somehow cheated in not feeling this pressing desire to find a niche with my name on it...'[89] The question was rhetorical. Bob had no time for the narcissism of identity politics because he knew very well what his niche was—'working class to the soles of my safety boots'. But what this meant politically was no longer clear.

At the time of the Rushdie affair Bob, like many others, was outraged by the spectacle of Muslim immigrants who, rather than seeking to integrate, 'want us to rearrange *our* country so that they fit'.[90] But he was resistant to the xenophobic racism of the far right and appreciative of Afro-Caribbean immigrants who, in taking up 'our culture', had given us 'bits of theirs'. Nevertheless it was patriotism which was to provide the last refuge for his shrinking sense of political agency. After Blair's triumph in the 1997 election, in which Bob had deserted Labour and voted for the anti-European Referendum Party, he confided to MO that in future he would only vote:

if a candidate is put up who supports the views of Henry V, the Duke of Wellington, the Old Contemptibles and the BEF and wants to keep us out of the hands of the French and Germans...If it's only the others I won't bother and save the pencil lead.[91]

When I met him in the autumn of 2014 he was intending to vote for the anti-European UK Independence Party in the general election. In Basildon, he explained, UKIP was run by one-time Labour Party activists and had a good record in resisting the ultra-Thatcherite policies of the Tory council. Although passionate in his hostility to the European Union, Bob's support for UKIP was essentially tactical. He had rejoined the Labour Party in 2010, briefly hopeful that its new leader Ed Miliband would bring the party back to its working-class roots. UKIP, he told me, was 'never going to get real power nationally, I'm hoping it will be the "stone in the shoe" and produce a Labour Party I can think about re-joining.'[92] A year later, his tactic apparently vindicated, he joined again following the surprise election of a leader, Jeremy Corbyn, 'preaching the sort of Labour party that I joined in 1964'.[93]

7

Despite political disappointments Bob never lost his zest for life. Presenting himself for the MO website in 2000 he wrote: 'I am sixty-six and feel about eighteen. As I am now a widower what I need is a nubile eighteen year old female to move in with me to complete the illusion.'[94] Not content with illusions, he started visiting 'working girls'. Matter-of-fact about what he saw as 'just the way men are made', he spoke publicly as a punter in a radio programme on prostitution.[95] Chatting to the working girls he became knowledgeable about the sex trade, and encouraged them to participate in an action research project which successfully established a sex workers' union, subsequently affiliated to the General and Municipal Workers Union.[96] He saw no need to hide his behaviour from his children: 'I think it says something for my family's attitude to sex that I was able to tell all my children that I have been going to working girls since their mother died and that they accepted it without question.'[97] When I interviewed him in 2014 he remarked that his daughter, who lived next door, had 'met one of the young ladies half way down the garden path and said good afternoon to her'.[98]

Despite his impatience with the narcissism of people delving into themselves to find out 'who they were', he was nevertheless fascinated by his own family history and, in retirement, he joined the thriving amateur research community of family historians, not only tracking his own ancestors, but also using his spare time to transcribe census records for the benefit of his fellow researchers. Alongside writing the memoir of his working life, he encouraged others to write for the newsletter of his vintage lorry club, and worked with a group of academics on an encyclopaedic *Companion to British Road Haulage History*.[99] His continuing relationship with Mass Observation involves not only responding to directives, but also attending, and speaking at, conferences and using his newly acquired computing skills to transcribe some of the early directives. In all this activity Bob continues to display a commitment to collective endeavour which belies any simple reading of his later life as a retreat from political activism into private life. His hope that by voting UKIP he can recall the Labour Party to its socialist purpose may be quixotic, but through the range of his own activities he continues to uphold the values he learned as a child when national pride and working-class solidarity appeared to go hand in hand.

9

Banker

In the late 1980s Michael Roper interviewed thirty senior executives in the British manufacturing industry.[1] Born between the two world wars, they belonged to what he defined as an 'in-between' generation of managers who saw themselves as pioneers of professionalism but lacked the formal management training of their successors. They brought a rational, analytic approach to their work at odds with the more subjective and intuitive managerial style of the older generation. But they retained an old-fashioned company loyalty, in contrast to the more mobile and aggressively entrepreneurial generation which succeeded them. In the sociological literature of the 1950s and 60s they were described as 'organization men', unemotional, calculating, rational bureaucrats.[2] In reality, the corporation, no less than the family, was a place where passions ran high, where action was driven by emotion as much as by reason. Roper's interviews were designed to probe behind the public face of business leadership, to reveal 'the fears and desires which lay behind the seemingly methodical actions of organization men',[3] and to challenge accounts which artificially separated the public rhetoric of managerial professionalism from the interpersonal, private, and psychic lives of his subjects.

Although my final subject, Sam, was a banker, not an industrial manager, his career in the City, spanning the period from 1960 to 1987, shared many of the characteristics of the in-between generation explored by Roper. He was a modernizer, impatient with the conservatism of many of his older colleagues, but he was also a loyal company man who stayed with the same bank throughout his career, a choice hardly available to his successors. The life of the banker, even more than that of the industrialist, was to change radically from the 1980s, when the gentlemanly capitalism of the 'Old City' was transformed by

Thatcher's deregulation and the influx of American banks.[4] Those
changes, particularly as they appeared to Sam's generation of leading
City men, were documented in a major oral history project—122
interviews deposited in the British Library's National Sound Archive.[5]
This evidence, extracts from which were published in 1996, chimes
with much of Sam's experience; although the interviews were no
doubt subject to the more or less conscious self-censorship that one
would expect from public testimony delivered by people at the apex
of successful careers.

Roper, whose main interest was in analysing versions of elite masculinity, relied on a close and subtle analysis of interview tapes—and
body language—to get behind the public face of his subjects. With
Sam we have instead the mass observer's commitment to revealing on
paper one's innermost thoughts and feelings. Looking back after twelve
years with Mass Observation he wrote:

> I often reflect that if all my various contributions were examined together they
> would present a detailed autobiography covering not only the facts of my life,
> but my thoughts, hopes, fears, my prejudices and hatreds—and of course all my
> stupidities and weaknesses. My guard is down when I write about myself for
> Mass Observation—because of the anonymity—so that I have I believe sup-
> plied a truer picture than if I were carefully sieving the detail for publication,
> when perhaps I would present the man that I would like others to see.[6]

And a few years later, responding 'after much anxious thought' to one
of MO's most intrusive directives ('Having an Affair'), he 'decided to
bare my soul on this subject to our archive. Social History has been a
lifelong study of mine, and I am now anxious to contribute to our
archive by describing fully my personal experiences.'[7] Sam's sense of
shared ownership of 'our archive' underpinned his determination to
'bare his soul' as fully and honestly as he could.

Sam wrote for MO from 1982 until 2008, four years before his
death. From much earlier, however, he had been keeping a diary—
continuously from 1959—which his widow has deposited in the Mass
Observation archive.[8] The comparison between his autobiographical
writing for MO, most of it written in retirement and looking back to
earlier times in his life, and the diaries, in which he wrote (usually at
bedtime) an account of each day, provide a salutary reminder of the
limitations of even the most conscientiously honest autobiographical
writing. Of course, even diaries cannot provide an unmediated window
on the soul—who can account for the pull and push of unconscious

fears and desires?—but the daily practice of diary-writing leaves behind a jagged record of emotional fluctuations and intellectual confusions that tends to be ironed out by the smoother contours of autobiographical composition. Even a night's sleep made a difference: after he retired, when Sam took to writing his diary in the morning rather than at the end of the day, he noticed that it became more 'bland' and lost 'that instant freshness'.[9] Writing for MO, Sam may not have been presenting 'the man I would like others to see', but he was engaging in the endless process by which we construct narratives of our lives acceptable to *ourselves*. A major function of autobiography, which we all undertake every time we tell and re-tell stories from our pasts, is to find composure, to come to terms with how we have lived.[10] The reflective autobiographical voice brings a measure of composure where the diaries, so much closer to the raw experience, record moments of triumph, joy, wonder, pride, and fulfilment, alongside irritation, anxiety, doubt, confusion, and despair. Taken together, the two sources give us an unusually complete picture of the inner life of a public man.

I

As a young man starting his first professional job, Sam had done his best to get fat. He thought it would make him look older, and that this would make it easier to cultivate the image of reliability and trustworthiness expected of a small-town solicitor.[11] Fortunately metabolism defeated misplaced ambition, and however much he ate he could not put on weight. But the instrumentalism towards his own body revealed by the attempt, and the underlying belief that he could make of himself whatever he willed, was indicative of qualities that were to take him a very long way from the premature aging into the modest professional security which he had initially sought.

Respectability and financial security were what Sam's parents were seeking for him, financing the Victorian pattern of professional formation that was still common as a route into the law, accountancy, or banking for the children of aspiring middle-class parents. This 'disgraceful system of five years...service as a solicitor's unpaid clerk' required self-discipline, self-denial, self-exploitation, and a degree of deferred gratification that, as he tried to eat his way into the job, threatened to crystallize into permanent subordination of the man to the conventions of his status.[12] What he learned as an articled clerk working full time in the office could have been picked up in three months in a classroom, and the serious study necessary to pass the solicitors' exams was done in the evenings after work on a correspondence course supplemented by two six-month periods at law school. For five years Sam 'did almost nothing but work and study late into every night...a dreadful unhappy period in which I missed out on my youth, grew old beyond my years', and developed a duodenal ulcer which plagued him throughout his working life.[13]

Not only was he unpaid, but his parents had to pay the solicitor for the privilege—as well as finding the money for smart clothing, commuting to work, law books, and fees for the correspondence course and the law school. They did the same for his brother, two years younger, articled to a chartered accountant; and they struggled to pay the bills. Throughout his clerkship Sam was aware that the money might run out before he qualified. His father, who had acquired a master mariner's certificate in the 1920s, lost his job in the slump, and at the time of Sam's birth was reduced to working as a dock labourer and living in his own mother's Merseyside council house. When, forty-six years later, as a successful City man, Sam revisited the house he took a rags-to-riches photograph with his Daimler and his uniformed chauffeur posed outside. But that exaggerated his upward mobility. Swiftly promoted to foreman on the docks, his father had left Merseyside when Sam was three years old for a well-paid job managing shipping for the same company in London. Although Sam's mother did her best to stay in touch with their northern working-class relatives, the family had moved into an entirely different world. At the outbreak of war, Sam's father signed up for naval service, and the family left London for a pleasantly leafy town within commuting distance of the city. Sam, now aged six, was to live there (with one brief interval) for the rest of his life.

From 1945 Sam was educated at a minor local public school geared to sport and character formation rather than academic achievement. The school nurtured the masculine leadership qualities which, Sam believed, did much to help him succeed in later life. By supporting their sons into their mid-20s through private education and professional apprenticeships, the parents not only denied themselves comforts—the only fire in the house, Sam recalled, was reserved for weekends: during the week they just put on more clothes—but also stretched their finances to breaking point. Although his father had commanded warships during the war, back in civilian life his career stalled and he was unable match his pre-war salary. His mother, drawing on childhood experience of working in her father's business (he had been a milk roundsman), set up a shop to supplement the family income. When the money ran out the parents took on a second mortgage and borrowed from relatives and friends, relying on their sons to clear the debts once they were earning—a risky strategy since, if the boys were to fail their qualifying exams (as many did), they might never have been able to meet this obligation.

Within six years of qualifying as a solicitor, Sam had catapulted himself from provincial obscurity into the higher echelons of the City of London. Bored by his work as a small-town solicitor, and anxious to pay off his parents' debts as soon as possible, he turned his attention to making money on the side. During their training years he and his brother had invented a variety of 'wheezes for making a little money', including organizing Thames river parties with hired bands on rented boats, and buying up advance tickets for the local cricket club's New Year's Eve parties and then selling them on at a profit.[14] After qualifying he continued the Thames boat scheme with larger boats, better bands, and bigger profits. And, with help from a friend who had become a West End theatre producer, he extended his range as a ticket tout. Tipped off about forthcoming productions, he borrowed money from the bank, bought advance tickets, and sometimes made a substantial profit—notably on the opening of *My Fair Lady* in 1958.

These activities involved a lot of work, but, turning his attention to the stock exchange, he discovered that he could sell shares at a profit before he had to pay the broker for buying them. By this time he was working for a friend's father who ran a small practice in the City specializing in financial law, and (with helpful advice from his new employer) was using his lunch breaks to play the market. He was instrumental in setting up an investment club with other young professional City men meeting once a month to discuss what shares to buy. While insider dealing was not then illegal, the club sailed close to the margins of what was ethically acceptable at the time: 'Of course they never blatantly stated that a certain "takeover" was imminent, but there were often implications between the lines of a likely sharp rise in price—and I acted on this.'[15] But the biggest risk he took was in the run-up to the 1959 election when, gambling on a Tory victory which would dispel fears of re-nationalization, he borrowed heavily to buy shares in steel companies. Macmillan won, and the gamble paid off. These speculative activities usefully supplemented his solicitor's salary, enabling him to clear his parents' debts within two and half years of qualifying, and, most importantly, teaching him 'a trade on which my future career in the bank became based'.[16]

In 1960, dissatisfied with his prospects, he cast around for a more rewarding position. Although tempted by the security offered by civil service employment, he wanted to be closer to the money-making action and applied instead to the legal department of one of Britain's largest public companies, a 'financial conglomerate' with many overseas subsidiaries controlling 'a huge group of other banks, insurance companies, and other financial and even industrial companies'.[17] The reason he got the job, he later discovered, had less to do with his legal expertise than with the entrepreneurial skill he had demonstrated in his extra-curricular money-raising initiatives: 'a flair for modest business ventures', commented the deputy chairman, 'that could be developed for the benefit of the Bank'.[18] Within two years, promoted from the legal department, he had become company secretary with a seat on the boards of several of its subsidiary companies. In 1968 he became joint managing director of the group's largest subsidiary, and a year later, aged only thirty-five, he was appointed to the board of the parent company.

How to explain this dizzying ascent? From the outset he impressed his superiors as a forceful and ambitious young man endowed with 'a precise and analytical way of seeing problems'.[19] Unwilling to accept that established ways of doing things were necessarily the best, he demonstrated, when given his head, the determination and political skills needed to push through change against the resistance of more conservative colleagues. Sam did not see himself as exceptionally intelligent: 'Working, as one does in a merchant bank, with people who are double-firsts from Oxford, I saw that my brain was not in that class.'[20] But what he lacked in intellect he made up for in practical good sense and, above all, in decisiveness. Better-educated colleagues might impress with their brilliance, but too often they hesitated to act.

While working in the legal department he had drawn up a rationalization plan involving significant redundancies and substantial savings for the bank. When his boss, a brilliant and charming lawyer but an ineffective manager, declined to implement the plan Sam caused a sensation, breaking protocol to appeal up the hierarchy directly to the deputy chairman, 'a fierce, tough Scotsman' he knew only by reputation. Summoned to account for themselves at a stormy meeting, the upstart held his own against the incumbent; convinced the deputy chairman of the merits of his plan; and emerged, relieved of his routine legal duties, and transferred to the company secretary's office with responsibility for overseeing the implementation of his plan.[21] Subsequently, as company secretary, he oversaw the bank's computerization, and played a significant role in persuading Parliament to make computerized records admissible in court. He reorganized the personnel department, introducing systems of appraisal, objective-setting, and performance-related pay characteristic of the new management professionalism. As an executive director in the early 1970s he took the initiative in promoting trade-union organization among the staff, persuading reluctant colleagues to recognize the National Union of Bank Employees in order to forestall attempts by Clive Jenkins' far more militant Association of Scientific, Technical and Managerial Staffs to establish itself in the company. His promotion to the board in 1969 had been clinched by his success in managing the takeover of a major competitor, implementing big cuts in staffing with no reduction in activity and a major growth in profits. 'Much of my work', he wrote later, 'lay in identifying companies which could be taken over, improved, perhaps merged with another business also acquired, and then resold at a profit. This is a difficult business involving high risk, but high profit if successful.'[22] Acquiring a reputation as an expert on mergers, he was gratified during the 1970s to be invited to give an annual lecture on the subject at one of Britain's leading business schools. Behind the scenes he took the leading role among his fellow directors in plotting the downfall of a chairman, a high-flying outsider whose impatience with City conservatism had contributed significantly to Sam's early career but who now appeared to have lost his grip. By the early 1970s Sam was well in line to become the next chairman but one.

Like Michael Roper's industrial managers, Sam saw himself as a pioneer of modern management techniques in a rather old-fashioned business. He later found it incredible that 'one of Britain's very largest companies, trading internationally with subsidiaries all round the world', should have had no formal discipline of long-term corporate planning when he joined it in 1960. 'Planning the company's future

was a low key, informal matter' and the introduction of formal procedures had to be pushed through against strong opposition from many of
the older, more senior, managers, one of whom protested that: 'Any
fool can go in for long term planning, but it takes real management
expertise to just leap from crisis to crisis.'[23] From 1974, when the
banking system came close to collapse and 'international banking
became a roller-coaster ride', Sam's own capacity for managing crisis
was to be put to the test.[24]

Sam spent ten or more hours a day in the City, sometimes working
late into the night and catching a few hours' sleep in his office. His
account of the start of a typical working day gives a glimpse of his disciplined approach. While shaving he would list the decisions he needed
to make on issues put to him by senior executives the previous day. At
6.30 a.m. his chauffeur arrived with the Daimler—a perk acquired on
his appointment to the board—'and I would sit in the back of the car
deep in thought, ticking off each decision, for most of the journey ... the
first decision had to be made by a certain point in my journey (e.g. the
end of my lane), the second by another point (e.g. a certain round-
about), etc.'[25] There was, however, plenty of variety in his working day,
including—often several times a week—a two-hour lunch in the directors' dining room, 'on the eighth floor with the most excellent view
over the City and the river'.[26] Here, served by a chef, a butler, and
two maids, the directors cultivated the company's public image by
entertaining 'a continuous list of the famous and successful'[27]—top
businessmen and civil servants, professional men, judges, and politicians
including Heath, Wilson, Callaghan, and (three times) Thatcher. At
other times, when entertaining mere customers invited 'for stark business reasons', they called in famous writers, sportsmen, and artists to add
glamour to the occasion. Sam loved these events, and shone at them as
a witty conversationalist—a talent recognized early on by his superiors
who, most unusually, had regularly invited him to 'lunch upstairs' before
he had the right to attend as a director: 'I am gratified', he noted in his
diary in 1966, 'to find that I am usually brought in when there is an
important guest'.[28] There was nothing unusual about Sam's lunches.
Two hours of fine dining well fuelled with alcohol was a common
mid-day practice in the City. No business was talked about during
what one banker described as his 'restaurant work', at least until the
dessert, but personal affinities were established, characters assessed,
judgements made about the integrity and reliability of potential clients

and partners.[29] The City ran on personal chemistry and an extrovert and sociable personality was as important as training and analytical skills to making a career in these gentlemanly institutions.

As he rose in the hierarchy, Sam felt at home among the directors, 'a scintillating, brilliant crowd...intelligent wide-thinking men', although, to his regret, it proved impossible to develop deep friendships with men who were competitors as much as they were colleagues: 'in the commercial, profit-making world...the maxim is the higher you are the closer you are to the door. I was surrounded by bright, ambitious men who would be glad to have my job if I could be got out.'[30] Such insecurity notwithstanding, he luxuriated in the masculine sociability of the City, proud in his late twenties to be moving among the 'well dressed and substantial looking' members of his investment club, or amongst his peers at a gathering of commercial lawyers, where 'everyone looked a first class type of man...I would say, quite object-ively, that this is the cream of the Law Society.'[31] Later, having gained a reputation as an amusing after-dinner speaker, he enjoyed frequent invitations 'to perform at white-tie-and-tails banquets' in the City.[32] The company of well-turned-out men was important to his sense of well-being, whether they were colleagues, his uniformed chauffeur, or the staff at Brown's—'the most magnificent hotel in London'—where 'every servant looks as though he has just returned from a senior ambassadorial appointment'.[33] He himself took care to cut an arresting figure—tall, slim, elegant in bowler hat, navy coat with velvet collar, rolled umbrella, dark-blue suit, waistcoat, watch and chain, and, as late as 1980, when most of his colleagues had given them up as too much trouble, still wearing a detachable stiff collar. On one occasion, arriving late for a meeting in Lazard's bank to discuss a takeover, he was delighted to record in his diary that 'I must have an impressive pres-ence', since the assembled gathering of lawyers and bankers had risen to their feet as he entered, an honour not accorded to a fellow director who arrived a little later.[34]

2

Despite long hours in the City, work was far from being the whole of Sam's life. On weekday evenings he sang in a choir and he was a regular performer with the local amateur dramatic society, particularly

in Gilbert and Sullivan operettas and in musicals. Often he waxed
lyrical in his diary about the pleasure he derived from 'the company of
these good-natured, sociable, singer-players', so different from the
competitive atmosphere of the office, but no less intense:

> What a joy it is to go out at 6.30, excited at going on the stage: the smell of
> greasepaint, sweat and beer in the men's changing room...singing...Cwm
> Rhonda always, and Jerusalem; the warmth, after the cold men's room, of the
> ladies changing room; the intimacy of seeing the girls in underwear; all drinking
> together and—harmlessly—kissing, standing with arms around waists, sitting
> on knees in the dressing room; the thrill of...waiting in the wings to go on;
> the smell of scenery, warmth of the lights and closeness of all the chorus,
> crowded together...and then the great excited sense of achievement at the
> end, taking our bows, above all the enormous camaraderie of the...cast.[35]

He filled his weekends with outdoor pursuits—beagling, riding, and
fox-hunting with his wife, sailing with a friend from his schooldays
with whom he jointly owned a small boat. Addicted to adrenalin, he
justified the hunting, sailing, motor-cycling, and his annual skiing trip
on the grounds that leisure activities 'which frightened me and which
demanded instant decisions' served to hone those powers of 'nerve and
decisiveness' so essential in his working life.[36]

And there was family. During his penultimate year as an articled
clerk he met his future wife. Daughter of a retired farmer, Alison was
two years younger than him and about to start a degree course at the
London School of Economics and Political Science. They became
engaged, but were not intending to marry until she had completed her
degree and Sam had done his two years of National Service, deferred
during his clerkship. Three days before his call-up Sam broke several
bones in a motor-cycle accident and, despite his best efforts to per-
suade them otherwise, the army turned him down on medical grounds.
Alison, who had interrupted her degree course to care for an epileptic
younger brother, dropped it altogether and they were married in
April 1957.

They had got to know each other as part of a group of friends
playing tennis, walking, and singing together, but, looking back, Sam
reflected that they were less than perfectly suited:

> I am an extrovert enjoying a wide variety of activities out and about with a
> wide variety of people, and I am very energetic both physically and mentally,
> whereas my wife is shy of people and is her happiest when alone at home

reading a good book. She has a higher intellect than me. But she has less physical energy.[37]

That difference could be lived with. What proved to be more difficult was their sexual incompatibility. They were both virgins when they married and he quickly found 'that while I had a hearty appetite for sex, my bride did not'. This was a big disappointment, but in the late 1950s sexual ignorance was still widespread and Sam concluded that this was just the way women were. 'So... I gritted my teeth in frustration and devoted myself to my work.'[38] Within five years of the marriage, he had a top job in the bank, a large house, and two children, a girl and a boy. Indifferent to his children as babies, he bonded closely with them as they learned to talk and they became his pride and joy for the rest of his life.

'I would have been happy', he wrote many years later and not entirely convincingly, 'to settle permanently into solid Victorian virtue'. As an aspiring small-town solicitor he had needed to be careful about his sex life, but as City banker he lived in an altogether looser moral environment. Moreover a man 'always keen to widen [his] experience of life' was not going to be untouched by 'the excitement of the new ethos engulfing... society' in the 1960s:

I was perhaps slow to notice it, but by about 1965 I saw that the tide of morality had changed, and was ebbing fast. The serious newspapers were now printing articles amazingly explicit about sex. Wow! My friends began different behaviour; parties became amazingly erotic and I heard tales of 'wife-swapping'. Adultery, I heard, was going on all around me. I felt I was missing out.

His first affair, with a divorced member of his choral society, served to dispel his dim view of female sexuality: 'My eyes were opened wide with amazement when I discovered that [she] had a voracious appetite for sex. I simply had not thought women could be like that... If there is such a thing as a nymphomaniac [she] was one—bless her!' But they had little else in common and the liaison was short-lived. Her chaotic lifestyle 'grated upon my organised, planned life', and, horrified by a (false) scare that she had become pregnant, he put an end to the affair and resolved to stray no more.

'But I had tasted honey...', and within months he had embarked on a new affair with a woman in his theatre group, 'beautiful—tall, slim and elegant... fine brain... witty conversationalist... an energetic, ambitious woman' who, like Sam, 'was impelled by the need not to be left out of the new exciting experience of the 60s'. Helen was married with three children and a 'delightful husband', and for two years after the affair began the two couples spent a good deal of time socializing together, taking the kids out, and, in the summer of 1969, holidaying together abroad.[39] But what had begun as a 'light hearted sexual romp' quickly got out of hand. 'We both fell, plunged, crashingly in love. I have never known anything like it. We became obsessed with each other . . . ' Thirty years later he could still write that 'the proudest thing in my life is that I was once loved by [Helen]. She simply was, is, the most beautiful and charming woman I have ever met.' Despite their mutual passion, however, he resisted her desire for divorce and remarriage, 'convinced that two people simply did not have the right, for their own happiness, to wreck the lives of seven others [the two partners and five young children]'. By the beginning of 1970 their respective partners had become aware of what was going on, and during the months that followed Sam divided many of his weekends between Saturdays out with Helen and Sundays with the family. Unusually, much of his diary during this year consists of blank pages, interrupted only by terse records of his time spent with Helen; until, in November, there is an entry in another hand (presumably Alison's): '[Sam] told me he had decided to resolve the situation. Hoping that trust is still possible, I have promised to try to appear calm and neutral.'[40] It took, however, an ultimatum from Alison three months later to bring matters to a head—she would divorce him unless he put an end to the affair. Alone in a hotel room for two days, Sam agonized between desire and duty, finally concluding that duty—and the calmer joys of his family life—had the prior claim. But his diary entries during the months that followed breaking things off with Helen plumb the depths of bewilderment and despair.

It did not end there. Within six months they had resumed the relationship, 'but now the need for secrecy was so utterly vital that' they seldom met:

And when we did the strains on us often resulted in unhappiness and an acrimonious parting—so that we believed each time that that was definitely the end—until a few months later we couldn't resist meeting again . . .

Meanwhile Sam and Alison struggled to sustain their marriage. In 1971 they moved out of town into a house with stables and enough land to keep their own horses, and for two years Sam buried his sorrows in heavy manual labour, creating a garden. By the summer of 1973, aware that her husband was again seeing Helen, Alison (he believed) had come to accept that divorce was probably inevitable. But the distress of their twelve-year-old daughter when she overheard her father talking of living separately persuaded them to postpone things, and they agreed to stay together for the sake of the children for the next three years.

During the mid-1970s, unhappy with both his wife and his mistress, Sam cheered himself up with a series of casual affairs. Frequently abroad on business, he discovered a novel use for art galleries, where he found it easy to meet 'educated women of about my own age' who were game for light-hearted weekend flings. Although, after two years, he had still been intending divorce, the three-year deadline appears to have passed without further discussion and in 1978, ten years after his affair with Helen began, they finally agreed to bring it to an end, Sam writing laconically in his diary: 'spoke to [Alison] of my intent to clear up certain irregularities in my private life.'[41] There was no more talk of divorce.

By the early 1980s Sam was surprised to find that he could have 'completely non-sexual' friendships with women, a discovery he put down to advancing age:

the sexual urge is no longer a constant over-riding preoccupation. By my late 40s it had ceased to obtrude continuously into my conscious thoughts and had receded to a back seat from which it came forward on appropriate occasions only. This is a welcome relief. It also means that at last I can regard women as friends rather than as potential targets.[42]

But despite his declared intention never again to 'stray from the family fold', his sexual urge refused to stay long on the back seat and 'appropriate occasions' continued to arise, driven by his 'insatiable desire to live life to the full' and his love of 'the company of fine women'.

Drawing up a balance sheet in response to Mass Observation's 1998 directive which asked people to write about extra-marital affairs, Sam believed that in staying with Alison he had made the right choice. He did not regret his escapades: 'my nature is to lead a life crammed full of different experiences, and clearly the romantic love of women is too fine a country to remain unexplored'. And although, in the end, his relationship with Helen caused him more unhappiness than happiness,

'I would not have missed this great experience of life. My life would not have been complete had I never loved so passionately.' While it was clear to him that Alison and he would probably never have married had they experimented, in modern fashion, with premarital sex, he nevertheless felt that this 'would have been a pity. I might have married a girl whose attractions were superficial, lacking the sterling qualities I have come over the years to admire in my dear wife.' He was devoted to his family and expressed no regret for having (eventually) sacrificed the love of his life to hold it together.[43]

Some years earlier, in 1990, he had given voice to views which he had never revealed to anyone, and which he thought his future readers would find 'very strange indeed—in fact quite ungrateful'. Marriage, he wrote, was an outdated institution. In Victorian times it was death that prevented most marriages from lasting too long. Now, with the pill, the ability of women (he asserted) to support themselves and their children economically, and public acceptance of unmarried relationships and illegitimacy, the notion of marrying for life would become a rarity. 'Marriage is an economic convenience— but a biological disaster', since men are biologically programmed for polygamy:

The fact is that if I was a young man, with the wider choice of life styles available today, I do not think I would plan to marry at all. Instead of spending a great deal of time, effort and money on family matters—and I have always done everything I could for my family—I would spend my time when not working in the many active pursuits that I enjoy. I would also have taken business risks not acceptable with my family's need for security in mind. I would have had a succession of girlfriends. And now that I'm retired I would live abroad.[44]

It was a nice fantasy—the dashing City gent free from family responsibilities, able to give free rein to his connoisseurship of 'fine women', while, presumably, avoiding long-term emotional entanglements. He should have been grateful that his times and his circumstances denied him the opportunity to try to live this impossible masculine dream. And perhaps, eventually, he was. 'Love is more complicated than sex', Alison told me after we met, reflecting that the longevity that required marriages to last so much longer than in the past, which Sam had seen as a problem, turned out to be a bonus—'a chance to put things right before death intervened'.[45]

3

It was not only his sex life that made the 1970s a difficult time for Sam. In 1974, amidst international financial upheavals triggered by the ending of fixed exchange rates and the oil-price hike, Britain's secondary banking sector, over extended during the lending and property boom of the early 70s, came close to collapse and Sam's company was one of many which had to be rescued by a 'lifeboat' organized by the Bank of England with funds from the clearing banks.[46] To restore profitability the company's activity was drastically slimmed down, and it fell to Sam to plan and implement the resulting reorganization and redundancies. One of the things which had attracted him when he joined the company fifteen years earlier was an 'esprit de corps' rooted, he believed, in the fact that many of the staff had followed their parents into the business and felt a strong sense of loyalty to the company. It was a loyalty he shared, defining himself as 'a company man' and resisting offers from headhunters (though careful to alert those deciding his salary from year to year that such offers had been made). Now, he found himself responsible for sacking nearly a third of the staff, many of them mid-level managers who had come into the company as young men and risen through the ranks with every expectation of a career for life. These men were likely to have started their working lives in much the same way as Sam himself had entered the law: bank clerks also endured apprenticeships paid for by years of self-denial and parental sacrifice. For those who made it up the hierarchy, the eventual reward was a respectable middle-class income and, above all, security of employment:[47]

And so my involvement in throwing them out of their jobs—out of their social life as well as their income, out of their membership of an organisation which they had all their lives believed in—was more distressing than I can say. Indeed, at the end of one appalling week, in 1975, when I had myself broken the bad news to many of our London managers in a series of tragic interviews going on almost continuously for a whole week, I spent most of the weekend in tears and thought I was beginning a nervous breakdown...it was a very difficult time to be a top manager of a large company.[48]

More redundancies followed as the company struggled unsuccessfully to regain independence and profitability. Throughout the later 1970s

Sam battled with a new chairman imposed by the Bank of England, a top man from one of the big four clearing banks who, in Sam's view, had little understanding of the nature of the business and even less concern for the welfare of its long-serving staff. The two-hour lunches in the directors' dining room, earlier such a delight, were given over to the chairman's egocentric monologues—'a disgusting, vulgar man' whose 'tyrannical idiocy' Sam was forced to endure.[49] Eventually, in the early 1980s, the company was taken over by a larger bank, though only after a nerve-wracking contest between rival takeover bids in which Sam, 'vilified [at a board meeting] for saying that our people count more than a few extra pence on the share price', risked dismissal by leaking information to his favoured bidder and even contemplated encouraging the union to threaten strike action.[50] Sam's relationship with the union bore testimony to his leadership skills. He prided himself on his effectiveness in explaining the situation facing the company to his staff with an appropriate mixture of frankness and authority: 'I am at my best on these occasions. How I would have loved to have commanded a regiment!'[51] Throughout the cutbacks the union's leaders had proved 'exceedingly co-operative', fully vindicating his earlier initiative in granting them recognition.[52] Following the take-over battle they invited Sam and his personnel staff to dinner 'in recognition of our keeping them so closely informed' during the crisis: 'what a nice gesture', he wrote in his diary, 'and I dare say unique in industrial relations'.[53] Sam won the takeover battle, and the new owners proved to be benign masters. But, by then, his appetite for the job had all but vanished.

During the late 1970s Sam had fallen into a decline, physical and mental: 'I became depressed and lacking in enthusiasm and self-confidence. I felt anxious and insecure. Soon I became a chain smoker and, for the first time, I began drinking alcohol for its mind-changing properties.'[54] On one occasion, returning to work after a holiday, he 'took a good tot of whisky before setting out to work, which suitably anaesthetised me against the possible horrors and the strain'.[55] No longer blithely confident of his own judgement, increasingly anxious about the consequences of making a bad decision, he felt he was 'working with a potential time bomb ticking in my desk drawer'.[56] In this run-down state the death of both of his parents in 1978 hit him much harder than he had expected, forcefully reminding him of his own mortality: 'At the age of 42 I was still young, full of youthful vigour and ambition. But four years later I was middle aged.'[57]

Early in 1979 a hernia operation gave him four weeks off work and an opportunity to reassess his life. Because he was forbidden to ride in the aftermath of his operation, Alison gave him a brochure on walking holidays. Lured by the idea of high-altitude walking in the Himalayas, he gave up smoking, decided to get fit, got his weight down to normal, and extended his usual fortnight's annual holiday to three weeks. Enthused by this first 'wilderness experience', he subsequently took instruction in rock climbing and Nordic skiing, establishing an annual routine of adventures in 'distant frozen wilds', including the Andes, the High Atlas, and the Greenland ice cap. Physically restored, he found his ambitions 'reoriented'. He had always intended to retire before he was too old to enjoy himself in vigorous physical activity, but now, 'lowering [his] gaze from the sunlit peaks' and abandoning his ambition to become chairman of the bank—'with a knighthood thrown in'—he began to plan seriously for an early retirement.[58]

4

Sam's difficulties at the bank were part of a wider crisis in which the cultural optimism of the 1960s gave way to apparently irresolvable social conflict. Although Sam always voted Conservative, there had been a moment in the early 1960s when his modernizing drive at work spilled over into a flirtation with radical ideas. He was excited by the new anti-establishment political satire—*Beyond the Fringe, That Was the Week That Was*—and not altogether displeased when Labour won the 1964 election. Harold Wilson's technocratic rhetoric was more to his taste than the patrician culture represented by the 14th Earl of Home. He found the *Daily Telegraph* 'ridiculously right wing', took to balancing his weekly diet of the *Spectator* with the *New Statesman,* and declared himself 'of semi-socialist conviction'.[59] Writing in his diary shortly after the election he favoured the abolition of 'ancient customs' which bred complacency—the monarchy, hereditary peers, and, most surprisingly given his own educational background, the public schools which, by encouraging nepotism, contributed to the 'appalling' quality of British management. He supported Labour's plan to introduce a tax on capital gains, and wanted resources put into management training and vocational education. Arts degrees, on the other hand, should be 'discarded', along with the theatre, which had become obsolete with the invention of cinema.[60]

The philistine excesses of this technocratic moment were soon abandoned: theatre played an important part in Sam's life; he read poetry and novels (and at one time even planned to write a novel of his own); was interested in painting; enjoyed classical music; respected, and was widely read in, academic history. Although he continued to berate monarchy, he soon regained his belief in the value of private education, active in support of his old school, and delighting in his son's successes at a leading public school (and later in an arts degree programme). Wilson's promise of a technocratic new dawn soon lost its appeal, and in the 1970s Sam fully shared conventional right-wing City ideology, supporting Edward Heath in his battles with the unions and anticipating disaster when Labour was returned to office. 'For the first time Britain suffered hyper-inflation ... The trade unions ... became increasingly militant and violent, so that our TV screens showed frequent scenes of rioting...' The talk was of 'ungovernability...it seemed that the whole fabric of British society was crumbling'.[61] Much of the blame for this 1970s 'trend towards anarchy' was placed by Sam (and, he added, by the 'successful business or professional people' with whom he associated) on schoolteachers, whose 'liberal' and 'subversive' attitudes had 'been a major cause of the decline in respect for law and order.'[62] And things could only get worse, he wrote in 1977, because 'the remedy, tougher measures on demonstrations, harsher punishment, tougher education, etc., will be unpalatable to any political party'.[63] With tax on top incomes rising to 86 per cent, Sam became convinced that 'the country is bound upon a course leading to extreme socialism such as will offer no prospects to the middle classes, and that therefore our sons should go abroad, and our daughters too if possible'.[64] As many of the 'bright young men' in the company chose to do just that, Sam toyed with the idea of emigrating himself—to Germany, where he had good business connections—but desisted because he did not want to disrupt the children's education.[65]

Mrs Thatcher's achievement in 'ending socialism', breaking trade-union power, 'turning our country back from the brink of the abyss', and substantially enhancing Sam's income by cutting the top rate of income tax, was little short of miraculous and he was filled with admiration for her courage and determination.[66] Later on he was appreciative of Tony Blair's attempts to wean the Labour Party off socialism, and confident that even if Labour reverted to bad old habits in government they would be unable to do too much damage since the abolition of exchange controls—one of the first acts of the Thatcher government in 1979—meant that investors were free to move their capital overseas: 'at the first sign of serious trouble in the economy there would be a flight from sterling—with disastrous effects for the Government.'[67]

When it came to his feelings about Britain's long-term future, however, he was far from being a conventional Thatcherite. Unimpressed by the flag-waving of the Falklands War, he wrote in his diary:

The fact is... that we cannot afford to defend hundreds of remote islands, [we] should acknowledge what Suez taught us—we are not a world power now... we must learn to be a second class European state.[68]

He disapproved of the fortieth anniversary celebrations in 1985 of Allied victory in the Second World War, fearing that they would jeopardize European unity while feeding the public nostalgia for Britain's 'finest hour' which, despite having witnessed the Battle of Britain in the sky above his home town as a boy, he condemned as a refusal to face up to post-war realities. Despite Thatcher's best efforts, the future for enterprising Britons lay in Europe—quite literally. In the long term, as Britain became 'part of a United States of Europe', the middle-class emigration he had advocated in the 1970s would become a fact:

the more able inhabitants will go elsewhere... leaving the poor and the blacks here in England... There will be only disadvantages in trading from an off-shore island, and living in our grim climate... Just as the Irish came to England, and as Northerners who are bright came to the South [as Sam's father had done], so eventually England will, I believe, be very poor and rundown—and black.[69]

Thatcher could do nothing to halt what he saw as the disastrous consequences of immigration from the Commonwealth, and inner-city rioting in the mid-1980s confirmed his belief that unemployment and alienation among young black men would remain an intractable social problem. Where others might react to such visions of national decline by embracing a blood-and-soil nationalism, the banker's fantasy, in line with the magical capacity of money to abstract value from its social context, was to up sticks and move abroad.

But it was only a fantasy. In reality Sam was as attached as the next
man to his English acres, the town he had lived in all his life, and his
various social networks. What he turned to for comfort 'during my
years of struggle and stress' was a spiritual, not a material, means of
escape.[70] Sam had been brought up as a Christian Scientist and had
remained 'a fervent religious believer' until shortly before he joined
the bank, at which point becoming a 'committed company man' did
something to 'fill the gap' left by his loss of religious faith.[71] By the
mid-1960s he was describing himself as a convinced atheist, but in the
aftermath of the crisis in his marriage in the early 1970s he turned again
to his religious inheritance. Not to churchgoing, but to private meditation informed by the writings of Joel Goldsmith, a dissident Christian
Scientist to whose works he had been introduced by his father.
Throughout the 1970s and early 1980s he frequently noted in his diary
the benefits he derived from reading and mediating upon Goldsmith's
reassuring message that by 'exchanging...our material sense of existence for the understanding and consciousness of life as spiritual', we can
not only rise above everyday anxieties but do so in a way which will
enable us to 'taste the full joys of home, companionship, and successful
enterprise'.[72] As his work became more and more stressful in the later
1970s he found that his regular reading of Goldsmith brought him
peace of mind, and helped him to maintain a positive attitude both in
the office and at home. 'Thank heavens I have my religion to help me
through these difficult times...greatly buoyed up and in good spirits as
a result of Joel reading...I wonder how ever I managed without it.'[73]

But manage he had. And, as ambition faded and retirement beck-
oned, he again lost interest in religion, and as 'a born again atheist'
came to understand his previous engagement with the spiritual as a
therapeutic rather than a religious experience. As with the Christian
Scientist belief in power of the mind to heal bodily illness, he never
doubted the efficacy of meditation; but he no longer believed 'that this
power comes from God: I believe it results from a certain method of
using the brain, in which a fervent religious belief may be a useful
mechanism'. And however useful religion had been to him in difficult
times he realized that he 'had no further need of it when I later felt that
my life was comfortably under my own control'.[74]

Looking back from 1997, Sam reflected that as his salary mounted
to levels far exceeding what he could spend, his personal financial
concerns had more to do with status than with material acquisitiveness:

'I ceased to be very interested in the actual rate of pay, as long as I knew it was the going rate for my kind of job.'[75] In fact, as the diary shows, he had been far from indifferent to the actual rate of pay. Until he had a secure, inflation-proofed package set in stone on the eve of his retirement, he suffered periodic bouts of extreme anxiety about his long-term finances and job security, despite the fact that from 1971 onwards he had a rolling five-year service contract that guaranteed a substantial payout in the event of redundancy. The anxiety, he eventually acknowledged, was irrational; a hangover from the insecurity of his years as an articled clerk. But the notion of 'the going rate' played an important part in his sense of self. Unlike the unfortunate subordinates he was forced to make redundant, he could still appeal to the operation of market forces to provide an objective measure of his own worth. Each pay rise, each renewal of his service contract, served to reassure him; and he continued to believe that the high levels of pay at the top of companies was justified by ability, hard work, and successful risk-taking. When asked by Mass Observation whether people's worth was recognized by society, he acknowledged that neither 'free market forces' nor 'public morality' had secured 'a proper balance [of] financial reward between, say, skills and qualifications on the one hand, and hard, unsociable drudgery on the other'. But he did not believe that such a balance would ever be found: 'so, although dissatisfied with what I see about me, I believe that, give or take occasional adjustments, we shall have to settle with what we have'.[76]

While the notion of 'the going rate' helped him to sidestep larger questions of distributive justice, he was not indifferent to the lives of the less fortunate. On one occasion he thought about spending a week living as a tramp in London: 'it would be an interesting experience to view life from the under-dog's point of view'. But Alison was afraid he would 'get knifed in a doss house' and the plan was dropped.[77] The closest he got to life on the street was the walk through Billingsgate market on his way to work, exoticized in an uncharacteristically poetic passage in a 1963 diary entry:

The fat, cheesy costers rolled about the streets littered with old fish and broken ice, barrows and carts stood scattered about, the perky porters lounged in warehouse doorways shouting raucous quips at each other, and two nuns walked by stepping carefully through the litter. What a bustling, alive scene. And less than 100 yards away stand the [company] offices ... where quiet, shrewd, cold, careful men sedately pass quite a different existence. How strange.[78]

Strange indeed—but this was literary pastoral. As he well knew, and documents extensively in his diary, he and his colleagues were far from being 'cold, careful men'—the office, no less than the street, was a hotbed of emotional turmoil, and even 'raucous quips' were not unknown during a well-oiled lunch. More prosaically, as we have seen, he had a genuine concern for the staff for whom he was responsible, and notably for his chauffeur, whom he relied on not only to drive him to and from work but also to mow the lawn, fix the mower, and pick up his son from boarding school. When the chauffeur was caught driving over the alcohol limit, Sam organized his legal defence, and ensured that the company kept him employed during the year that his licence was suspended.

The chauffeur, however, also represented what might have been seen as an ethical problem. Supplementing his salary, Sam received an array of tax-free fringe benefits. The first thing the directors did when they ousted their chairman in 1974 was to award themselves a clutch of new perks including longer holidays, interest-free loans for investment, and private use of chauffeurs at evenings and weekends. Nearly ten years later, when the Inland Revenue investigated the company's tax affairs, Sam feared that if they unravelled the chauffeur arrangements he could be landed with a tax bill of anything up to £30,000. 'Terribly worried', Sam turned again to Joel: 'my religion helps a lot in these awful situations'.[79] In the end the tax inspector required nothing more than that in future their lunches should be counted for tax purposes. Religion helped, then as at other times, because engagement with the spiritual allowed merely material anxieties to fade into the background. He looked to his meditative practice to relieve anxiety, not for the forgiveness of sin.

Nevertheless, Sam saw himself as a man living by a coherent ethical code. The efficacy of the old City maxim—'my word is my bond'—depended on the figuring out of 'character' (over lunch, maybe) and the exercise of informal sanctions by City leaders blackballing 'the wrong kind of chap'. 'I, and my friends,' wrote Sam, 'will have no truck with those who are dishonest or unreliable or generally of poor character . . . I believe that [we] have an exacting standard of integrity and honesty, and will not tolerate contravention.'[80] Contravention of course occurred, and much wrongdoing was swept under the carpet. Sam was genuinely shocked by the behaviour of one chairman—a man whose public reputation remained unblemished—who refused to take action against a senior executive caught by the auditors defrauding the bank because both men were Freemasons. And, as Sam freely admitted, his 'exacting standards' could be surprisingly flexible. Looking back at the 1970s, when taxes for the rich had risen to 'farcical levels', he remarked that these same friends 'would do almost anything to evade tax: the only question was whether you'd be found out'. Under Mrs Thatcher, on the other hand, tax rates were considered reasonable, 'and I note that my friends would now frown on any form of illegal avoidance'. Similarly, he wrote, 'businessmen are usually aware that even the large insurance companies are engaged in widespread petty trickery . . . and consequently will not hesitate to "redress the balance" by inflating insurance claims'. The existence of such a 'grey area around the fringe of integrity'—an area he knew well not only from his business life, but also from his changing attitudes to 'a certain degree of marital misbehaviour'—suggested that 'there are no absolutes in financial or moral integrity—there are simply levels of behaviour found acceptable by groups within society at particular times'. To behave ethically was to conform to the norms of one's social grouping, and although these norms might vary with time and circumstance, this lack of absolutes did not mean that anything goes. 'The difference between honesty and dishonesty', he concluded, 'is like the rhinoceros—difficult to define, but you know it when you see it'. Sam and his associates were confident that they could detect the 'fundamentally rotten' even when it hid itself behind the most impeccable of self-presentations.[81] In the end it was mutual recognition among men of character that provided Sam with his defence against a slide into moral relativism, an ethical approach well adapted to a privileged elite's functional need to cultivate trust amongst themselves while evading any searching critique of the moral implications of systemic social inequality.

Sam retired, aged fifty-four, in 1987 and continued to write for Mass Observation until 2008. He died four years later. In retirement he continued to live life to the full: 'an active life devoted entirely to pleasure', he wrote in his mid-60s, 'a wonderful success—I doubt if you could meet a happier man.'[82] His pleasures were many and varied. As a non-executive director of a new investment bank he kept in touch with old colleagues, and he was well known as an after-dinner speaker in the City. He served as a school governor and used his expertise to give financial advice to the Mass Observation trustees. He acted in plays with the local theatre group, sang in operas and musicals, and performed as a comedian and compère of a regular evening of music hall. He also hired himself out, sometimes as often as four times a week, as an after-dinner speaker on topics including Florence Nightingale, Tennyson's poetry, 'the history of food, drink and table manners', and 'An Anatomy of Humour: a hilarious 30 minute talk…suitable for both ladies and gentlemen—very funny, in constant demand.'[83] During one year in his mid-60s he earned about £4000 from exactly 100 speaking engagements, but turned down offers from professional agencies to perform for much higher fees as a cabaret comedian since this would have meant spending nights away from home, and he had no need for the money.

On top of all this he kept up his regime of vigorous physical activity. Up at 6 a.m., he would, in summer, 'take a dawn walk round my fields'.[84] Several mornings a week he obliged friends by exercising their nervous and highly strung thoroughbred horses. When not on a horse he liked to ride his motorbike fast around the local lanes, or take off on it to France for a few days. There were more wilderness walks, and sometimes, back home, he would go off by himself on long walks for two or three days, carrying only water and a waterproof sleeping bag, and buying food wherever he could find it. As more of his friends retired, he established a routine of fast 12–15-mile walks every Thursday, an occasion to exercise not only their bodies but also their shared contempt for the fatuousness of the civil liberties lobby, the whingeing of the *Guardian*-reading liberal intelligentsia, and what they saw as left-wing bias in the BBC. Sam had always enjoyed 'all-male company and outdoor life': while an articled clerk he had joined the Territorials and loved his two-week annual 'holiday' on Salisbury Plain, and he had been genuinely disappointed when the army refused to let him do his National Service.[85] Now, chatting in the pub after a strenuous day's walking, 'the blend of beer…hard exercise [and] good male company' was 'indeed a joyous delight.'[86]

But so was mixed company. Twice a year he went touring and camping in France with his wife, and back home he revelled in the companionship of the theatre, and in a regular round of dinner parties:

The enjoyment of food and drink reaches its apogee for me at a sophisticated dinner party for say 10 people in a private house—preferably my own, where I have been able to choose both the company and the menu…My wife and I choose only guests who are good intelligent conversationalists, preferably witty and humorous; our male guests have usually achieved much and the women will usually be charming and attractive.[87]

Thinking, perhaps, of the sensibilities of his audience at Mass Observation, he added a conciliatory afterthought: 'Mine is the last generation in which few English women have achieved much outside the home.'

5

Sam knew the world was changing—but he was not forced to change with it. Equally comfortable in the company of intelligent men and attractive women, he had no need to question the version of masculinity he had inherited as a child. Nothing in his life prompted him to question the propriety of the established division of labour between the sexes. In the City, dressed to kill, he fought manfully for power and authority, deploying the full range of masculine weaponry, the passions alongside his professional analytical skills. At home he was fully cognizant of both his rights and his duties. His job was to provide a secure financial basis for family life; hers was to be a mother to the children and to provide the comforts of a clean and tidy home. When occasionally he thought that she fell down on the latter (never the former), he used his diary to vent the righteous anger of a breadwinner denied his due.

The diffusion of feminist ideas from the 1970s had little impact in Sam's world. When, in 1991, Mass Observation confronted him with a directive designed to encourage respondents to think critically about their gender identities, provocatively entitled 'Women and Men', Sam declined to participate—this was one of the few directives to which he failed to respond. Nevertheless he had registered MO's interest in the topic and in subsequent directive replies went out of his way to make his standpoint clear:

I scorn those men who spend most of their leisure performing a 'deputy-mother' role, changing nappies, dandling infants, helping with the housework and shopping. The modern idea of fathers being present at birth and taking paternity leave appals me. Better by far for the father…to concentrate his efforts on working harder…to increase the family income. And better still if he can also spend some time in activities which will keep him healthy, broaden his experience and perhaps even develop his nerve and decisiveness—to the benefit of his earning capacity and job satisfaction.[88]

Sam would give no quarter to feminist demands for a new kind of man.

Of course, as with all gender identities, there were contradictions. For all their power and authority in the world of work, men like Sam remained highly dependent on the services of their female secretaries. Inefficient secretaries were a frequent source of irritation and efficient ones a treasure to be retained at all costs. But falling for one's secretary was a potential disaster, one which in his early thirties Sam fought off only after several months of obsessive (but undeclared) desire. It was not feminism which, for Sam, laid bare the flaws in the established gender order, but the sexual permissiveness of the 1960s. Taking things to their logical conclusion in the privacy of his own head, he could imagine a world of unrestrained masculine promiscuity. But he knew very well that real life was not like that, and when confronted with the contradiction between sexual desire and the stability of his marriage and family, he chose the latter. However painful at the time, he came to believe that his choice had been for the best, a conclusion facilitated no doubt by the continuing operation of a classically male double standard in sexual matters.[89]

The City that Sam encountered between the 1960s and 80s served him well. By retiring at fifty-four he was able to avoid the transforming impact of Thatcher's 'Big Bang' on City life. Despite the economic difficulties of the 1970s he served out his time as a respected and well-rewarded company man before the influx of American banks and the takeover culture to whose development Sam himself had contributed put paid to the gentlemanly world he had joined in 1960. For the historian of the 'Old City' the worst crime of the Thatcher years was to promote an aggressively mobile entrepreneurialism which 'took the brightest and the best of a generation—and consumed them in a bonfire of the vanities'.[90] Totally focussed on the relentless pursuit of profit, devoid of company loyalty or concern for their staff, substituting a sandwich for the leisurely and (sometimes) cultivated lunches of their forebears, the new generation of high-flyers—according to one disenchanted witness—met the challenge of City life by focussing so narrowly on the service of money that all other aspects of their personalities 'just withered and died'.[91] No one could say that of Sam. Despite nearly thirty years of 'stimulating but straining life in the fast lane', he had always managed to live life to the full, his evenings and weekends packed with sporting, creative, and sociable activities; all the more so as his holidays lengthened and his working week shortened during his final years as the company's longest-serving director.[92]

Sam had done well as a modernizer within the established gentlemanly order, and his wealth eventually gave him the control over his life that he had always sought. Before illness set in he was able to develop to the full his many capacities and enjoy twenty years of delightfully active hedonism, untroubled by the physical problems and psychological needs which had plagued him periodically during his working life. Writing for Mass Observation in retirement, Sam found composure. His ulcer calmed down; he was no longer driven to religion to assuage his anxieties; and his friends told him that he was 'a master in the art of enjoyment of life'.[93] And, if at times he made his life sound too good to be true, he also left behind a daily record of his ups and downs, providing for the social historian a rounded portrait of the man behind the public face of a successful City gentleman in the closing years of the Old City.

10

Conclusion

In telling their stories the mass observers wanted to contribute to the ways in which the history of their times came to be understood. Confronted with individual life stories, the job of the professional historian is not simply to record, but to select, compare, and interpret them in ways which offer insights about past human behaviour that may be of use in our efforts to make sense of the contemporary world. In that respect this book represents no more than a beginning. These seven biographical essays are suggestive of the diversity of ways, even among members of the same pre-war generation, in which the changing culture of late-twentieth-century Britain was experienced. Other historians, when they read these essays, will no doubt find in these lives material to illustrate interpretations of the period quite different from those I sketched out in Chapter 2. History is always a debate.

As E. H. Carr pointed out long ago, information about the past becomes 'historical'—as against merely antiquarian—only to the extent that it is deployed by historians in support of particular interpretations.[1] My hope is that these essays will help to place their subjects, or some of them, among those iconic individuals used by historians to illuminate contested interpretations of the period—as historians of British society during the Second World War have done, for example, with an earlier mass observer, Nella Last. In both periods the life writing fostered by Mass Observation enables us to access something of the fullness, ambiguity, complexity, and confusion of the real lives of otherwise obscure individuals, material so much more stimulating to the historical imagination than the abstracted and partial traces that most ordinary people leave in the public record. In the meantime I can best conclude by summarizing some of the ways in which the stories told here illustrate the currents and cross-currents of cultural change during the late twentieth century.

Writing to the archive, the mass observers knew they were contributing to a collective historical project, but they did so in isolation from one another. The great majority of mass observers never knowingly met any of their colleagues, and this was true of all seven people with the exception of Bob Rust who, late in life, met some fellow observers when he participated in a Mass Observation conference. Had their paths crossed, it is difficult to imagine that their shared commitment would have evoked much fellow feeling. Sam, the banker, and Bob, the lorry driver, were the same age but it is unlikely they would have found much in common had they encountered one another in the flesh. In April 1963, returning from a funeral in his Rolls Royce, the chairman of Sam's bank, impeccably dressed, decided to stop for coffee in a transport café. Sam, imagining the event in his diary, infused it with pride of class: 'The coalheavers and lorrymen present goggled at the chauffeur in his peaked cap sitting next to the magnificent [chairman]. What a splendid thought.'[2] Had Bob been one of the 'lorrymen' it is unlikely that he would have recognized himself in Sam's complacent picture of the great unwashed awestruck by this unexpected apparition of privilege and power.

Sam was set apart by his wealth, one of those businessmen whom Janet, the 'scum class teacher', occasionally glimpsed commuting from leafy dormitory towns in 'their big smart cars, with teeth', while she nervously made her way to work in a rusty Ford Capri.[3] Had they been able to communicate, Janet and Sam might have shared some sympathy with the permissive discourses of the 1960s, although for Sam this stopped with personal sexual liberation while Janet, ready to take on any taboo, sought to press forward the liberalizing legislative agenda from sex to death (euthanasia). Stella also discovered sexual liberation in the 1960s, but the New Age humanistic psychology which she deployed against oppressive social norms was entirely foreign to the convention-bound world of Sam's City. Caroline, who clung to convention and remained trapped in a miserable marriage, deplored the permissive society, but she and Sam shared their Thatcherite sympathies, both believing that financially they stood to benefit from the neo-liberal experiment. Perhaps more fundamental to Caroline's politics was a sense that Thatcher's rhetoric spoke to her refusal to embrace victimhood and her gritty determination to stand on her own feet no matter what fate threw at her: characteristics she attributed to having grown up 'emotionally right wing'. Bob deplored neo-liberalism and was not right wing 'emotionally' or otherwise, but his gradual loss of sympathy with the labour movement he had earlier served may have owed as much to the independent spirit of the lorry driver as it did to the fact that he also benefitted from Thatcher's flagship policies, in his case council-house sales and privatization. Len, with whom Bob had so much in common, had nothing but anger and contempt for the self-serving profiteering involved in the privatization of local services. While at one with Caroline both in deploring 1960s permissiveness and in blaming the indiscipline of the young on foolishly 'progressive' schoolteachers, he was entirely in agreement with the 'scum class teacher' in identifying the evil consequences of the relentlessly expanding imposition of so-called managerial expertise at the expense of the proper autonomy of the skilled worker, whether mechanic or, in her case, teacher. Sam believed that the public sector suffered from the absence of the new managerial disciplines which he took so much pride in helping to introduce in the City; Janet and Len could have instructed him on the disastrous consequences of the ignorant and self-serving managerialism invading the public sector.

Although it is commonly assumed that most mass observers were *Guardian*-reading liberals, five of my seven observers were at one time or another drawn to the right in British politics—or indeed six, if one counts Helen, the RAF wife, before her 1960s conversion. For Sam and Caroline the appeal of the Conservative Party was straightforward. For Janet, who could curse *Guardian* readers, warmongering politicians, and establishment paedophile rings with equal vehemence, the flirtation with the UK Independence Party was perhaps no more than a random throw of the dice. For Len, and especially for Bob, on the other hand, UKIP seemed to offer a way of protesting against what they saw as the Labour Party's abandonment of working-class interests. Hostility to the European Union, seen as a capitalist plot against the workers, together with a British patriotism rooted in memories of the Second World War, were central to their attraction to UKIP.

Responses to race and immigration were complex. Caroline, well aware of immigrant culture through her sons' association with black and Asian youth, was determinedly anti-racist, bitterly resenting the assumptions people made about the views of the Tory lady in her hat. Janet, ferocious in her denunciation of both leftist and establishment

anti-racism, was proud to be accepted as an 'honorary wog' by her
Caribbean pupils, and an ally against patriarchy by her Asian ones. While
everyone who commented on the Rushdie affair shared alarm and
resentment against book-burning Pakistanis, Helen was exceptional in
interrogating her own instinctive reactions to the refusal of some immigrants to embrace Western values. Despite their shared dislike of racism,
it is difficult to imagine Helen and Caroline hitting it off, although that
may be to underestimate Helen's capacity for seeing things from the
other person's point of view. Canvassing a council estate in the run-up
to the 1987 election, Helen described her encounter with a home-
owning decorator's wife, whose six grown-up children were all in work,
'who regaled me for half an hour about her lazy, greedy neighbours
who took the dole and went potato picking on the side... We got along
wonderfully well, with our arguments and counter-arguments, neither
of us convincing the other.' Helen found herself admiring the woman's
'sheer energy and application', and, although her own pleas 'for compassion for people who weren't so strong and committed to self-help'
were met with derision, they parted on good terms. 'She was Thatcher
personified', Helen reflected, 'and one mustn't degrade some of these
qualities.'[4] She might well have felt the same about Caroline.

The most systematic contrast between the life experiences of the
mass observers lay across the fault line of gender. For most men of this
generation, gender was an unproblematic given—'men' was simply
what they were, and what they understood by 'manliness' was rooted,
they believed, in biology. When, from the 1970s, modern feminism
called into question such ahistorical understandings of gender difference,
these mass observers found it hard to scrutinize their own gender
identity and harder still to contemplate changing what it meant to live
'like a man'. Moreover, since all three were blessed with wives who
were themselves unresponsive to the new feminism, they had no
pressing need to do so. When Dorothy Sheridan took over the leadership of Mass Observation in 1990 she was keen to explore issues of
gender identity, but she was well aware that some mass observers would
be uncomfortable with the feminist agenda underpinning her enquiry.
The responses of the three men discussed in this book fully bore out
this expectation. Len, the mechanic, used the Autumn 1991 directive
on 'Women and Men' to express his indignation at feminist attempts
to undermine the 'natural' gender order, condemning 'women's lib. [as]
the biggest confidence trick ever played on women', and dismissing

so-called 'new men' as 'wimps' who had allowed 'modern ideas [to] undermine [their] masculine virtues'. Bob, the lorry driver, was also hostile to feminism, restoring propriety from the outset with a pointed reversal of Sheridan's directive title—'Men and Women (alphabetical order)'. And, although he knew that a new world was arriving, Sam was at one with Len in his contempt for the domesticated male, and he remained content to divide his friends between 'intelligent men and charming women'—and to divide his women between exciting mistresses and the children's devoted mother.

The relative stability of the male identities contrasts strikingly with the altogether more complicated processes by which the women constructed their sense of themselves. While the men tended to use their MO writing to express a confident, composed, achieved selfhood, the women's writing focussed more on the disjunctions, the obstacles, the paths not taken. Unlike the men, the women were fully paid-up members of what Christopher Lasch described as 'the therapeutic society'.[5] In 2008 Janet observed that 'there is now a category of "Painful Writings" in the bookshops and people can tell of their sad childhoods in an autobiographical way. Probably it's a way to catharsis and cheaper than a shrink.'[6] She herself felt scarred by an exceptionally sad childhood, and writing about it for MO helped her to manage the pain. A similarly therapeutic purpose was served by Caroline's stories of an evil stepmother and a pathetically murderous father, stories which helped to establish her adult self as her own creation, 'independent and beholden to no-one', until some tragic flaw of character led her into a loveless marriage. All four women dwell on their struggles to liberate themselves from families of origin in which they had been undervalued, their potential denied. Caroline, Stella, and Helen were all forced to leave school early by fathers who saw little purpose in educating their daughters; and Janet's father's opposition to her taking up the scholarship she won to Queen's University was overcome only by the pleading of her stepmother and a female neighbour. Denied opportunities early in life, the women made good with adult education. But a sense of unfulfilled potential remained, embodied for the older two—Caroline and Helen—in the memory of lost wartime lovers very different from their eventual partners and providing, perhaps, a consolatory myth of a possible alternative life. A lost lover, like a miserable childhood, could have a role to play in the construction of an acceptable 'theory of the self'.[7]

Throughout the writing of the book I had a working title which, in the end, I decided not to use. That title was 'My Times: Their Lives'. It expressed two salient facts about the enterprise. Firstly that, after many years submerged in the 1940s, I had finally managed to move forward into the period of my own adult life. Secondly that, not being ready for the degree of self-exposure involved in writing autobiographically, I was making use of these other, self-revealed, lives to gain greater understanding of the times I have lived through. At various points where there were overlaps between my own experience and that of the mass observers I attempted to insert myself into the text, if only to justify the working title—an eighth life interpolating the other seven. But, writing self-consciously for publication, I found it quite impossible to match the intimacy, honesty, and (relative) absence of self-censorship with which the other seven wrote for Mass Observation, and only the slightest traces of these attempts remain in the final version. When Jules Michelet, the French historian, warned that 'the historian who... undertakes to erase himself while writing... is not a historian at all', he was thinking not about the special hazards of contemporary history, but about those bonds of human sympathy that underpin the possibility of understanding other lives in any epoch.[8] In that sense I am not erased. And, although I have done my best to view each of these lives with empathy, my own values were bound to intrude. They are clear enough in the writing.

It is as a reader of these lives, not as a writer, that I have come closest to examining not only my times, but also my own life. Proust was thinking of the novel when he remarked that 'every reader is, while he is reading, the reader of his own self', but the dictum is equally applicable to the reader of Mass Observation's life writing. Explaining his meaning Proust added: 'The writer's work is merely a kind of optical instrument which he offers to the reader to enable him to discern what, without this book, he would perhaps never have perceived in himself.'[9] If, dear reader, the stories offered here have helped you—as they have me—to contemplate your own life and your own paths not taken then this writer's work will have been competently done.

Notes

1. MASS OBSERVATION

1. James Hinton, *The Mass Observers. A History, 1937–1949*, Oxford, 2013; Nick Hubble, *Mass Observation and Everyday Life*, Basingstoke, 2006; Tom Jeffery, *Mass Observation—A Short History*, Birmingham, 1978.

2. Luisa Passerini, 'Work ideology and consensus under Italian fascism', *History Workshop*, 8, 1979; Richard Johnson and Graham Dawson (Popular Memory Group), 'Popular memory. Theory, politics, method', in Richard Johnson et al. (eds.), *Making Histories: Studies in History-writing and Politics*, London, 1982; Ken Worpole, 'A ghostly pavement: The political implications of local working-class history', in Raphael Samuel (ed.), *People's History and Socialist Theory*, London, 1981; Stephen Yeo, 'The politics of community publications', in Raphael Samuel (ed.), *People's History and Socialist Theory*, London, 1981; Chris Waters, 'Autobiography, nostalgia and the changing practices of working-class selfhood', in George K. Behlmer and Fred M. Leventhal (eds.), *Singular Continuities. Tradition, Nostalgia and Identity in Modern British Culture*, Stanford, CA, 2000; Raphael Samuel, 'History Workshop, 1966–80', in Raphael Samuel (ed.), *People's History and Socialist Theory*, London, 1981; Paul Thompson, *The Voice of the Past. Oral History*, Oxford, 1978.

3. A. Kuhn, *Family Secrets. Acts of Memory and Imagination*, London, 2002, 9; Dorothy Sheridan, 'Writing to the archive: M-O as autobiography', *Sociology*, 27, 1, 1993, 27–40; Dorothy Sheridan, Brian Street, and David Bloome, *Writing Ourselves. Mass-Observation and Literacy Practices*, Cresskill, NJ, 2000; D. Sheridan, *Damned Anecdotes and Dangerous Confabulations. Mass-Observation as Life History*, M-O Archive Occasional Paper, 7, 1996.

4. Prue Chamberlayne, Joanna Bornat, and Tom Wengraf (eds.), *The Turn to Biographical Methods in the Social Sciences*, Abingdon, 2000; Daniel Bertaux (ed.), *Biography and Society. The Life History Approach to the Social Sciences*, London, 1981; Paul Thompson and Daniel Bertaux (eds.), *Pathways to Social Class*, Oxford, 1997; Ken Plummer, *Documents of Life*, London, 1983; Ken Plummer, *Documents of Life 2. An Invitation to a Critical Humanism*, London, 2001; Liz Stanley, 'On auto/biography in sociology', *Sociology*, 27, 1993.

5. Sheridan et al., *Writing Ourselves*, 49, 97–8, 100, 101.

6. Dorothy Sheridan, correspondence with Angus Calder, 1979–1993, SxMOA28. As well as being active in the women's liberation movement, Sheridan was involved in QueenSpark Books, a community publishing organization in Brighton, on which see Michael Hayler and Alistair Thomson, 'Working with words: Active learning in a community writing and publishing group', in Jane Mace (ed.), *Literacy, Language and Community Publishing: Essays in Adult Education*, Clevedon, 1995; Ben Jones, 'The uses of nostalgia', *Cultural and Social History*, 7, 3, 2010; Ben Jones, *The Working Class in Mid-twentieth-century England. Community, Identity and Social Memory*, Manchester, 2012, 107–10.

7. Sheridan, cited in Annebella Pollen, 'Using the Mass-Observation Archive', in Anne Jamieson and Christina Victor (eds.), *Researching Ageing and Later Life: The Practice of Social Gerontology*, Buckingham, 2002, 77.

8. Sheridan et al., *Writing Ourselves* has the fullest account. For a recent discussion of the nature of the MOP writing see Annebella Pollen, 'A hybrid heterogeneity hard to contain: Research methods and methodology in the post-1981 Mass Observation Project', *History Workshop Journal*, 75, 2013; see also Jenny Shaw, 'Intellectual property, representative experience and M-O', M-O Archive Occasional Paper, 9, 1998; Dorothy Jerome, 'Time, change and continuity in family life', *Ageing and Society*, 14, 1994.

9. Carol Smart, speaking at Mass Observation's 75th Anniversary Conference, July 2012.

10. Cited in Sheridan et al., *Writing Ourselves*, 135.

11. Shaw, 'Intellectual property', 4; another researcher suggests that 'testimonies gathered by the solitary and anonymous act of writing can be more intimate than that produced by an interview where the person being interviewed may seek to engage or deflect the interviewer, to please them or guard against them' (Louise Purbrick, 'Present life: Mass Observation and understanding the ordinary', *Qualitative Researcher*, 7, 2008, 11, cited in Pollen, 'Hybrid heterogeneity'). For a contrary view from an oral historian see Lynn Abrams, 'Liberating the female self: Epiphanies, conflict and coherence in the life stories of post-war British women', *Social History*, 39, 1, 2014. She argues that writing gives the respondent the opportunity to dissemble in ways that could not be hidden from a skilled interviewer.

12. Cited in Steph Lawler, *Identity: Sociological Perspectives*, Cambridge, 2008, 19. There are younger writers, people more likely to be at the cutting edge of cultural change in the later twentieth century, among the mass observers but I did not find enough of them to balance the depth of insight provided by my selection of people from the older generation. Perhaps, as they age, they will become subjects of a further volume of biographical essays.

13. For a valuable discussion of the formation, coexistence, and interaction of different social generations see Jane Pilcher, 'Mannheim's sociology of

generations: An undervalued legacy', *The British Journal of Sociology*, 45, 3, 1994, 481–95.

14. Johnson and Dawson, 'Popular memory'; Penny Summerfield, 'Culture and composure: Creating narratives of the gendered self in oral history interviews', *Cultural and Social History*, 1, 2004, 65–93; Jones, *Working Class*, 48–51. For a useful discussion of 'reflexivity' see Margaret Archer, *Making our Way through the World: Human Reflexivity and Social Mobility*, Cambridge, 2007.

15. On myths of the working class see Carolyn Steedman, *Landscape for a Good Woman. A Story of Two Women*, 1986. On myths of wartime unity see Angus Calder, *The Myth of the Blitz*, London, 1991; Malcolm Smith, *Britain and 1940. History, Myth and Popular Memory*, London, 2000; Sonia O. Rose, *Which People's War? National Identity and Citizenship in Britain 1939–1945*, Oxford, 2003; James Hinton, *Nine Wartime Lives. Mass Observation and the Making of the Modern Self*, Oxford, 2010.

16. On the role of historical myths in the creation of Thatcherism see E. H. H. Green, 'Thatcherism: An historical perspective', *Transactions of the Royal Historical Society*, 9, 1999.

17. Johnson and Dawson, 'Popular Memory', 211.

18. Passerini, 'Work ideology and consensus'.

19. I owe this terminology to Tony Kushner whose *We Europeans? Mass-Observation, 'Race' and British Identity in the Twentieth Century*, Aldershot, 2004, includes a pioneering attempt to trace the evolution of individual mass observers' attitudes. One reason why surprisingly little use has been made of the biographical method with MO materials is the organization of the archive, which continues to inhibit its use as a source of biographical information. From the start responses to each directive were filed separately rather than under the identity of the author, and the same procedure has been followed since the revival of the panel in 1981. Although the archive catalogue can now be used to produce a list of all the responses sent in by any individual correspondent, the responses are stored in scores of different boxes, making access to the material laborious for both the researcher and the archive staff. These mundane organizational details probably go a long way to explain the otherwise surprising failure of researchers working on replies to a particular directive to deepen their understanding of the more interesting responses by seeking out relevant biographical information contained in responses made by the same individuals to other directives. Digitalization will eventually solve this problem, as it has already done for the original MO material.

20. Charles Madge and Tom Harrisson, *Mass-Observation*, London, 1937, 30.

21. Michael Rustin, 'Reflections on the biographical turn in the social sciences', in Prue Chamberlayne, Joanna Bornat, and Tom Wengraf (eds.), *The Turn to Biographical Methods in the Social Sciences*, Abingdon, 2000, 49.

22. As Paul Thompson says of oral history, such material can open up 'wholly new perspectives—interpretations from the previously ill-represented standpoints of ordinary men, women and children about what they believed had mattered most in their lives' (Paul Thompson, 'Life histories and the analysis of social change', in Daniel Bertaux (ed.), *Biography and Society. The Life History Approach to the Social Sciences*, London, 1981). For a splendid exemplification of Thompson's point see Steedman's 'defiant pleasure' in using her own mother's story to 'subvert' established accounts of working-class experience (Steedman, *Landscape for a Good Woman*, 8–9).
23. Observer R2143, 'Being Part of Research', 2004.
24. Cited by Annebella Pollen in a paper delivered to the 75th Anniversary Conference of Mass Observation, University of Sussex, July 2012.
25. Richard Holmes, *Footsteps: Adventures of a Romantic Biographer*, London, 1985, 66.
26. For a valuable discussion of these issues see Barbara Taylor, 'Historical subjectivity', in Sally Alexander and Barbara Taylor (eds.), *History and Psyche. Culture, Psychoanalysis and the Past*, New York, 2012.

2. HISTORIES

1. Michael Rustin, 'Reflections on the biographical turn in the social sciences', in Prue Chamberlayne, Joanna Bornat, and Tom Wengraf (eds.), *The Turn to Biographical Methods in the Social Sciences*, Abingdon, 2000, 49.
2. Arthur Marwick, *The Sixties: Cultural Revolution in Britain, France, Italy, and the United States*, Oxford, 1998. For the weaknesses of this book see the review by Jim Obelkevich in *Twentieth Century British History*, 11, 3, 2000, 333–6.
3. Frank Mort, 'The permissive society revisited', *Twentieth Century British History*, 22, 2, 2011, 286–8.
4. Martin P. M. Richards and B. Jane Elliott, 'Sex and marriage in the 1960s and 1970s', in David Clark (ed.), *Marriage, Domestic Life and Social Change*, London, 1991; Claire Langhamer, 'Adultery in post-war England', *History Workshop Journal*, 62, 1, 2006; B. Jane Elliott 'Demographic trends in domestic life, 1945–1987', in Clark (ed.), *Marriage, Domestic Life and Social Change*, 1991.
5. At least in the short term. For a balanced account of the longer-term impact of the pill on sexual behaviour see Hera Cook, 'The English sexual revolution: Technology and social change', *History Workshop Journal*, 59, 2005, 109–28.
6. Jane Lewis, *Women in Britain since 1945*, Oxford, 1992; Penny Summerfield, 'Women in Britain since 1945: Companionate marriage and the double burden', in James Obelkevich and Peter Catterall (eds.), *Understanding Post-War British Society*, London, 1994; Janet Finch and Penny Summerfield, 'Social reconstruction and the emergence of companionate marriage,

1945–69', in David Clark (ed.), *Marriage, Domestic Life and Social Change*, London, 1991; Lesley Hall, *Sex, Gender and Social Change in Britain since 1880*, Basingstoke, 2000; Rebecca Jennings, 'Sexuality', in F. Carnevali and J.-M. Strange (eds.), *20th Century Britain*, London, 2007.

7. Jane Lewis, 'Public institution and private relationship: Marriage and marriage guidance, 1920–1968', *Twentieth Century British History*, 1, 3, 1990; Claire Langhamer, *The English in Love. The Intimate Story of an Emotional Revolution*, Oxford, 2013; Deborah Cohen, *Family Secrets: Shame and Privacy in Modern Britain*, Oxford, 2013; A. Barlow, S. Duncan, J. Grace, and A. Park, *Cohabitation, Marriage and the Law: Social Change and Legal Reform in the 21st Century*, Oxford, 2005.

8. Paul Byrne, *Social Movements in Britain*, London, 1997; Nick Crossley, *Making Sense of Social Movements*, Buckingham, 2002; Paul Bagguley, 'Social change, the middle class and the emergence of "New Social Movements"', *Sociological Review*, 40, 1, 1992, 26–48; Stephen Buechler, 'New social movement theories', *Sociological Quarterly*, 36, 3, 1995; Holger Nehring, 'The growth of social movements', in Paul Addison and Harriet Jones (eds.), *A Companion to Contemporary Britain, 1939–2000*, Oxford, 2005; Meredith Veldman, *Fantasy, the Bomb, and the Greening of Britain. Romantic Protest, 1945–1980*, Cambridge, 1994. See also Frank Musgrove, *Ecstasy and Holiness. Counter Culture and the Open Society*, London, 1974 for a sympathetic study of counter-cultural behaviour in North-West England.

9. Paul Heelas, *The New Age Movement: Religion, Culture and Society in the Age of Postmodernity*, Oxford, 1996; Steve Bruce, *Religion in Modern Britain*, Oxford, 1995; Callum Brown, *The Death of Christian Britain: Understanding Secularisation 1800–2000*, London, 2000.

10. Sheila Rowbotham, *Promise of a Dream: Remembering the Sixties*, Harmondsworth, 2001; Lynne Segal, 'Jam today: Feminist impacts and transformations in the 1970s', in Lawrence Black, Hugh Pemberton, and Pat Thane (eds.), *Reassessing 1970s Britain*, Manchester, 2013; Lewis, *Women in Britain*; Byrne, *Social Movements*; Martin Pugh, *Women and the Women's Movement in Britain, 1914–1999*, Basingstoke, 2000; Sasha Roseneil, *Common Women, Uncommon Practices: The Queer Feminism of Greenham*, London, 2000.

11. Sarah Perrigo, 'Women and change in the Labour Party, 1979–1995', in Joni Lovenduski and Pippa Norris (eds.), *Women in Politics*, Oxford, 1996; Hilary Wainwright, *Labour. A Tale of Two Parties*, London, 1987; Stephen Brooke, *Sexual Politics: Sexuality, Family Planning, and the British Left from the 1880s to the Present Day*, Oxford, 2011.

12. Matthew Hilton, 'Politics is ordinary: Non-governmental organizations and political participation in contemporary Britain', *Twentieth Century British History*, 22, 2, 2011; Matthew Hilton, James McKay, Nicholas Crowson, and Jean-Francois Mouhot, *The Politics of Expertise: How NGOs Shaped Modern Britain*, Oxford, 2013.

13. Peter A. Hall, 'Social capital in Britain', *British Journal of Politics*, 29, 1999.

14. Richard Crossman, 'The role of the volunteer in the modern social service,' in A. H. Hasley (ed.), *Traditions of Social Policy: Essays in Honour of Violet Butler*, Oxford, 1976.

15. Pat Thane, 'Women and the 1970s. Towards liberation?', in Lawrence Black, Hugh Pemberton, and Pat Thane (eds.), *Reassessing 1970s Britain*, Manchester, 2013; Catriona Beaumont, *Housewives and Citizens: Domesticity and the Women's Movement in England, 1928–1964*, Manchester, 2013.

16. Lawrence Black, *Redefining British Politics: Culture, Consumerism and Participation, 1954–70*, Basingstoke, 2010, ch. 5; Amy C. Whipple, 'Speaking for whom? The 1971 Festival of Light and the search for the "Silent Majority"', *Contemporary British History*, 24, 3, 2010.

17. Chris Waters, 'Dark strangers in our midst: Discourses of race and nation in Britain, 1947–1963', *Journal of British Studies*, 36, 1997; Bill Schwarz, '"The only white man in there": The re-racialization of Britain, 1956–68', *Race and Class*, 38, 1996; Paul Gilroy, *'There Ain't No Black in the Union Jack'*, London, 1987; Colin Holmes, *A Tolerant Country? Immigrants, Refugees and Minorities in Britain*, London, 1991.

18. There is an enormous literature. Notable interventions include, from the left, Perry Anderson, 'Origins of the present crisis', *New Left Review*, 23, 1964; from the right, Martin Wiener, *English Culture and the Decline of the Industrial Spirit: 1850–1980*, Cambridge, 1981 and Correlli Barnett, *The Audit of War: The Illusion and Reality of Britain as a Great Nation*, London, 1986; and, from the centre, David Marquand, *The Unprincipled Society*, London, 1988 and Will Hutton, *The State We're In*, London, 1995.

19. Steve Fielding, '"White heat" and white collars: The evolution of "Wilsonism"', in R. Coopey, S. Fielding, and N. Tiratsoo (eds.), *The Wilson Governments, 1964–1970*, London, 1993.

20. Jim Tomlinson, 'The politics of declinism', in Lawrence Black, Hugh Pemberton, and Pat Thane (eds.), *Reassessing 1970s Britain*, Manchester, 2013; Jim Tomlinson, 'Thrice denied: "Declinism" as a recurrent theme in British history in the long twentieth century', *Twentieth Century British History*, 20, 2, 2009; David Edgerton, *Warfare State. Britain 1920–1970*, Cambridge, 2006; Jose Harris, 'Tradition and transformation: Society and civil society in Britain, 1945–2001', in Kathleen Burk (ed.), *The British Isles since 1945*, Oxford, 2003; Lawrence Black and Hugh Pemberton, Introduction, in *An Affluent Society?: Britain's Post-War 'Golden Age' Revisited*, Aldershot, 2004; Barry Supple, 'Fear of falling: Economic history and the decline of Britain', in P. Clarke and C. Trebilcock (eds.), *Understanding Decline. Perceptions and Realities of British Economic Performance*, Cambridge, 1997.

21. Nick Crafts, 'The British economy', in F. Carnevali and J.-M. Strange (eds.), *20th-Century Britain*, London, 2007, 9–18.

22. Edgerton, *Warfare State*; Mike Savage, *Identities and Social Change in Britain since 1940. The Politics of Method*, Oxford, 2010; Nikolas Rose, *Governing the Soul. The Shaping of the Private Self*, London, 1999.

23. Harold Perkin, *The Rise of Professional Society. England since 1880*, London, 1989.
24. David Lockwood, 'Marking out the middle class(es)', in Tim Butler and Mike Savage (eds.), *Social Change and the Middle Classes*, London, 1995.
25. Jose Harris, 'Enterprise and welfare states: A comparative perspective', *Transactions of the Royal Historical Society*, 40, 1990, 179–92. Harris convincingly shreds the contrary claims made by Correlli Barnett's key New Right account, *The Audit of War*. See also Edgerton, *Warfare State*, 65–70.
26. Marquand, *Unprincipled Society*; Samuel Beer, *Britain against Itself: The Political Contradictions of Collectivism*, London, 1982.
27. Tara Martin López, *The Winter of Discontent: Myth, Memory and History*, Liverpool, 2014; John McIlroy and Alan Campbell, 'The high tide of trade unionism: Mapping industrial politics, 1964–1979', in John McIlroy, Nina Fishman, and Alan Campbell (eds.), *British Trade Unions and Industrial Politics*, Vol. 2, Aldershot, 1999.
28. Colin Hay, 'Narrating crisis: The discursive construction of the "winter of discontent"', *Sociology*, 30, 2, 1996.
29. Andrew Gamble, *The Free Economy and the Strong State: The Politics of Thatcherism*, Durham, NC, 1994.
30. W. D. Rubinstein, *Capitalism, Culture and Decline in Britain, 1750–1990*, London, 1993, 154.
31. E. J. Hobsbawm, *The Age of Extremes*, London, 1994.
32. Michael Roper, *Masculinity and the British Organization Man since 1945*, Oxford, 1994; Hutton, *The State We're In*.
33. N. Deakin, 'The perils of partnership. The voluntary sector and the state, 1945–1992', in J. Davis Smith, et al. (eds.), *An Introduction to the Voluntary Sector*, London, 1995.
34. Avner Offer, 'British manual workers, from producers to consumers, c. 1950–2000', *Contemporary British History*, 22, 4, 2008; Rosemary Compton, *Class and Stratification*, Cambridge, 2008; Supple, 'Fear of falling'.
35. Offer, 'British manual workers'; Patrick Seyd and Paul Whiteley, *Labour's Grass Roots. The Politics of Party Membership*, Oxford, 1992; Bagguley, 'New Social Movements'; Crossley, *Making Sense of Social Movements*, 164; Hilton et al., *Politics of Expertise*, 17–18; Klaus Eder, *The New Politics of Class. Social Movements and Cultural Dynamics in Advanced Societies*, London, 1993. The fact that many campaigning organizations were conducted on behalf of the less fortunate does not lessen the point: '... even actions which are not driven by struggle for advantage over others, indeed, even those that have egalitarian motives, are likely to be twisted by the field of class forces in ways which reproduce class hierarchy' (Andrew Sayer, *The Moral Significance of Class*, Cambridge, 2005, 169).
36. Ben Jones, *The Working Class in Mid Twentieth-century England. Community, Identity and Social Memory*, Manchester, 2012, 208.
37. Supple, 'Fear of falling', 25; Gamble, *The Free Economy*, 194–5.

38. Offer, 'British manual workers'; Rose, *Governing the Soul*, 230–2.
39. Selina Todd, *The People. The Rise and Fall of the Working Class, 1910–2010*, London, 2014, 275, 277, 284; E. J. Hobsbawm, 'The 1970s: Syndicalism without syndicalists?', in *Worlds of Labour*, London, 1984; Martin Jacques and Francis Mulhern (eds.), *The Forward March of Labour Halted?*, London, 1981.
40. Heelas, *New Age Movement*.
41. J. O'Neill, cited in Compton, *Class and Stratification*, 26; Nancy Fraser, 'Feminism, capitalism, and the cunning of history', *New Left Review*, 56, March–April 2009.
42. Thus David Harvey, *A Brief History of Neoliberalism*, Oxford, 2005, sees the new individualism as a consequence of neo-liberalism, while Hobsbawm, *Age of Extremes*, gives more weight to cultural shifts since the 1960s.
43. Anthony Giddens, *Modernity and Self-identity: Self and Society in the Late Modern Age*, Cambridge, 1992; Richard Sennett, *The Fall of Public Man*, London, 1977; Alisdair MacIntyre, *After Virtue: A Study on Moral Theory*, London, 1985.
44. James Hinton, *Nine Wartime Lives. Mass Observation and the Making of the Modern Self*, Oxford, 2010.
45. Charles Taylor, *Sources of the Self. The Making of the Modern Identity*, Cambridge, 1989; Roy Porter (ed.), *Rewriting the Self: Histories from the Renaissance to the Present*, London, 1997.
46. Lynn Jamieson, *Intimacy. Personal Relationships in Modern Societies*, Cambridge, 1998. For a nuanced account see Carol Smart, *Personal Life. New Directions in Sociological Thinking*, Cambridge, 2007. Simon Duncan, 'Personal life, pragmatism and bricolage', *Sociological Research Online*, 16, 4, 2012 is a useful clearing of the conceptual decks for empirical investigation of these issues.
47. Although the soliciting and archiving is itself a product of shifts in the relationship between self and society. Caroline Steedman, 'State sponsored autobiography', in Becky Conekin, Frank Mort, and Chris Waters (eds.), *Moments of Modernity. Reconstructing Britain, 1945–1964*, London, 1999.

3. HOUSEWIFE

1. DR 1984 Spring.
2. DR 1994 Spring/2.
3. DR 1992 Spring/2.
4. DR 1984 Spring.
5. DR 1983 Spring/1.
6. DR 1984 Winter.
7. DR 1993 Spring/1.
8. DR 1984 Spring.
9. DR 1994 Spring/1.

10. DR 1993 Spring/1.
11. DR 1993 Spring/1.
12. DR 1994 Spring/1.
13. DR 1993 Spring/1.
14. On the role of spinster teachers in fostering young female talent see Lynn Abrams, 'Liberating the female self: Epiphanies, conflict and coherence in the life stories of post-war British women', *Social History*, 39, 1, 2014, 17.
15. DR 1991 Spring/1.
16. Memoir of her grandmother written for a book published in 1983, enclosed with DR Winter 1984.
17. DR 1983 Summer.
18. DR 1985 Spring/1.
19. DR 1990 Summer/1.
20. DR 1990 Summer/1.
21. DR 1993 Summer/1.
22. DR 1984 Spring.
23. DR 1990 Summer/1.
24. DR 1985 Spring/1.
25. DR 1990 Summer/1.
26. DR 1990 Summer/1.
27. DR 1990 Summer/1.
28. DR 1993 Spring/1.
29. DR 1983 Summer.
30. DR 1993 Spring/1.
31. DR 1993 Spring/1.
32. DR 1985 Spring/1.
33. DR 1994 Spring/1.
34. DR 1993 Spring/1.
35. DR 1993 Spring/1.
36. DR 1991 Autumn/1.
37. DR 1992 Spring/2.
38. DR 1988 Autumn/1.
39. DR 1983 Spring/1.
40. DR 1983 Summer.
41. DR 1983 Spring/1.
42. Memoir of her grandmother written for a book published in 1983, enclosed with DR Winter 1984.
43. DR 1983 Summer.
44. DR 1993 Spring/1.
45. DR 1990 Spring/1.
46. DR 1985 Spring/1.
47. DR 1994 Spring/2.
48. DR 1985 Spring/1.
49. DR 1994 Spring/2.

50. DR 1992 Winter/1.
51. DR 1994 Spring/2.
52. DR 1992 Spring/2.
53. DR 1983 Summer.

4. TEACHER

1. DR 1988 Summer/1, and *passim*.
2. DR 1993 Summer/1.
3. DR 1985 Spring/1.
4. DR 1992 Spring/3.
5. DR 1993 Spring/3.
6. DR 2010 Autumn/3.
7. DR 1997 Summer/1.
8. DR 2000 Autumn/1.
9. DR 1984 Winter.
10. DR 2009 Summer/1.
11. DR 2001 Summer/1; DR 1985 Spring/1; DR 1991 Spring/1.
12. DR 1985 Spring/1.
13. DR 2008 Spring/2.
14. DR 2005 Autumn/1.
15. DR 2008 Spring/2; DR 1990 Summer/1.
16. DR 1990 Summer/1.
17. Wladyslaw Sikorski, *The Dark Side of the Moon*, with preface by T. S. Eliot, London, 1946.
18. DR 1994 Spring/1.
19. DR 2010 Summer/2.
20. DR 1990 Autumn/2.
21. DR 1985 Spring/1.
22. DR 1993 Summer/1.
23. DR 1992 Spring/3.
24. DR 1990 Summer/1.
25. The 400 figure comes from Janet. His conviction was based on seven cases.
26. DR 1990 Summer/1.
27. Details of the crisis from the VES *Newsletter*, 1979–1984.
28. DR 1987 May Special.
29. DR 1990 Autumn/2; DR 1992 Summer/1.
30. DR 2008 Winter/1.
31. DR 1987 May Special.
32. DR 1990 Spring/1.
33. DR 1987 May Special.
34. DR 2001 Spring/2.
35. DR 1990 Spring/1.
36. DR 1992 Spring/2.

37. DR 1987 May Special.
38. DR 1990 Autumn/2.
39. DR 1989 Summer/1.
40. DR 1990 Summer/2.
41. In her seventies, however, irritated by letters from MO warning her against mentioning identifiable people in a defamatory way (on one occasion she named a man alleged to be a paedophile living in her street), she complained that MO offered less freedom of expression than the letters pages of the newspapers, and threatened that 'as you have a censorship policy, I'll not write what I truly think' (DR 2010 Spring/3). I doubt that she carried out this threat: more characteristic was her remark: 'Now I'm old I'll write what I think fit. Holloway here I come' (DR 2009 Winter/3; Holloway is a women's prison).
42. DR 1987 May Special.
43. DR 1990 Autumn/2.
44. DR 1990 Autumn/3.
45. DR 1985 Spring/1.
46. DR 1991 Autumn/1.
47. DR 1992 Spring/2.
48. DR 1991 Autumn/1.
49. DR 1996 Summer/2.
50. DR 1985 Spring/1.
51. DR 1990 Autumn/2.
52. DR 1991 Autumn/1.
53. DR 1996 Summer/2.
54. DR 2001 Summer/1.
55. DR 1990 Summer/1.
56. DR 1984 Winter.
57. DR 1990 Summer/1.
58. DR 1992 Spring/2.
59. DR 1990 Summer/1.
60. DR 1991 Autumn/1.
61. DR 1987 May Special.
62. DR 1990 Autumn/2.
63. DR 1990 Summer/1.
64. DR 1990 Spring/1.
65. DR 1989 Summer/1.
66. DR 1994 Spring/1.
67. DR 1990 Spring/1. *Blue Peter* is a BBC TV show for children. The much-coveted badge is awarded to children who appear on the show.
68. DR 1990 Autumn/2.
69. DR 1992 Spring/3.
70. Said during an interview in 1997. I cannot give the reference without disclosing her identity.

71. DR 2009 Winter/2.
72. DR 1990 Spring/1; DR 2003 Spring/3.
73. DR 1997 Summer/1; DR 1990 Autumn/2.
74. DR 1991 Spring/1.
75. DR 1992 Spring/3.
76. DR 2003 Autumn/1.
77. DR 1993 Spring/3.
78. DR 1993 Spring/1.
79. DR 2001 Autumn/2.
80. DR 1984 Winter.
81. DR 1992 Summer/1.
82. DR 1991 Autumn/1; DR 1990 Autumn/3.
83. DR 1990 Summer/1.
84. DR 1992 Spring/3.
85. DR 2008 Spring/2.
86. She discussed these issues in an interview conducted in 1997. I cannot give the reference without disclosing her identity.
87. DR 1992 Spring/3.
88. DR 1990 Summer/2.

5. SOCIAL WORKER

1. DR 1992 Spring/2.
2. DR 2008 Summer/2.
3. DR 1993 Spring/1.
4. DR 2008 Summer/2.
5. DR 2008 Summer/2.
6. DR 2000 Autumn/1.
7. DR 2005 Autumn/1.
8. DR 1998 Spring/2.
9. DR 2000 Autumn/1. 'Sent to Coventry', i.e. ostracized, her parents refusing to talk to her. 'Sixth form' is the British term for the non-compulsory post-sixteen final two years at school.
10. DR 2005 Autumn/1.
11. DR 2005 Autumn/1.
12. DR 2005 Autumn/1.
13. S. H. Foulkes, *Introduction to Group-analytic Psychotherapy*, London, 1948. In 1952 Abercrombie became a founder member of the Group Analytic Society, and president of the society in 1981.
14. M. L. J. ('Jane') Abercrombie, *An Anatomy of Judgement*, London, 1960, 17. In 1970 the Society for Research into Higher Education published a booklet by Abercrombie on *Aims and Techniques of Group Teaching*, which she dedicated to Foulkes.
15. DR 2004 Autumn/1.

16. DR 1993 Autumn/2.
17. DR 2004 Spring/3.
18. DR 2008 Winter/3.
19. DR 1998 Spring/2.
20. DR 2005 Autumn/1.
21. DR 2005 Autumn/1.
22. As Claire Langhamer points out, Stella's fear was quite realistic. Claire Langhamer, 'Adultery in post-war England', *History Workshop Journal*, 62, 1, 2006, 142.
23. DR 1990 Summer/1.
24. Catherine Fletcher, 'The crisis in morality—A question of conscience', *Learning for Living*, 10, 2, 1970, 31. He had set up a Centre for Spiritual and Psychological Studies, and, in 1973, was a founder member of The Scientific and Medical Network, established 'to reconcile scientific investigation and scientific models of reality with the spiritual dimension of life, and so to open dialogue between scientists and spiritual luminaries of all backgrounds'. The thoroughly 'New Age' aims of the Network are spelled out as:

    To provide a safe forum for the critical and open-minded discussion of ideas that go beyond conventional paradigms in science, medicine, and philosophy.
    To integrate intuitive insights with rational analysis in our investigations.
    To encourage a respect for Earth and community which emphasizes a spiritual and holistic approach.
    To challenge the adequacy of 'scientific materialism' as an exclusive basis for knowledge and values.

25. University of Surrey, *Understanding the Real World* (a history of the University of Surrey), no date, ch. 1 (<http://www.surrey.ac.uk/files/pdf/chapter1.PDF>, accessed in February 2016).
26. John Heron, 'My early engagement with humanistic psychology', *Self & Society*, 40, 1, 2012, 50. On the origins of humanistic psychology see Paul Heelas, *The New Age Movement: Religion, Culture and Society in the Age of Postmodernity*, Oxford, 1996, 53.
27. After seven years at Surrey, Heron was recruited by the British Postgraduate Medical Federation (a London University institution in charge of medical education) to run their Education Department—which suggests an intriguing connection with Abercrombie's earlier work with medical students.
28. Tom Scheff. In 1974 Heron was among the founders of Co-counselling International, a breakaway from the mainstream Re-evaluation Counselling which he saw as 'theoretically rigid and internally authoritarian'. John Heron, *Co-Counselling Manual*, Auckland, 1998.
29. *Understanding the Real World*, 33.
30. DR 2005 Autumn/1.
31. DR 2005 Autumn/1.

32. DR 1998 Spring/2.
33. DR 1998 Spring/2.
34. DR 2009 Winter/1.
35. DR 2005 Autumn/1.
36. DR 2000 Autumn/1.
37. DR 2005 Autumn/1.
38. An account of the development of the unit she worked in is given in Kirstie Maclean, 'Towards a fee-paid fostering service', *Adoption & Fostering*, 13, 1989, 25–9.
39. Nancy Hazel, *A Bridge to Independence*, Oxford, 1981; Martin Shaw and Tony Hipgrave, *Specialist Fostering*, London, 1983.
40. DR 1993 Spring/1.
41. On the diploma course see Heron, 'My early engagement with humanistic psychology', 53. Once again Stella was fortunate to be in the right place. Yorkshire was the only place outside Southern England where such a course was taught, run by another inspirational teacher, Bryce Taylor (Bryce Taylor, *Learning for Tomorrow: Whole Person Learning for the Planetary Citizen*, Boston Spa, 2007; obituary, *Yorkshire Post*, 26 March 2010).
42. DR 1997 Summer/1.
43. DR 2004 Spring/3.
44. DR 2008 Winter/3.
45. DR 1996 Summer/2.
46. DR 1992 Spring/2.
47. DR 2001 Summer/1.
48. DR 2001 Summer/1.
49. DR 1993 Summer/1.
50. DR 1990 Spring/1.
51. DR 1990 Spring/1.
52. DR 1993 Summer/1.
53. DR 2005 Autumn/1.
54. DR 2005 Autumn/1.
55. Interview, 4 October 2014.
56. DR 1991 Autumn/1.
57. DR 2001 Summer/1.
58. DR 2000 Autumn/1.
59. DR 2006 Autumn/3.
60. DR 1988 Autumn/1. *The Archers* is a fictional 'everyday story of country folk' still broadcast in the early evening six days a week.
61. DR 1997 Spring/2.
62. Richard Sennett, *The Fall of Public Man*, London, 1977; Christopher Lasch, *The Culture of Narcissism*, New York, 1979. The latter (p. 9) cites Peter Marin ('The new narcissism', *Harpers*, 1975): 'The new therapies spawned by the human potential movement…teach that "the individual will is all

powerful and totally determines one's fate"; thus they intensify the "isolation of the self".'

63. Nikolas Rose, *Governing the Soul: The Shaping of the Private Self*, London, 1999.
64. DR 2005 Autumn/1; DR 2000 Autumn/1.
65. DR 2005 Autumn/1.
66. Heron, 'My early engagement with humanistic psychology', 51. A notion, interestingly, which was not entirely unlike that which had inspired the founders of Mass Observation back in 1937.
67. DR 1997 Summer/1.
68. Heron, 'My early engagement with humanistic psychology', 53.
69. DR 1992 Spring/2. Lines from Rudyard Kipling's poem, *If...*
70. DR 1992 Spring/2.
71. DR 1996 Summer/2.
72. DR 1996 Summer/2.
73. DR 2009 Summer/2. She is quoting from memory a line from Edward Fitzgerald's translation of the *Rubaiyat of Omar Khayyam*.

> Myself when young did eagerly frequent
> Doctor and Saint, and heard great Argument
> About it and about: but evermore
> Came out by the same Door as in I went.

74. Interview, 4 October 2014.
75. DR 2009 Summer/2. She is writing of an occasion when she tried, and failed, to induce an out-of-body experience through self-hypnosis. But the remark has wider relevance.
76. DR 1996 Summer/2.
77. DR 2009 Summer/2.
78. DR 2009 Summer/2.

6. RAF WIFE

1. Richard Broad and Suzie Fleming (eds.), *Nella Last's War: A Mother's Diary, 1939–45*, Bristol, 1981.
2. DR 2004 Summer/1.
3. DR 2009 Spring/1.
4. DR 2006 Summer/1.
5. DR 1991 Spring/1.
6. DR 1990 Summer/1.
7. DR 1993 Spring/1; DR 1995 Autumn/2. Helen appears as 'Brenda' in Jane Mace, *Playing with Time: Mothers and the Meaning of Literacy*, London, 1998, 52–5.
8. DR 2005 Autumn/1.
9. DR 1991 Autumn/1.
10. DR 1993 Spring/1.

11. DR 1988 Autumn/1.
12. DR 1991 Spring/1.
13. DR 1992 Winter/1.
14. DR 1994 Spring/1.
15. DR 2001 Summer/1.
16. DR 1990 Summer/1.
17. DR 2001 Summer/1.
18. DR 2013 Spring/2.
19. DR 2001 Summer/1; DR 1992 Winter/1.
20. DR 1991 Spring/1.
21. DR 2000 Autumn/1.
22. DR 1992 Winter/1.
23. DR 1991 Spring/1.
24. O-levels: public exams normally taken aged sixteen.
25. He told me this in an email on 6 March 2015.
26. DR 2009 Winter/1.
27. DR 1992 Winter/1.
28. DR 2009 Winter/1.
29. Interview, 1 March 2014.
30. DR 2009 Winter/1.
31. DR 1991 Spring/1.
32. E. J. Hobsbawm, *The Age of Extremes*, London, 1994, 328. Dorothy Jerome, 'Time, change and continuity in family life', *Ageing and Society*, 14, 1994 uses Mass Observation material to raise questions about the ways in which children influence their parents' adaptation to cultural change.
33. British 'public' schools are private and fee-paying. 'A-levels' are public exams normally taken aged eighteen.
34. DR 1991 Spring/1.
35. Interview, 1 March 2014.
36. DR 2008 Spring/2; interview, 1 March 2014.
37. DR 1991 Spring/1.
38. DR 2009 Winter/1.
39. DR 2011 Autumn/3.
40. DR 1993 Spring/2.
41. DR 1996 Autumn/2; DR 1992 Winter/2.
42. DR 1996 Autumn/2.
43. DR 1997 Spring/2.
44. DR 2011 Autumn/3.
45. DR 1990 Autumn/2. Her extensive Gulf War diary spans November 1990 to March 1991.
46. DR 1990 Autumn/2.
47. DR 2003 Spring/3.
48. DR 1990 Summer/1; DR 2008 Winter/3; interview, 1 March 2014.
49. DR 1998 Spring/2.
50. DR 2008 Winter/3.

51. DR 1997 Spring/2.
52. DR 2008 Winter/3.
53. DR 2008 Winter/3.
54. DR 1990 Summer/1; DR 1991 Autumn/1.
55. DR 1991 Autumn/1.
56. DR 1998 Spring/2.
57. DR 2009 Summer/2; DR 2013 Spring/2.
58. DR 1991 Autumn/1.
59. DR 1990 Summer/1.
60. DR 1990 Spring/1.
61. DR 1992 Winter/1.
62. DR 1992 Winter/1.
63. DR 1990 Autumn/2.
64. DR 2011 Autumn/3.
65. DR 2011 Autumn/3.
66. DR 1992 Winter/1.

7. MECHANIC

1. DR 1991 Spring/2.
2. DR 2010 Autumn/3.
3. DR 1990 Summer/1; DR 1993 Spring/1.
4. DR 1997 Summer/1.
5. DR 1993 Spring/1.
6. 11-plus: public exam used to determine which children went to selective grammar schools.
7. DR 1992 Winter/1. Indentures: a contract governing the apprenticeship.
8. DR 2010 Summer/2; DR 2008 Spring/2.
9. DR 1989 Summer/1.
10. DR 1993 Spring/1.
11. DR 2010 Spring/1.
12. DR 1991 Spring/1.
13. DR 1990 Spring/1.
14. DR 2008 Spring/2.
15. DR 1997 Summer/1.
16. DR 2009 Winter/1.
17. DR 1997 Summer/1.
18. DR 1992 Winter/1.
19. DR 1997 Summer/1. Unless otherwise noted all quotations in the remainder of Section 2 are from this directive reply.
20. DR 1992 Winter/1.
21. DR 2004 Autumn/1.
22. Interview, 28 February 2014; DR 1997 Summer/1.
23. DR 1997 Summer/1.
24. DR 2004 Autumn/1.

25. DR 1997 Summer/1.
26. DR 1991 Autumn/1.
27. DR 1991 Autumn/1.
28. DR 1993 Spring/1.
29. DR 1991 Autumn/1.
30. DR 1990 Summer/1.
31. DR 1991 Autumn/1.
32. DR 1998 Spring/2.
33. DR 1998 Spring/2.
34. DR 1990 Summer/1.
35. DR 1992 Spring/3.
36. DR 1990 Spring/1.
37. DR 2000 Autumn/1.
38. DR 1997 Spring/2.
39. DR 1993 Summer/1.
40. Chris Waters, 'Autobiography, nostalgia and the changing practices of working-class selfhood', in George K. Behlmer and Fred M. Leventhal (eds.), *Singular Continuities. Tradition, Nostalgia and Identity in Modern British Culture*, Stanford, CA, 2000. But contrast Ben Jones, 'The uses of nostalgia', *Cultural and Social History*, 7, 3, 2010.
41. DR 1996 Autumn/2.
42. DR 1998 Spring/2.
43. DR 1993 Spring/1.
44. DR 1996 Autumn/2.
45. DR 1989 Summer/1.
46. DR 2008 Winter/3.
47. DR 1996 Autumn/2.
48. DR 1990 Spring/1.
49. DR 2010 Summer/2.
50. DR 2009 Summer/2.
51. DR 2009 Summer/2.
52. DR 1991 Spring/2.
53. DR 2004 Autumn/1.
54. DR 1991 Spring/2.
55. DR 1994 Spring/2.
56. DR 1994 Spring/2.
57. DR 1991 Spring/2.
58. DR 1991 Spring/1.

8. LORRY DRIVER

1. Bob declined the offer of anonymity, so, uniquely among my subjects, he is referred to by his real name.
2. DR 2004 Autumn/1.

3. Paul Smith, *Unionization and Union Leadership. The Road Haulage Industry*, London, 2001.
4. These tensions between individualism and solidarity are well explored in Peter G. Hollowell, *The Lorry Driver*, London, 1968.
5. Bob Rust, *Where Do You Want This Lot?*, Manchester, 2007.
6. DR 1993 Spring/1.
7. DR 1991 Spring/1.
8. DR 1991 Spring/1.
9. Rust, *Where Do You Want This Lot?*, 5.
10. DR 1991 Spring/1.
11. DR 1991 Spring/1.
12. DR 2004 Spring/3.
13. DR 1991 Spring/1.
14. DR 1991 Spring/1.
15. Cited in Selina Todd, *The People. The Rise and Fall of the Working Class, 1910–2010*, London, 2014, 218.
16. Interview, 6 October 2014.
17. Rust, *Where Do You Want This Lot?*, 38.
18. DR 1997 Summer/1.
19. DR 1984 Winter.
20. DR 1991 Spring/2.
21. DR 1991 Spring/2. The North Circular is the inner-London ring road.
22. DR 2008 Winter/3.
23. Ted Murphy, *The Big Load*, London, 1963, cited in Hollowell, *Lorry Driver*, 189.
24. Rust, *Where Do You Want This Lot?*, 164.
25. DR 1996 Summer/2.
26. DR 1996 Summer/2.
27. DR 1984 Winter.
28. DR 1987 Summer/1.
29. DR 1987 Summer/1.
30. DR 1987 Summer/1.
31. DR 1998 Spring/2.
32. DR 1989 Autumn/1.
33. DR 2000 Autumn/1.
34. DR 1994 Spring/1.
35. DR 2008 Winter/3.
36. DR 1988 Autumn/1.
37. DR 2000 Autumn/1.
38. DR 2000 Autumn/1. *Coronation Street* is a British TV soap opera, and Ena Sharples was a particularly forceful character.
39. DR 1992 Winter/1.
40. DR 2001 Summer/1.
41. DR 2000 Autumn/1.

42. Interview, 6 October 2014; Bob Rust to Mrs Field, 15 December 1999, in Bob's personal file, MOP archive.
43. DR 1985 Spring/1.
44. Interview, 6 October 2014.
45. DR 2000 Autumn/1.
46. Simon Szreter and Kate Fisher, *Sex before the Sexual Revolution: Intimate Life in England 1918–1963*, Cambridge, 2010.
47. DR 1989 Summer/1.
48. Special report, July 1988.
49. DR 1987 May Special.
50. DR 1991 Autumn/1.
51. DR 1991 Autumn/1.
52. DR 1991 Spring/2.
53. DR 1988 Autumn/1; DR 1984 Spring; DR 1983 Summer.
54. DR 1988 Autumn/1.
55. Karen Harrison and Derek McGhee, 'Reading and writing family secrets: Reflections on mass-observation', *Auto/Biography*, 11, 1 and 2, 2003, 25–36.
56. Bob Rust to Dorothy Sheridan, 3 July 2004, in Bob's personal file, MOP archive. Bob is quoting from George Bernard Shaw's *Man and Superman*, 1903: 'Those who can, do; those who can't, teach.'
57. DR 1991 Spring/1.
58. DR 1988 Autumn/1.
59. Interview, 6 October 2014; Rust, *Where Do You Want This Lot?*, 65.
60. He discovered this in 1991, when the left-wing journalist Paul Foot got hold of a copy of the blacklist and the *Daily Mirror* raised funds for the Labour Party by inviting members, in return for a small fee, to enquire whether they were on it (Mike Hughes, *Spies at Work*, Bradford, 1994, 216). The blacklist was mainly used in the construction industry, and it does not seem to have affected Bob's employability, even after he left BRS in 1983.
61. DR 1996 Autumn/2; Bob Rust to author, 8 October 2014.
62. DR 1996 Autumn/2.
63. Interview with Anna Green, 2000, cited in <http://www.mmhistory.org.uk/anna_green_2000/web4.htm> (accessed in July 2015).
64. Special report, July 1984.
65. Special report, February 1984.
66. DR 1986 Autumn/2.
67. Interview, 6 October 2014.
68. Hollowell, *Lorry Driver*, 224.
69. Special report, April 1989.
70. DR 1996 Autumn/2.
71. DR 2011 Autumn/2.
72. DR 1996 Autumn/2.
73. Dennis Hayes and Alan Hudson, *Basildon. The Mood of the Nation*, London, 2001, 11, 27. See also Brendan Evans, 'Thatcherism and the British people',

in Stuart Ball and Ian Holliday (eds.), *Mass Conservatism. The Conservatives and the Public since the 1880s*, London, 2002.

74. DR 1990 Spring/2.
75. Special report, January 1985.
76. DR 2004 Autumn/1.
77. DR 1996 Autumn/2.
78. DR 1986 Autumn/2.
79. Interview, 6 October 2014; special report on Falklands, 1982.
80. Special report on Falklands, 1982.
81. DR 1983 Summer.
82. DR 1983 Summer.
83. Special report, August 1985.
84. DR 2000 Autumn/1.
85. Special report, August 1985.
86. DR 1992 Winter/1.
87. DR 1996 Autumn/2.
88. DR 1992 Winter/1.
89. DR 1986 Autumn/2.
90. DR 1990 Spring/1.
91. DR 1987 May Special. The 'Old Contemptibles' was the proudly ironic name adopted by survivors of the British Expeditionary Force who fought Germany in the First World War.
92. Bob Rust to author, 9 October 2014.
93. Bob Rust to author, 12 October 2015.
94. Interview with Anna Green, 2000, cited in <http://www.mmhistory.org.uk/anna_green_2000/web4.htm> (accessed in July 2015).
95. DR 2005 Autumn/1.
96. Ana Lopes, 'Sex workers of the world unite!', *Feminist Review*, 67, Spring 2001, 151–3; Ana Lopes and Jennifer Webber, 'Organising sex workers in the UK: What's in it for trade unions?', paper delivered to the 2013 Ruskin Conference on Critical Labour Studies (accessed online in February 2016 at <http://www2.uwe.ac.uk/faculties/BBS/BUS/Research/CESR/July_2013_Lopes_Webber.pdf>); Gregor Gall, 'Sex worker unionisation: An exploratory study of emerging collective organisation', *Industrial Relations Journal*, 38, 1, 2007, 70–88.
97. DR 2005 Autumn/1.
98. Interview, 6 October 2014.
99. John Armstrong (ed.), *Companion to British Road Haulage History*, London, 2002.

9. BANKER

1. M. Roper, *Masculinity and the British Organization Man since 1945*, Oxford, 1994.
2. W. H. Whyte, *The Organization Man*, New York, 1956.

3. Roper, *Masculinity*, 11.
4. David Kynaston, *The City of London, Vol. 4, A Club no More, 1945–2000,* London, 2001; Philip Augar, *The Death of Gentlemanly Capitalism,* London, 2000.
5. Cathy Courtney and Paul Thompson, *City Lives. The Changing Voices of British Finance,* London, 1996.
6. DR 1994 Spring/2.
7. DR 1998 Spring/2.
8. I have been given privileged access to these diaries. They are closed to other researchers until 2065.
9. DR 1998 Spring/2.
10. Penny Summerfield, 'Culture and composure: Creating narratives of the gendered self in oral history interviews', *Cultural and Social History,* 1, 2004, 65–93.
11. Solicitor: a lawyer who is not a barrister, and may not plead cases in superior courts.
12. DR 1997 Summer/1.
13. DR 1990 Summer/1.
14. DR 2004 Spring/3.
15. DR 2004 Spring/3.
16. DR 1997 Summer/1.
17. DR 1997 Summer/1.
18. DR 2004 Spring/3.
19. Diary, 17 March 1966.
20. DR 1997 Summer/1.
21. DR 1997 Summer/1. This is how he told the story to Mass Observation forty years later, with considerable detail about the meeting with the deputy chairman. Oddly, the only stormy meeting with the deputy chairman recorded in his contemporary diary occurred a year earlier and concerned an entirely different matter. Moreover the diary suggests that the decision to promote him to the company secretary's department occurred ahead of the plan he produced for reorganizing the department. Perhaps events were telescoped in memory.
22. DR 1997 Summer/1.
23. DR 1997 Autumn/2.
24. DR 1992 Winter/1.
25. DR 1997 Autumn/2.
26. Diary, 15 February 1963.
27. DR 1997 Summer/1.
28. Diary, 11 March 1966.
29. Kynaston, *A Club no More,* 423–4, 558; Courtney and Thompson, *City Lives,* xxiv, 172, 194–9.
30. DR 1997 Summer/1.
31. Diary, 25 May 1961, 21 March 1962.

32. DR 1997 Summer/1.
33. Diary, 23 January 1973.
34. Diary, 18 April 1980.
35. Diary, 3 April 1974.
36. DR 1997 Summer/1.
37. DR 1998 Spring/2.
38. DR 1998 Spring/2.
39. DR 1990 Summer/1.
40. Diary, 26 November 1970.
41. Diary, 30 May 1978.
42. DR 1992 Winter/1.
43. Unless otherwise noted, all the above references to his affairs are from DR 1998 Spring/2.
44. DR 1990 Summer/1.
45. Sam's widow to author, 4 and 6 February 2015.
46. Margaret Reid, *The Secondary Banking Crisis, 1973–74. Its Causes and Course*, London, 1982.
47. Katherine Stovel, Michael Savage, and Peter Bearman, 'Ascription into achievement: Models of career systems at Lloyds Bank, 1890–1970', *American Journal of Sociology*, 102, 2, 1996, 58–99.
48. DR 1992 Winter/1.
49. Diary, 25 June and 20 October 1980. These judgements contrast strikingly with the chairman's contemporary public reputation as portrayed in Kynaston, *A Club no More*.
50. Diary, 8 December 1980.
51. Diary, 6 February 1981.
52. Diary, 25 May 1976.
53. Diary, 4 March 1981.
54. DR 1992 Winter/1.
55. Diary, 18 September 1978.
56. DR 1992 Winter/1.
57. DR 1992 Winter/1.
58. DR 1992 Winter/1.
59. Diary, 18 October and 30 December 1964.
60. Diary, 30 December 1964.
61. DR 1992 Winter/1.
62. Diary, 1 September 1975; DR 2001 Autumn/2.
63. Diary, 16 August 1977.
64. Diary, 18 June 1975.
65. Diary, 17 November 1978.
66. DR 2002 Spring/2.
67. DR 1997 Spring/2.
68. Diary, 3 April 1982.
69. Diary, 30 September 1985.

70. DR 1996 Summer/2.

71. DR 1998 Spring/2; DR 1997 Summer/1.

72. Joel Goldsmith, *The Infinite Way*, London, 1979 (first published 1961), 5, 9.

73. Diary, 15 January 1981.

74. DR 1996 Summer/2.

75. DR 1997 Summer/1.

76. DR 1984 Spring.

77. Diary, 17 February 1981. Doss house: a cheap lodging house for homeless people.

78. Diary, 11 July 1963.

79. Diary, 28 September 1983.

80. DR 1989 Summer/1.

81. DR 1989 Summer/1.

82. DR 1997 Autumn/2.

83. DR 1997 Autumn/2.

84. DR 2001 Autumn/2.

85. Diary, 31 October 1986. Roper notes that his industrial mangers had all progressed from 'one male-dominated institution to another, from public school, to national service, to the corporation', 35. They valued their time in National Service and what they learned there about masculine virtues of leadership and authority.

86. DR 1993 Summer/1.

87. DR 1993 Summer/1.

88. DR 1993 Spring/1.

89. Commenting on this story, Claire Langhamer notes how it was the persistence of the double standard which allowed Sam to reconcile 'claims to family duty' with 'self-actualisation' through 'romantic love and sexual pleasure'. For Helen, however, 'things did not work out so well'. Claire Langhamer, 'Adultery in post-war England', *History Workshop Journal*, 62, 1, 2006, 107–8.

90. Kynaston, *A Club no More*, 758.

91. Courtney and Thompson, *City Lives*, 142.

92. DR 1997 Autumn/2. It was Sam's good fortune to work for a company that tolerated this. More generally by the 1980s, as one of his contemporaries pointed out, the old custom that 'when you got promoted it meant you could arrive later and leave earlier' had been stood on its head (Courtney and Thompson, *City Lives*, 73).

93. DR 1994 Spring/2.

10. CONCLUSION

1. E. H. Carr, *What is History?*, Cambridge, 1961, 5–7.

2. Diary entry, 8 April 1963.

3. DR 1992 Spring/3.

4. DR 1987 May Special.
5. Christopher Lasch, *The Culture of Narcissism*, New York, 1979.
6. DR 2008 Winter/3.
7. Agnes Hankiss, 'Ontologies of the self. On the mythological rearranging of one's life-history', in Daniel Bertaux (ed.), *Biography and Society. The Life History Approach to the Social Sciences*, London, 1981, 203: 'Everyone builds his or her own theory about the history and the course of his or her life by attempting to classify his or her particular successes and fortunes, gifts and choices...[by endowing] certain fundamental episodes with symbolic meaning, often to the point of turning them almost into myths, by locating them at a focal point of the explanatory system of the self.'
8. Cited in Linda Orr, 'Intimate images: Subjectivity and history—Staël, Michelet and Tocqueville', in Frank Ankersmit and Hans Kellner (eds.), *The New Philosophy of History*, Chicago, 1995, 106–7.
9. Cited in P. N. Furbank, *Unholy Pleasure. The Idea of Social Class*, Oxford, 1985, 141.

Bibliography

I. MASS OBSERVATION ARCHIVE, THE KEEP, SUSSEX

\<http://www.thekeep.info/collections/mass-observation-archive/\>

SxMOA28 Dorothy Sheridan, correspondence with Angus Calder, 1979–1993 Mass Observation Project Directive Replies and Special Reports

The Directive Replies listed below are cited in the endnotes. Those marked with an asterisk were read for all seven mass observers, if they responded to them. Individual replies to other directives, and 'special reports' sent in by some of the observers, have been consulted where it seemed appropriate.

DR 1983 Spring/1   General Election
DR 1983 Summer   *Work
DR 1984 Spring   *Social Well Being
DR 1984 Winter   *Relatives, Friends and Neighbours
DR 1985 Spring/1   *Morality and Religion
DR 1986 Autumn/2   Major Events
DR 1987 May Special   *General Election
DR 1987 Summer/1   Holidays
DR 1988 Summer/1   Time
DR 1988 Autumn/1   *Regular Pastimes
DR 1989 Summer/1   *Rules of Conduct
DR 1989 Autumn/1   Relaxants and Stimulants
DR 1990 Spring/1   *Social Divisions
DR 1990 Spring/2   Retrospective on the 1980s
DR 1990 Summer/1   *Close Relationships
DR 1990 Summer/2   *Your Views on MO
DR 1990 Autumn/2   *Gulf Crisis (this box contains Gulf War diaries, 1990–91)
DR 1990 Autumn/3   *Organisations
DR 1991 Spring/1   *Education
DR 1991 Spring/2   *The Uses of Reading and Writing and Diaries
DR 1991 Autumn/1   *Women and Men
DR 1992 Spring/2   *The Pace of Life

DR 1992 Spring/3   *One Day Diary
DR 1992 Summer/1   *Nature and the Environment
DR 1992 Winter/1   *Growing Older
DR 1992 Winter/2   Looking Back at 1992
DR 1993 Spring/1   *Growing Up
DR 1993 Spring/2   Reading
DR 1993 Spring/3   Community/Foreigners
DR 1993 Summer/1   *Pleasure
DR 1994 Spring/1   *Death, Bereavement and Serial Killers
DR 1994 Spring/2   *Autobiography and Diaries
DR 1995 Autumn/2   Mothers and Literacy
DR 1996 Summer/2   *The Supernatural
DR 1996 Autumn/2   *Unpaid Work
DR 1997 Spring/2   *General Election
DR 1997 Summer/1   *Doing a Job
DR 1997 Autumn/2   The Future
DR 1998 Spring/2   *Having an Affair
DR 2000 Autumn/1   *Gays and the Family
DR 2001 Spring/2   General Election
DR 2001 Summer/1   *Courting and Dating
DR 2001 Autumn/2   September 11th
DR 2002 Spring/2   The Royal Family
DR 2003 Spring/3   *The War in Iraq
DR 2003 Autumn/1   Public and Private Spaces/Places
DR 2004 Spring/3   *Going to University
DR 2004 Summer/1   Letters
DR 2004 Autumn/1   *Being Part of Research
DR 2005 Autumn/1   *Sex
DR 2006 Summer/1   History Matters
DR 2006 Autumn/3   *Age
DR 2008 Spring/2   *Your Life Line
DR 2008 Summer/2   War: Experience and Reflections
DR 2008 Winter/1   The World Financial Crisis
DR 2008 Winter/3   *The Ups and Downs of Friendship
DR 2009 Spring/1   The Second World War
DR 2009 Summer/1   Animals and Humans
DR 2009 Summer/2   *Heaven and Hell
DR 2009 Winter/1   *Mid-life Transitions
DR 2009 Winter/2   Books and You
DR 2009 Winter/3   Predicting the Future
DR 2010 Spring/1   A Working Day
DR 2010 Summer/2   Belonging
DR 2010 Autumn/3   Taking Part in Mass Observation
DR 2011 Autumn/2   Civil Disobedience

DR 2011 Autumn/3   You and the 1980s
DR 2013 Spring/2   Spiritualism

2. BOOKS AND ARTICLES

Abercrombie, M. L. J. ('Jane'), *An Anatomy of Judgement*, London, 1960
Abrams, Lynn, 'Liberating the female self: Epiphanies, conflict and coherence in the life stories of post-war British women', *Social History*, 39, 1, 2014
Anderson, Perry, 'Origins of the present crisis', *New Left Review*, 23, 1964
Archer, Margaret, *Making our Way through the World: Human Reflexivity and Social Mobility*, Cambridge, 2007
Armstrong, John (ed.), *Companion to British Road Haulage History*, London, 2002
Augar, Philip, *The Death of Gentlemanly Capitalism*, London, 2000
Bagguley, Paul, 'Social change, the middle class and the emergence of "New Social Movements"', *Sociological Review*, 40, 1, 1992, 26–48
Barlow, A., Duncan, S., Grace, J., and Park, A., *Cohabitation, Marriage and the Law: Social Change and Legal Reform in the 21st Century*, Oxford, 2005
Barnett, Correlli, *The Audit of War: The Illusion and Reality of Britain as a Great Nation*, London, 1986
Beaumont, Catriona, *Housewives and Citizens: Domesticity and the Women's Movement in England, 1928–1964*, Manchester, 2013
Beer, Samuel, *Britain against Itself: The Political Contradictions of Collectivism*, London, 1982
Bertaux, Daniel (ed.), *Biography and Society. The Life History Approach to the Social Sciences*, London, 1981
Black, Lawrence, *Redefining British Politics: Culture, Consumerism and Participation, 1954–70*, Basingstoke, 2010
Black, Lawrence, and Pemberton, Hugh, Introduction, in *An Affluent Society?: Britain's Post-War 'Golden Age' Revisited*, Aldershot, 2004
Broad, Richard, and Fleming, Suzie (eds.), *Nella Last's War: A Mother's Diary, 1939–45*, Bristol, 1981
Brooke, Stephen, *Sexual Politics: Sexuality, Family Planning, and the British Left from the 1880s to the Present Day*, Oxford, 2011
Brown, Callum, *The Death of Christian Britain: Understanding Secularisation 1800–2000*, London, 2000
Bruce, Steve, *Religion in Modern Britain*, Oxford, 1995
Buechler, Stephen, 'New social movement theories', *Sociological Quarterly*, 36, 3, 1995
Byrne, Paul, *Social Movements in Britain*, London, 1997
Calder, Angus, *The Myth of the Blitz*, London, 1991
Carr, E. H., *What is History?*, Cambridge, 1961
Chamberlayne, Prue, Bornat, Joanna, and Wengraf, Tom (eds.), *The Turn to Biographical Methods in the Social Sciences*, Abingdon, 2000

Cohen, Deborah, *Family Secrets: Shame and Privacy in Modern Britain*, Oxford, 2013

Compton, Rosemary, *Class and Stratification*, Cambridge, 2008

Cook, H., 'The English sexual revolution: Technology and social change', *History Workshop Journal*, 59, 2005, 109–28

Courtney, Cathy, and Thompson, Paul, *City Lives. The Changing Voices of British Finance*, London, 1996

Crafts, Nick, 'The British economy', in F. Carnevali and J.-M. Strange (eds.), *20th-Century Britain*, London, 2007

Crossley, Nick, *Making Sense of Social Movements*, Buckingham, 2002

Crossman, Richard, 'The role of the volunteer in the modern social service,' in A. H. Hasley (ed.), *Traditions of Social Policy: Essays in Honour of Violet Butler*, Oxford, 1976

Deakin, N., 'The perils of partnership. The voluntary sector and the state, 1945–1992', in J. Davis Smith, et al. (eds.), *An Introduction to the Voluntary Sector*, London, 1995

Duncan, Simon, 'Personal life, pragmatism and bricolage', *Sociological Research Online*, 16, 4, 2012

Eder, Klaus, *The New Politics of Class. Social Movements and Cultural Dynamics in Advanced Societies*, London, 1993

Edgerton, David, *Warfare State. Britain 1920–1970*, Cambridge, 2006

Elliott, B. Jane, 'Demographic trends in domestic life, 1945–1987', in David Clark (ed.), *Marriage, Domestic Life and Social Change*, London, 1991

Evans, Brendan, 'Thatcherism and the British people', in Stuart Ball and Ian Holliday (eds.), *Mass Conservatism. The Conservatives and the Public since the 1880s*, London, 2002

Fielding, Steve, ' "White heat" and white collars: The evolution of "Wilsonism"', in R. Coopey, S. Fielding, and N. Tiratsoo (eds.), *The Wilson Governments, 1964–1970*, London, 1993

Finch, Janet, and Summerfield, Penny, 'Social reconstruction and the emergence of companionate marriage, 1945–69', in David Clark (ed.), *Marriage, Domestic Life and Social Change*, London, 1991

Fletcher, Catherine, 'The crisis in morality—A question of conscience', *Learning for Living*, 10, 2, 1970, 31

Foulkes, S. H., *Introduction to Group-analytic Psychotherapy*, London, 1948

Fraser, Nancy, 'Feminism, capitalism, and the cunning of history', *New Left Review*, 56, March–April 2009

Furbank, P. N., *Unholy Pleasure. The Idea of Social Class*, Oxford, 1985

Gall, Gregor, 'Sex worker unionisation: An exploratory study of emerging collective organisation', *Industrial Relations Journal*, 38, 1, 2007, 70–88

Gamble, Andrew, *The Free Economy and the Strong State: The Politics of Thatcherism*, Durham, NC, 1994

Giddens, Anthony, *Modernity and Self-identity: Self and Society in the Late Modern Age*, Cambridge, 1992

Gilroy, Paul, *'There Ain't No Black in the Union Jack'*, London, 1987

Goldsmith, Joel, *The Infinite Way*, London, 1979

Green, E. H. H., 'Thatcherism: An historical perspective', *Transactions of the Royal Historical Society*, 9, 1999

Hall, Lesley, *Sex, Gender and Social Change in Britain since 1880*, Basingstoke, 2000

Hall, Peter A., 'Social capital in Britain', *British Journal of Politics*, 29, 1999

Hankiss, Agnes, 'Ontologies of the self. On the mythological rearranging of one's life-history', in Daniel Bertaux (ed.), *Biography and Society. The Life History Approach to the Social Sciences*, London, 1981

Harris, Jose, 'Enterprise and welfare states: A comparative perspective', *Transactions of the Royal Historical Society*, 40, 1990, 179–92

Harris, Jose, 'Tradition and transformation: Society and civil society in Britain, 1945–2001', in Kathleen Burk (ed.), *The British Isles since 1945*, Oxford, 2003

Harrison, Karen, and McGhee, Derek, 'Reading and writing family secrets: Reflections on mass-observation', *Auto/Biography*, 11, 1 and 2, 2003

Harvey, David, *A Brief History of Neoliberalism*, Oxford, 2005

Hay, Colin, 'Narrating crisis: The discursive construction of the "winter of discontent"', *Sociology*, 30, 2, 1996

Hayes, Dennis, and Hudson, Alan, *Basildon. The Mood of the Nation*, London, 2001

Hayler, Michael, and Thomson, Alistair, 'Working with words: Active learning in a community writing and publishing group', in Jane Mace (ed.), *Literacy, Language and Community Publishing: Essays in Adult Education*, Clevedon, 1995

Hazel, Nancy, *A Bridge to Independence*, Oxford, 1981

Heelas, Paul, *The New Age Movement: Religion, Culture and Society in the Age of Postmodernity*, Oxford, 1996

Heron, John, *Co-Counselling Manual*, Auckland, 1998

Heron, John, 'My early engagement with humanistic psychology', *Self & Society*, 40, 1, 2012

Hilton, Matthew, 'Politics is ordinary: Non-governmental organizations and political participation in contemporary Britain', *Twentieth Century British History*, 22, 2, 2011

Hilton, Matthew, McKay, James, Crowson, Nicholas, and Mouhot, Jean-Francois, *The Politics of Expertise: How NGOs Shaped Modern Britain*, Oxford, 2013

Hinton, James, *Nine Wartime Lives. Mass Observation and the Making of the Modern Self*, Oxford, 2010

Hinton, James, *The Mass Observers. A History, 1937–1949*, Oxford, 2013

Hobsbawm, E. J., 'The 1970s: Syndicalism without syndicalists?', in *Worlds of Labour*, London, 1984

Hobsbawm, E. J., *The Age of Extremes*, London, 1994

Hollowell, Peter G., *The Lorry Driver*, London, 1968

Holmes, Colin, *A Tolerant Country? Immigrants, Refugees and Minorities in Britain*, London, 1991

Holmes, Richard, *Footsteps: Adventures of a Romantic Biographer*, London, 1985

Hubble, Nick, *Mass Observation and Everyday Life*, Basingstoke, 2006

Hughes, Mike, *Spies at Work*, Bradford, 1994

Hutton, Will, *The State We're In*, London, 1995

Jacques, Martin, and Mulhern, Francis (eds.), *The Forward March of Labour Halted?*, London, 1981

Jamieson, Anne, and Victor, Christina (eds.), *Researching Ageing and Later Life: The Practice of Social Gerontology*, Buckingham, 2002

Jamieson, Lynn, *Intimacy. Personal Relationships in Modern Societies*, Cambridge, 1998

Jeffery, Tom, *Mass Observation—A Short History*, Birmingham, 1978

Jennings, Rebecca, 'Sexuality', in F. Carnevali and J.-M. Strange (eds.), *20th Century Britain*, London, 2007

Jerome, Dorothy, 'Time, change and continuity in family life', *Ageing and Society*, 14, 1994

Johnson, Richard, and Dawson, Graham (Popular Memory Group), 'Popular memory. Theory, politics, method', in Richard Johnson, et al. (eds.), *Making Histories: Studies in History-writing and Politics*, London, 1982

Jones, Ben, 'The uses of nostalgia', *Cultural and Social History*, 7, 3, 2010

Jones, Ben, *The Working Class in Mid Twentieth-century England. Community, Identity and Social Memory*, Manchester, 2012

Kuhn, A., *Family Secrets. Acts of Memory and Imagination*, London, 2002

Kushner, Tony, *We Europeans? Mass-Observation, 'Race' and British Identity in the Twentieth Century*, Aldershot, 2004

Kynaston, David, *The City of London, Vol. 4, A Club no More, 1945–2000*, London, 2001

Langhamer, Claire, 'Adultery in post-war England', *History Workshop Journal*, 62, 1, 2006, 86–115

Langhamer, Claire, *The English in Love. The Intimate Story of an Emotional Revolution*, Oxford, 2013

Lasch, Christopher, *The Culture of Narcissism*, New York, 1979

Lawler, Steph, *Identity: Sociological Perspectives*, Cambridge, 2008

Lewis, Jane, 'Public institution and private relationship: Marriage and marriage guidance, 1920–1968', *Twentieth Century British History*, 1, 3, 1990

Lewis, Jane, *Women in Britain since 1945*, Oxford, 1992

Lockwood, David, 'Marking out the middle class(es)', in Tim Butler and Mike Savage (eds.), *Social Change and the Middle Classes*, London, 1995

Lopes, Ana, 'Sex workers of the world unite!', *Feminist Review*, 67, Spring 2001

Lopes, Ana, and Webber, Jennifer, 'Organising sex workers in the UK: What's in it for trade unions?', paper delivered to the 2013 Ruskin Conference on Critical Labour Studies (accessed online in February 2016 at <http://www2.uwe.ac.uk/faculties/BBS/BUS/Research/CESR/July_2013_Lopes_Webber.pdf>).

López, Tara Martin, *The Winter of Discontent: Myth, Memory and History*, Liverpool, 2014

Mace, Jane, *Playing with Time: Mothers and the Meaning of Literacy*, London, 1998

MacIntyre, Alisdair, *After Virtue: A Study on Moral Theory*, London, 1985

Maclean, Kirstie, 'Towards a fee-paid fostering service', *Adoption & Fostering*, 13, 1989

Madge, Charles, and Harrisson, Tom, *Mass Observation*, London, 1937

Marquand, David, *The Unprincipled Society*, London, 1988

Marwick, Arthur, *The Sixties: Cultural Revolution in Britain, France, Italy, and the United States*, Oxford, 1998

McIlroy, John, and Campbell, Alan, 'The high tide of trade unionism: Mapping industrial politics, 1964–1979', in John McIlroy, Nina Fishman, and Alan Campbell (eds.), *British Trade Unions and Industrial Politics*, Vol. 2, Aldershot, 1999

Mort, Frank, 'The permissive society revisited', *Twentieth Century British History*, 22, 2, 2011, 286–8

Musgrove, Frank, *Ecstasy and Holiness. Counter Culture and the Open Society*, London, 1974

Nehring, Holger, 'The growth of social movements', in Paul Addison and Harriet Jones (eds.), *A Companion to Contemporary Britain, 1939–2000*, Oxford, 2005

Obelkevich, James, review of Marwick, *The Sixties*, in *Twentieth Century British History*, 11, 3, 2000, 333–6

Offer, Avner, 'British manual workers, from producers to consumers, c. 1950–2000', *Contemporary British History*, 22, 4, 2008

Orr, Linda, 'Intimate images: Subjectivity and history—Staël, Michelet and Tocqueville', in Frank Ankersmit and Hans Kellner (eds.), *The New Philosophy of History*, Chicago, 1995

Passerini, Luisa, 'Work ideology and consensus under Italian fascism', *History Workshop*, 8, 1979

Perkin, Harold, *The Rise of Professional Society. England since 1880*, London, 1989

Perrigo, Sarah, 'Women and change in the Labour Party, 1979–1995', in Joni Lovenduski and Pippa Norris (eds.), *Women in Politics*, Oxford, 1996

Pilcher, Jane, 'Mannheim's sociology of generations: An undervalued legacy', *The British Journal of Sociology*, 45, 3, 1994, 481–95

Plummer, Ken, *Documents of Life*, London, 1983

Plummer, Ken, *Documents of Life 2. An Invitation to a Critical Humanism*, London, 2001

Pollen, Annebella, 'Using the Mass-Observation Archive', in Anne Jamieson and Christina Victor (eds.), *Researching Ageing and Later Life: The Practice of Social Gerontology*, Buckingham, 2002

Pollen, Annebella, 'A hybrid heterogeneity hard to contain: Research methods and methodology in the post-1981 Mass Observation Project', *History Workshop Journal*, 75, 2013

Porter, Roy (ed.), *Rewriting the Self: Histories from the Renaissance to the Present*, London, 1997

Pugh, Martin, *Women and the Women's Movement in Britain, 1914–1999*, Basingstoke, 2000

Reid, Margaret, *The Secondary Banking Crisis, 1973–74. Its Causes and Course*, London, 1982

Richards, Martin P. M., and Elliott, B. Jane, 'Sex and marriage in the 1960s and 1970s', in David Clark (ed.), *Marriage, Domestic Life and Social Change*, London, 1991

Roper, Michael, *Masculinity and the British Organization Man since 1945*, Oxford, 1994

Rose, Nikolas, *Governing the Soul. The Shaping of the Private Self*, London, 1999

Rose, Sonia O., *Which People's War? National Identity and Citizenship in Britain 1939–1945*, Oxford, 2003

Roseneil, Sasha, *Common Women, Uncommon Practices: The Queer Feminism of Greenham*, London, 2000

Rowbotham, Sheila, *Promise of a Dream: Remembering the Sixties*, Harmondsworth, 2001

Rubinstein, W. D., *Capitalism, Culture and Decline in Britain, 1750–1990*, London, 1993, 154

Rust, Bob, *Where Do You Want This Lot?*, Manchester, 2007

Rustin, Michael, 'Reflections on the biographical turn in the social sciences', in Prue Chamberlayne, Joanna Bornat, and Tom Wengraf (eds.), *The Turn to Biographical Methods in the Social Sciences*, Abingdon, 2000

Samuel, Raphael, 'History Workshop, 1966–80', in Raphael Samuel (ed.), *People's History and Socialist Theory*, London, 1981

Savage, Mike, *Identities and Social Change in Britain since 1940. The Politics of Method*, Oxford, 2010

Sayer, Andrew, *The Moral Significance of Class*, Cambridge, 2005

Schwarz, Bill, ' "The only white man in there": The re-racialization of Britain, 1956–68', *Race and Class*, 38, 1996

Segal, Lynne, 'Jam today: Feminist impacts and transformations in the 1970s', in Lawrence Black, Hugh Pemberton, and Pat Thane (eds.), *Reassessing 1970s Britain*, Manchester, 2013

Sennett, Richard, *The Fall of Public Man*, London, 1977

Seyd, Patrick, and Whiteley, Paul, *Labour's Grass Roots. The Politics of Party Membership*, Oxford, 1992

Shaw, Jenny, 'Intellectual property, representative experience and M-O', M-O Archive Occasional Paper, 9, 1998

Shaw, Martin, and Hipgrave, Tony, *Specialist Fostering*, London, 1983

Sheridan, Dorothy, 'Writing to the archive: Mass-Observation as autobiography', *Sociology*, 27, 1, 1993

Sheridan, Dorothy, 'Damned anecdotes and dangerous confabulations. Mass Observation as life history', M-O Archive Occasional Paper, 7, 1996

Sheridan, Dorothy, Street, Brian, and Bloome, David, *Writing Ourselves. Mass-Observation and Literacy Practices*, Cresskill, NJ, 2000

Sikorski, Wladyslaw, *The Dark Side of the Moon*, London, 1946

Smart, Carol, *Personal Life. New Directions in Sociological Thinking*, Cambridge, 2007

Smith, Malcolm, *Britain and 1940. History, Myth and Popular Memory*, London, 2000

Smith, Paul, *Unionization and Union Leadership. The Road Haulage Industry*, London, 2001

Stanley, Liz, 'On auto/biography in sociology', *Sociology*, 27, 1993

Steedman, Carolyn, *Landscape for a Good Woman. A Story of Two Women*, London, 1986

Steedman, Carolyn, 'State sponsored autobiography', in Becky Conekin, Frank Mort, and Chris Waters (eds.), *Moments of Modernity. Reconstructing Britain, 1945–1964*, London, 1999

Stovel, Katherine, Savage, Michael, and Bearman, Peter, 'Ascription into achievement: Models of career systems at Lloyds Bank, 1890–1970', *American Journal of Sociology*, 102, 2, 1996, 58–99

Summerfield, Penny, 'Women in Britain since 1945: Companionate marriage and the double burden', in James Obelkevich and Peter Catterall (eds.), *Understanding Post-War British Society*, London, 1994

Summerfield, Penny, 'Culture and composure: Creating narratives of the gendered self in oral history interviews', *Cultural and Social History*, 1, 2004, 65–93

Supple, Barry, 'Fear of falling: Economic history and the decline of Britain', in P. Clarke and C. Trebilcock (eds.), *Understanding Decline. Perceptions and Realities of British Economic Performance*, Cambridge, 1997

Szreter, Simon, and Fisher, Kate, *Sex before the Sexual Revolution: Intimate Life in England 1918–1963*, Cambridge, 2010

Taylor, Barbara, 'Historical subjectivity', in Sally Alexander and Barbara Taylor (eds.), *History and Psyche. Culture, Psychoanalysis and the Past*, New York, 2012

Taylor, Bryce, *Learning for Tomorrow: Whole Person Learning for the Planetary Citizen,* Boston Spa, 2007

Taylor, Charles, *Sources of the Self. The Making of the Modern Identity*, Cambridge, 1989

Thane, Pat, 'Women and the 1970s. Towards liberation?', in Lawrence Black, Hugh Pemberton, and Pat Thane (eds.), *Reassessing 1970s Britain*, Manchester, 2013

Thompson, Paul, *The Voice of the Past. Oral History*, Oxford, 1978

Thompson, Paul, 'Life histories and the analysis of social change', in Daniel Bertaux (ed.), *Biography and Society. The Life History Approach to the Social Sciences*, London, 1981

Thompson, Paul, and Bertaux, Daniel (eds.), *Pathways to Social Class*, Oxford, 1997

Todd, Selina, *The People. The Rise and Fall of the Working Class, 1910–2010*, London, 2014

Tomlinson, Jim, 'Thrice denied: "Declinism" as a recurrent theme in British history in the long twentieth century', *Twentieth Century British History*, 20, 2, 2009

Tomlinson, Jim, 'The politics of declinism', in Lawrence Black, Hugh Pemberton, and Pat Thane (eds.), *Reassessing 1970s Britain*, Manchester, 2013

University of Surrey, *Understanding the Real World* (a history of the University), no date, (<http://www.surrey.ac.uk/files/pdf/chapter1.PDF/>, accessed in February 2016).

Veldman, Meredith, *Fantasy, the Bomb, and the Greening of Britain. Romantic Protest, 1945–1980*, Cambridge, 1994

Wainwright, Hilary, *Labour. A Tale of Two Parties*, London, 1987

Waters, Chris, 'Dark strangers in our midst: Discourses of race and nation in Britain, 1947–1963', *Journal of British Studies*, 36, 1997

Waters, Chris, 'Autobiography, nostalgia and the changing practices of working-class selfhood', in George K. Behlmer and Fred M. Leventhal (eds.), *Singular Continuities. Tradition, Nostalgia and Identity in Modern British Culture*, Stanford, CA, 2000

Whipple, Amy C., 'Speaking for whom? The 1971 Festival of Light and the search for the "Silent Majority"', *Contemporary British History*, 24, 3, 2010

Whyte, W. H., *The Organization Man*, New York, 1956

Wiener, Martin, *English Culture and the Decline of the Industrial Spirit: 1850–1980*, Cambridge, 1981

Worpole, Ken, 'A ghostly pavement: The political implications of local working-class history', in Raphael Samuel (ed.), *People's History and Socialist Theory*, London, 1981

Yeo, Stephen, 'The politics of community publications', in Raphael Samuel (ed.), *People's History and Socialist Theory*, London, 1981

Index

1960s 9–14, 20–1, 85, 101, 143, 144, 149, 158, 162, 163

Abercrombie, Jane 64, 66, 67, 69
abortion 12, 31, 44–5, 90, 121
Abortion Law Reform Association 14, 51
Althusser, Louis 49
Androgen Insensitivity Syndrome 70, 72
Archers, The 76
Association of Scientific, Technical and Managerial Staffs 139

Bank of England 147, 148
Barnardo's 14, 42, 57, 72
Basildon 113, 119, 123, 126, 130–1
Beatles, The 10, 78
Beckett, Samuel 52
Belfast 43, 44, 53
Benn, Tony 129
Beyond the Fringe 149
Billingsgate 153
Blair, Cherie 56
Blair, Tony 76, 87, 91, 130, 151
Bob vi, 109–32
    childhood 109, 110, 118–19
    children 109, 118, 122, 131
    class 109, 111–12, 124, 126, 129
    education 109, 110–12
    employment 109–10, 113–17
    friendship 114, 116–17, 118, 120
    marriage 111, 112, 119–21
    MO writing vii, 114, 120, 122–3, 124, 131–2

politics 13, 109, 112, 121, 123–32, 163, 165
    religion 116, 120
    volunteering 123–4
Bournemouth 61
Bradford 69, 71
Bristol 62, 63
British Road Services 113, 123, 125
British Sociological Association 51
Brown, Gordon 48
Brown's Hotel 141
Buddhism 77, 78

Callaghan, Jim 140
Caroline vi, 25–40
    childhood 26–8, 41
    children 32–5, 39
    class 37–8
    education 28, 35–6, 38, 165
    employment 36–7, 39
    friendship 35–6, 40
    marriage 25–6, 31–5, 39
    MO writing vii, 39–40
    politics 37, 53, 162–3, 164
    religion 38–9
    volunteering 37
Carr, E. H. 161
Castle, Barbara 101
Catcher in the Rye 84
Catholicism 27, 44, 46, 50
Cathy Come Home 101
Central School of Speech and Drama 61
Chamberlain, Neville 128
Christian Science 152